LOGIC, METAPHYSICS, AND THE NATURAL SOCIABILITY OF MANKIND

NATURAL LAW AND
ENLIGHTENMENT CLASSICS

Knud Haakonssen
General Editor

Francis Hutcheson

NATURAL LAW AND
ENLIGHTENMENT CLASSICS

Logic, Metaphysics, and the Natural Sociability of Mankind

Francis Hutcheson

Edited by James Moore and Michael Silverthorne

Texts translated from the Latin by Michael Silverthorne

Introduction by James Moore

*The Collected Works and Correspondence
of Francis Hutcheson*

LIBERTY FUND
Indianapolis

This book is published by Liberty Fund, Inc., a foundation established
to encourage study of the ideal of a society of free and responsible individuals.

The cuneiform inscription that serves as our logo and as the design motif for
our endpapers is the earliest-known written appearance of the word
"freedom" (*amagi*), or "liberty." It is taken from a clay document written
about 2300 B.C. in the Sumerian city-state of Lagash.

Frontispiece: Detail of a portrait of Francis Hutcheson by Allan Ramsay (ca. 1740–45),
oil on canvas, reproduced courtesy of the Hunterian Art Gallery, University of Glasgow.

10 09 08 07 06 C 5 4 3 2 1
10 09 08 07 06 P 5 4 3 2 1

Library of Congress Cataloging-in-Publication Data

Hutcheson, Francis, 1694–1746.
[Logicae compendium. English] Logic, metaphysics, and the natural sociability of mankind/
Francis Hutcheson; edited by James Moore and Michael Silverthorne;
texts translated from the Latin by Michael Silverthorne; introduction by James Moore.
p.   cm.—(The collected works and correspondence of Francis Hutcheson)
(Natural law and enlightenment classics)
Includes bibliographical references (p.   ) and index.
ISBN-13: 978-0-86597-446-3 (alk. paper)   ISBN-10: 0-86597-446-2 (alk. paper)
ISBN-13: 978-0-86597-447-0 (pbk.: alk. paper)   ISBN-10: 0-86597-447-0 (pbk.: alk. paper)
1. Logic—Early works to 1800.   2. Metaphysics—Early works to 1800.
I. Moore, James, 1934–   . II. Silverthorne, Michael.
III. Hutcheson, Francis, 1694–1746.   Synopsis metaphysicae. English.
IV. Title.   V. Series: Hutcheson, Francis, 1694–1746.   Works. 2002.
B1500.E5S55 2006
192—dc22   2005024558

LIBERTY FUND, INC.
8335 Allison Pointe Trail, Suite 300
Indianapolis, Indiana 46250-1684

CONTENTS

INTRODUCTION

Francis Hutcheson's *A Compend of Logic* and *A Synopsis of Metaphysics* represent his only systematic treatments of logic, ontology, and pneumatology, or the science of the soul. They were considered indispensable texts for the instruction of students in the eighteenth century. There were six (posthumous) editions of his *Logic*[1] and seven editions of his *Metaphysics* (five of them posthumous).[2] Any serious study of Hutcheson's philosophy must take into account his understanding of logic: of ideas and terms, judgments and propositions, reasoning and discourse, topics, fallacies, and method; and metaphysics: of being, substance, cause and effect, the intellect, the will, the soul, the attributes of God.

Notwithstanding the importance of the subject matter, Hutcheson's texts on logic and metaphysics have not figured prominently in studies of his philosophy. This may be explained in part by the circumstance that they were written in Latin; the present volume provides the first complete translation of these writings into English. The relative neglect of Hutcheson's *Logic* and *Metaphysics* may also be linked to the fact that they were composed for the use of students. Unlike his English-language works, published in the 1720s and written for adult readers,[3] but like *A Short Introduction to*

---

1. *Logicae Compendium. Praefixa est Dissertatio de Philosophiae Origine, Ejusque Inventoribus aut Excultoribus Praecipuis* (Glasgow, 1756; reprinted 1759, 1764, 1772, 1778, and 1787).

2. *Metaphysicae Synopsis: Ontologiam, et Pneumatologiam, Complectens* (Glasgow, 1742); *Synopsis Metaphysicae, Ontologiam et Pneumatologiam, Complectens,* editio altera auctior (Glasgow, 1744); *Synopsis Metaphysicae, Ontologiam et Pneumatologiam Complectens,* editio tertia, auctior et emendatior (Glasgow, 1749). There were four more editions in 1756, 1762, 1774, and 1780.

3. *An Inquiry into the Original of Our Ideas of Beauty and Virtue; in Two Treatises. In which the Principles of the late Earl of Shaftesbury are Explain'd and Defended against the*

Moral Philosophy (1747; originally composed in Latin as *Philosophiae Moralis Institutio Compendiaria,* 1742, 1745), his logic and metaphysics were intended for classroom use.[4] Thus, the significance of his academic or Latin writings can be best appreciated by recognizing their derivative character: they belong to a textbook tradition of commentary on the writings of others. Some of the most distinctive and central arguments of Hutcheson's philosophy—the importance of ideas brought to mind by the internal senses, the presence in human nature of calm desires, of generous and benevolent instincts—will be found to emerge in the course of these writings. But the direction of the arguments, the structure of the books, the questions he found it necessary to address can be best understood and appreciated by recognizing that they derive from texts assigned to students by his predecessors and his contemporaries at the University of Glasgow in the first half of the eighteenth century.

A Compend of Logic

Two approaches to the study of logic were combined in the teaching of Hutcheson and his colleagues. One was the logic of ideas: the logic of Port Royal as in *The Art of Thinking* by Arnauld and Nicole (1662), Locke's *An Essay Concerning Human Understanding* (1690), and Jean Le Clerc's *Logica; sive Ars Ratiocinandi* (1692). The second approach was the logic of Aristotelian scholasticism: the texts that appear to have been most often consulted were those of Franco Burgersdijk, *Institutiones Logicae* (1632), Robert Sanderson, *Logicae Artis Compendium* (1672), and Henry Aldrich, *Artis Logicae Compendium* (1692).

In Hutcheson's *A Compend of Logic* (*Logicae Compendium,* 1756), the

---

Author of the Fable of the Bees (London, 1725); and *An Essay on the Nature and Conduct of the Passions and Affections, with Illustrations on the Moral Sense* (London, 1728).

4. Hutcheson asked his friend Thomas Drennan to send a copy of *Synopsis Metaphysicae* to Bishop Edward Synge, who "is wanting such Elementary books for his Son." Letter of Hutcheson to Drennan, 29 October 1743, Glasgow University Library MS Gen. 1018, fol. 14. And in the dedication to *A Short Introduction to Moral Philosophy,* addressed "to the students in universities," he wrote, "these elementary books are for your use who study at Universities, and not for the learned."

logic of ideas provided the structure and point of departure for his exposition. His first concern, which he shared with the logicians of Port Royal,
Locke and Le Clerc, was to account for the formation of ideas: how ideas
are conceived or apprehended (Part I); how judgments are formed by comparisons of ideas (Part II); how inferences are made by reasoning or by
judgments which depend upon a third idea or discourse (Part III); how
ideas should be ordered to avoid fallacious reasoning, or method (appendix). It will also be evident, however, that while the logic of ideas provided
the form or framework of the presentation, the substance of Hutcheson's
Logic was drawn very largely from scholastic discussions of terms (Part I);
of propositions (Part II); of the rules of syllogism (Part III); and topics
(appendix).

This combination of the way of ideas and of scholastic or Aristotelian
logic was a characteristic of the teaching of Hutcheson's former professor
and senior colleague at the University of Glasgow, John Loudon. Loudon
taught philosophy at the University of Glasgow from 1699 until his death
in 1750; from 1727 to 1750 he was Professor of Logic (and metaphysics). In
his elementary course, Compendium Logicae, he lectured on scholastic or
Aristotelian logic.[5] In his more advanced course, or Logica, he expanded
on the logic of ideas.[6] In his advanced treatment of logic, Loudon introduced a class of ideas that would have particular significance for Hutcheson. Following Antoine Arnauld and Nicholas Malebranche, Loudon
maintained that our ideas of spiritual things do not originate in sensation
or imagination; such ideas are better understood as ideas of pure intellect,
inspired in us directly by God. And Loudon went on to argue that spiritual
ideas are not the only ideas conceived in this way. Ideas of pure intellect
also include universal ideas, ideas of affirmation and negation, ideas of
truth and virtue.[7]

Hutcheson would employ ideas of pure intellect to comprehend and
account for an even wider range of mental phenomena. He included among

5. John Loudon, "Compendium Logicae."
6. John Loudon, "Logica, Pars Prima." See Emily Michael, "Francis Hutcheson's
Logicae Compendium and the Glasgow School of Logic."
7. Loudon, "Logica," fol. 6.

pure intellections all ideas of its own operations formed by the understanding; all judgments and reasonings; abstract ideas; ideas of primary qualities; ideas of certainty and doubt, of desire and aversion, of virtue and vice. Hutcheson did not discover the origin of these ideas of pure intellect in divine inspiration, as Loudon did.[8] He proposed instead that such ideas are brought to mind by an internal sense. The importance of ideas of internal sensation, which he also called concomitant ideas, has been recognized by students of Hutcheson's moral philosophy.[9] It will be evident in what follows that ideas of internal sensation were of central significance for Hutcheson's metaphysics.

The second and third parts of *A Compend of Logic,* on judgment and discourse, derive very largely from the scholastic logics of Sanderson and Aldrich.[10] And it is remarkable that Hutcheson did not avail himself of the opportunity (as Loudon did) to illustrate his logic by lessons drawn from his metaphysics and his moral philosophy. The lack of originality that characterizes the latter part of *A Compend of Logic* may explain why it was not published in Hutcheson's lifetime. It would appear, however, that there was a demand among students at the University of Glasgow for the text. A student's transcription of the *Logic* was made in 1749 and bound with the *Synopsis Metaphysicae* in a duodecimo volume entitled "Logica et Metaphysica Hutcheson."[11] This transcription has been used in this edi-

8. James Clow, Professor of Logic at the University of Glasgow from 1752 to 1774, who used Hutcheson's *A Compend of Logic* as his text, and who had studied logic with Loudon in 1730, considered that Hutcheson was in error in not deriving ideas of pure intellect from divine inspiration: "for they are a power bestowed upon us by the Author of our Being. . . ." "A System of Logic," fol. 92.

9. See David Fate Norton, "Hutcheson's Moral Sense Theory Reconsidered," "Hutcheson on Perception and Moral Perception," and "Hutcheson's Moral Realism." Also see Kenneth Winkler, "Hutcheson's Alleged Realism" and "Hutcheson and Hume on the Color of Virtue."

10. See Kenneth Winkler, "Lockean Logic," p. 176, n. 27: "Much of Hutcheson's material is cribbed from Henry Aldrich's *Compendium.*"

11. Francis Hutcheson, "Logica et Metaphysica," GUL MS Gen. 872: this transcription of Hutcheson's "Logica" was made by Jo[annes] Macneal, who entered the University of Glasgow in November 1747. *The Matriculation Albums of Glasgow from 1728 to 1858,* p. 36.

tion to clarify some anomalies in the published version of the *Logicae Compendium.*[12]

A Synopsis of Metaphysics

Hutcheson's *A Synopsis of Metaphysics* is a work of much greater significance than *A Compend of Logic* for an appreciation of Hutcheson's philosophy. Every part of the book exhibits Hutcheson's distinctive cast of mind. But *A Synopsis of Metaphysics* was also a derivative work. It was based upon the text regularly assigned students of metaphysics at the University of Glasgow during the first half of the eighteenth century: the *Determinationes Pneumatologicae et Ontologicae* of the Dutch metaphysician Gerard de Vries. John Loudon informed the faculty that his lectures on metaphysics were based on the work of de Vries.[13] He supplemented that work with arguments of his own, designed to counter "wrong notions some authors endeavour to infuse . . . [and] the unreasonable pains they are at to introduce skepticism in their Metaphysics. . . ." He had in mind the writings of Jean Le Clerc, which were, he thought, "industriously stuff'd with doctrines of a very dangerous tendency. . . ."[14] Loudon continued to base his lectures on metaphysics on the work of de Vries to the end of his long career. As late as the 1740s, students recalled much later, Loudon "used in solemn peripatetic step to illustrate his own mysterious Compend [of logic] and the still more metaphysical subtleties of de Vries."[15]

Hutcheson designed his metaphysics to serve as a counterpart to the work of de Vries. He wrote to Thomas Drennan, of *A Synopsis of Metaphysics:* "I am sure it will match de Vries, and therefore I teach the 3rd part of it De Deo."[16] In the first part of *A Synopsis,* he provided a critical commentary on de Vries's ontology. In opposition to de Vries, for whom the

12. See below, Part I, p. 15, n. 7; Part III, p. 35, n. 5; appendix, p. 50, n. 2 and p. 54, n. 6.

13. See John Loudon's report on his teaching (1712), Glasgow University Archives 43228.

14. *Ibid.*

15. Jas. Wodrow to the Earl of Buchan, 27 April 1808, Mitchell Library (in Glasgow) MSS Baillie 32225 fol. 55–57.

16. Hutcheson to Thomas Drennan, 29 October 1743, GUL MS Gen. 1018 fol. 14.

immediate concern of ontology was the traditional Aristotelian preoccupation with being or entities or things, Hutcheson explained being and its modes in terms of ideas. He objected to the identification by scholastics of essence and existence as equivalent terms: existence is suggested to the mind by every sensation and reflection, whereas essences are ideas abstracted from existence and denote the primary attributes of things. Hutcheson's ontology consisted very largely in the translation of scholastic terms of being into the language of ideas. He considered it a great mistake on the part of scholastic metaphysicians that they had often attributed real or objective existence to their terms: "We must be careful . . . not to attribute to external things or to objects of ideas those things that belong only to ideas or to words."[17] He reviewed the various entities or things which were supposed by metaphysicians like de Vries to stand between being and nothing: relations, possibles, entities of reason. Hutcheson argued that these things are nothing but ideas; they may or may not signify objects external to the mind.[18] Hutcheson was working his way through the ontology of de Vries and scholastic metaphysicians to his own distinctive theory of concomitant ideas or ideas of internal sensation which accompany perceptions of the external senses. He would attempt to align his theory of ideas with Locke and use it to counter skeptical uses of the theory of ideas that would deny reality to objects external to the mind.[19]

Finally, he examined the principal divisions of being: independent and dependent; necessary and contingent; finite and infinite; substance and accident; cause and effect. The last particularly requires comment. Hutcheson

17. See *A Synopsis of Metaphysics,* I, i, 1, p. 67.
18. *Ibid.,* I, i, 4, pp. 70–72.
19. John Locke, *An Essay Concerning Human Understanding,* II, 8, 15, p. 137. Hutcheson objected to Berkeley's critique of primary qualities. In a letter to William Mace, 6 September 1727, printed in the *European Magazine* for September 1788, and reprinted in part in David Berman, "Francis Hutcheson on Berkeley and the Molyneux Problem," he wrote, "I was well apprized of the scheme of thinking you are fallen into, not only by our Dr. Berkly's [*sic*] books, and by some of the old academics, but by frequent conversations with some few speculative friends in Dublin." Hutcheson considered that the apposite response to Berkeley and others could be found in concomitant ideas of primary qualities of extension, figure, and so on. "I own I cannot see the force of the arguments against external objects, i.e. something like or proportional to our concomitant ideas, as I call extension, figure, motion, rest, solidity."

dispensed with the fourfold classification of causes taken over from the philosophy of Aristotle. He objected to the classification of formal and material causes as causes. He considered efficient causes to include, in effect, both formal and material causes. But he also left a place for final causation that could be best determined by an internal or external sense.[20] He rejected the possibility of an infinite series of causes. And he found no place for contingency in the physical or the moral world. He invoked the Stoic idea that all things, including human actions, were "set and foreseen by God himself."[21] These were some of the most notable of Hutcheson's arguments concerning ontology in the first edition of his *Metaphysics*. He would find other uses for the categories of being that were identified by Aristotle and the scholastics in the second edition of his *Metaphysics*.[22]

In Part II of his metaphysics, Hutcheson turned to the study of the mind or the spirit or soul, the subject of pneumatics or pneumatology, as it was called by de Vries and other early modern metaphysicians. It was of the first importance in the study of pneumatics to demonstrate that spirits or souls are different from bodies, that the immateriality of the soul provides reasons to believe in the soul's immortality. Hutcheson rehearsed those arguments the self consciousness, the simplicity, the capacity for action of the soul, in contrast with the thoughtlessness, the disaggregation, the inertia of bodies—in the third (originally the first) chapter of Part II. But in order to appreciate the nature of the soul, Hutcheson thought, like Locke, that one must examine the distinctive powers of the human mind, which Hutcheson took to be the understanding and the will. He located the sources of human understanding, as Locke did, in the senses. He attached particular importance to what Locke had called ideas of reflection, which Hutcheson called ideas of internal sensation. Hutcheson liked to remind his readers that Locke too had called ideas of reflection ideas of internal sensation.[23] It is controversial, however, whether Locke would have en-

---

20. See below, p. xxvi, and *A Synopsis of Metaphysics*, I, 4, 5, p. 94.

21. *Ibid.*, I, 4, 6, p. 97.

22. In a new chapter, Part I, chap. 5, added to the second edition (1744); see below, pp. 101–10.

23. In *An Essay on the Nature and Conduct of the Passions and Affections* (3rd ed., 1742), preface, p. 205. Locke used the term "internal Sense" in *Essay*, II, I, 4, p. 105.

dorsed many of Hutcheson's uses for ideas of internal sensation. Locke had
been wary of distinguishing faculties of the understanding, on the grounds
that this had "misled many into a confused notion of so many distinct
agents in us."[24] Hutcheson entertained no such apprehension. He distinguished a bewildering variety of internal senses, including senses of beauty
and virtue, of praise and honor, of novelty, harmony, imitation, and humor. And he insisted that these several senses were all of them innate, although they may be cultivated and reinforced by habit.[25]

The same senses were complemented by desires, which Hutcheson distinguished, following the scholastic distinction employed by de Vries, between lower or sensual desires and higher or rational desires. The mind
always fastens upon the desire that is strongest. The will should not be supposed to be a power to turn or direct the mind in any direction it may
choose. All that can be meant by the liberty of the will is the liberty or
power to act on a desire or refrain from doing what we do not desire, a
position he attributed again to Locke. Hutcheson's idea of power was not,
however, like Locke's, the power to suspend desire; it was rather the importance of recognizing in the mind the presence of rational or calm desires, and of cultivating those desires, as opposed to the more violent desires
excited by the body. Hutcheson was careful not to assert that the soul has
command over the body (Part II, chapter 4). But he insisted that the cultivation of the internal senses and the calm desires offered the best assurance
of the immortality of the soul. While the external senses and the violent
desires expire with the body, the soul, reinforced by the nobler senses and
desires, may survive the death of the body. It had been accordingly the
conviction of the best men, as he considered them, that the imperfections,
hardships, and injustices of this life could be compensated in the next, and
so "the whole fabric and government of the world becomes fully worthy
of the great and good God."[26]

The concluding part of pneumatics or the science of the soul, Part III
of Hutcheson's *Metaphysics,* was natural theology or the study by reason,
unaided by revelation, of the existence, the attributes, and the providence

24. Locke, *Essay,* II, 21, 6, p. 237.
25. *A Synopsis of Metaphysics,* II, 1, 5, pp. 117–22.
26. *Ibid.,* II, 4, 3, p. 148.

or operations of God. Hutcheson's treatment of natural theology is remarkable for its rhapsodic evocation of the harmony, design, and beauty of the world. This way of demonstrating the existence of the creator stands in marked contrast to the revealed theology of Reformed theologians, who argued from the evidence of sin in our fallen human nature to the need for forgiveness of our sins by God. Reformed natural theologians, Gershom Carmichael among them, had attached particular importance to the glory of God, as contrasted with the fallibility of man; they revered especially those attributes of God that could not be shared with or communicated to man.[27] Hutcheson reviewed some of the incommunicable attributes: independence, necessary existence, immutability, incomprehensibility, in Part II, chapter 2; but the attributes of God that he chose particularly to celebrate, in chapters 3 and 4, were the communicable attributes: above all, the benevolence of God. The benevolence of the Creator was manifested in human nature, in our capacity for virtue and in our ability to recognize virtue by a moral sense. Hutcheson's metaphysics, his ontology and pneumatology, which eventuated in natural theology, provided, in his Latin writings, at least, a metaphysical foundation for his moral philosophy.[28] The latter included his arguments, in many ways distinctive, for the natural sociability of mankind.

On the Natural Sociability of Mankind

Hutcheson was elected Professor of Moral Philosophy at the University of Glasgow in December 1729. He delivered his inaugural lecture, "On the Natural Sociability of Mankind," almost a year later, in November 1730,

27. See "Synopsis of Natural Theology," chap. 2 in *Natural Rights on the Threshold of the Scottish Enlightenment*, pp. 248 ff.

28. It was characteristic of Hutcheson's Latin writings that moral distinctions were thought to be dependent upon a metaphysical foundation that included natural theology and the attributes of divinity. See *Philosophiae Moralis* (1745), pp. 111–12, and *A Short Introduction to Moral Philosophy* (1747), pp. 105–6. Such dependence appears to have been absent, however, from his *Inquiry, Essay,* and *Illustrations,* written not for scholars but for gentlemen. There, following the lead of Shaftesbury, Hutcheson considered metaphysical reasoning unnecessary and misleading. See *Inquiry* (1725), viii, 115, and *Illustrations* (1728), 339; Shaftesbury, *Characteristics*, 129–30, 137, 302, 427; and James Moore, "The Two Systems of Francis Hutcheson" and "Utility and Humanity: The Quest for the *Honestum* in Cicero, Hutcheson, and Hume."

on the occasion of his formal admittance to the university. Robert Wodrow, who attended the lecture, reported that "he delivered it very fast and low, being a modest man, and it was not well understood."[29] Wodrow also said that the subject of the lecture was "on a very safe and general topic," a judgment he might not have made had he heard it more distinctly. For Hutcheson's lecture was designed to challenge a number of widely accepted opinions: theological, juridical, and moral. The style of the lecture was engaging; it was written in a style that is conspicuously different from the scholastic idiom of the logic and most (not all) of the metaphysics. His students would later recall that Hutcheson spoke Latin "with abundant ease and fluency; and as his stile was formed on the very best models, particularly Cicero, so it was a pleasure to hear him speak in that language."[30] His inaugural oration is perhaps the best illustration of this tribute to his spoken Latin.

After some nostalgic recollections of his years as a student at the University of Glasgow—1710–11, as a student in the final undergraduate year; 1711–12, as a student of Greek and Latin literature; 1712–18, as a student of divinity—Hutcheson warmed to his theme. He would consider, first, what qualities of character are natural to man, with regard to moral life; second, whether society, in the absence of government, can be called natural; in each case, he would engage in rhetorical redescription of how the term "natural" should be used in theology and in jurisprudence. The last part of the lecture (more than a third of the text) was a response to his critics, to those moralists who maintained that all moral motivation may be reduced to self-love.

It was one of the dogmas of Reformed or Presbyterian theology that the natural condition of mankind was a state of sin, of fallen human nature. This natural state or condition was preceded by the state of innocence enjoyed by our first parents before the Fall; the state of nature was succeeded by the state of grace, in which the souls of some have been saved by the atonement made by Christ for our sins; and this progression from inno-

---

29. Robert Wodrow, *Analecta; or, Materials for a History of Remarkable Providences,* vol. 4, p. 187.

30. James Wodrow to the Earl of Buchan, 28 May 1808, Mitchell Library MSS Baillie 32225 fol. 59.

cence to sin to grace culminated in the fourth and final state, the eternal
state.[31] Hutcheson's metaphysics allowed him to offer an alternative vision
of human nature and the human condition. He had made provision for
final causes in his ontology, for internal sensibilities and calm desires in his
pneumatology, for the communication of divine attributes, notably benevolence, in his natural theology. He now drew upon his metaphysics to
redefine the meaning of the term "natural" as applied to human nature.
The nature of a thing, he proposed, can be understood only by considering
its final cause or end or purpose, that for which it was originally designed.
Human nature was designed to allow men to live in a manner consistent
with their internal sensibilities and higher desires. Although weakness and
imperfection may be found in the original design of human nature, such
weakness should not inhibit or divert us from acting in accordance with
our nature: "All our innate desires strive against that weakness and declare
that such weakness is not the end of our duties much less the goal which
nature has set for our actions."[32] Hutcheson had redefined the state of nature as it had been understood by the Reformed theologians; he had identified the state of nature with the state of innocence. And he did not hesitate
to declare that "Reformed theologians agree with all these doctrines, very
rightly pointing to the original fabric and construction of our nature as it
once was. . . . And evident signs of this design and workmanship are preserved, they acknowledge, in the very ruins of its fabric."[33]

Hutcheson's redescription of the Reformed doctrine of the state of nature had juridical implications. For not only Hobbes, but also Pufendorf,
"the grand Instructor in Morals to all who have of late given themselves to
that Study,"[34] as Hutcheson once called him, had depicted the natural condition of mankind in a most unflattering light. Pufendorf described the
state of nature as a state of poverty, weakness, and malice. Hutcheson proposed that writers on politics and jurisprudence would be best advised to

---

31. Thomas Boston, *Human Nature in Its Fourfold State.*
32. See p. 197.
33. See pp. 199–200.
34. *Dublin Weekly Journal,* no. 10, 5 June 1725, in *A Collection of Letters and Essays on
Several Subjects Lately Publish'd in the Dublin Journal* (London and Dublin, 1729), vol.
I, pp. 78–79.

discontinue use of the term "state of nature." The condition of mankind in the absence of civil government could be better described as a state of liberty, a usage Hutcheson maintained consistently in his later publications on natural rights and politics. Hobbes and Pufendorf had both fallen into the teachings of the Epicureans, that self-love or the pursuit of pleasure and utility is the source of justice and social life. Hutcheson juxtaposed against this view the opinion of modern critics of Hobbes (Cumberland and Shaftesbury) and of Pufendorf (Titius and Carmichael). Shaftesbury in particular had described social life as a condition sought not only for utility and pleasure but also for itself. We seek sociability not only for the peaceable living and other benefits sociability may afford: we delight in the company of family, friends, neighbors, and fellow citizens and rejoice in their happiness and good fortune.[35] Our natural sociability is reinforced by our internal senses of honor and decency, of the *honestum* and *decorum*. When human nature is considered in this light, we have many reasons to conclude that men are naturally sociable, that society is natural to man in the absence of government.

The last part of Hutcheson's lecture (pp. 206–14) was a response to critics who thought that he was mistaken in his understanding of moral motivation; in the judgment of these critics, the motives that prompt us to be virtuous and permit us to live in society are reducible to self-liking or desire for esteem. Two works, both critical of Hutcheson's moral philosophy on these grounds, were published in the months preceding the inaugural lecture. Bernard Mandeville had written a second volume of *The Fable of the Bees* (1729) in which he expanded upon his critique of Shaftesbury's theory of the natural sociability of man[36] and also invited Mr. Hutcheson to consider how much real benevolence and love of country men have, abstracted from their desire to be thought to have such benevolence, even though they feel none.[37] In the previous year (1728) Archibald Campbell's work *Arete-logia; or, An Enquiry into the Original of Moral Virtue* was published; the last third of Campbell's work was devoted to an

---

35. Shaftesbury, "Sensus Communis," in *Characteristics of Men, Manners, Opinions, Times,* pp. 51 ff.

36. Bernard Mandeville, *The Fable of the Bees,* vol. 2, 4th dialogue, p. 177 ff.

37. *Ibid.,* 6th dialogue, pp. 345–46.

extended critique of Hutcheson's moral psychology.[38] In Campbell's understanding of moral life, other persons are extensions of oneself: children, relatives, friends, persons distant from one in time and place are all perceived to be connected, if only in imagination or by sympathy, with oneself. It is this association, direct or indirect, of others with ourselves that is the source of virtue and morality; we approve of the virtue and good conduct of others because we perceive it to be advantageous to ourselves. And we depend upon the approval or esteem of others to provide a motive for us to be virtuous. It is self-love, as it exhibits itself in the desire for esteem, that is "the great commanding Motive" of moral life.[39] In this light, Campbell held that the benevolence or the instinctive determination to promote the good of others that Hutcheson claimed to find in human nature could be nothing but "an Occult Quality; which is a Part of Philosophy far beyond my Comprehension."[40]

In opposition to his critics, Hutcheson put before his listeners a number of considerations. He invited all in his audience to consider whether they do not have a natural desire for the happiness of others, even when they expect no advantage to themselves to follow from such a desire. He acknowledged that natural desires also include anger, desire for vengeance, avarice, and ambition, but he reminded his auditors that there are other desires, other senses, of the beautiful and the fitting, which direct and control our basic desires. He objected to the narrow characterization of sociality offered by Mandeville, who thought love of company a quality more likely to be found among fox hunters or sailors on leave than among men of sense; and Campbell, who insisted that each of us is properly selective about the company he keeps.[41] Hutcheson was dismissive of these reservations; he appears to have regarded these criticisms as a caricature of the position he defended: "As if we could be benevolent or have kind and so-

---

38. Archibald Campbell, *Arete-logia; or, An Enquiry into the Original of Moral Virtue* (London, 1728). This text was reprinted in 1739. A second revised edition was published in Edinburgh and in London in 1733 and 1734.

39. *Ibid.*, pp. 173, 320.

40. *Ibid.*, p. 271.

41. Mandeville, "A Search into the Nature of Society," *The Fable of the Bees*, vol. 1, p. 340. Campbell, *Arete-logia*, p. 316.

ciable dispositions only toward those whom we would wish to choose as companions and intimates."[42] It had been complained of Hutcheson's idea of virtue that it gives us "dark melancholy views of those Pursuits to which we are invited. . . ."[43] Not so, Hutcheson countered:

> Nor when we exhort men to live a good life, harmless, temperate, friendly and beneficent, should anyone think that there is laid upon him anything sour, vexatious, repulsive, or sorrowful, which nature shuns.[44]

He concluded with an appeal to students in his audience: "Go forward, then, in virtue, beloved young men, the hope of this generation and the glory, I trust, of the generation to come. . . ."[45]

The Dating of Hutcheson's *Logic* and *Metaphysics*

It is possible to date the month and the year of Hutcheson's inaugural lecture: November 1730. It seems clear that he composed the lecture sometime in the same year, subsequent to his election in December 1729 to the chair of moral philosophy at Glasgow. It is more difficult to fix the dates of composition of the *Logic* and *Metaphysics*. As the Professor of Moral Philosophy, Hutcheson did not teach logic and metaphysics (ontology and pneumatology) at the University of Glasgow. Those subjects were taught by the Professor of Logic, John Loudon, who continued to teach them until he died in December 1750, more than four years after Hutcheson's death in August 1746. Hutcheson taught only the third and last part of metaphysics, natural theology, at Glasgow; the more animated rhetorical style of that part of his metaphysics may reflect this circumstance.

Hutcheson had last taught logic and metaphysics at his academy, in Dublin, in the 1720s. He told Henry Home, in the spring of 1739, in a letter of thanks for the gift of David Hume's *A Treatise of Human Nature,* books I and II, that "these metaphysical subjects have not been much in my thoughts of late: tho a great many of these sentiments and reasonings had

42. See p. 215.
43. Campbell, *Arete-logia,* p. 309.
44. See p. 216.
45. See p. 216.

employed me 10 or 12 years ago."[46] As the master of a dissenting academy, Hutcheson was preparing students for study at a university in Scotland; for most Irish students, the university of choice was Glasgow. It seems most probable that Hutcheson composed *A Compend of Logic* and *A Synopsis of Metaphysics* in the 1720s for the instruction of students in his Dublin academy. Moreover, there is no argument in the text of the *Logic* (as distinct from the prefatory "Dissertation on the Origin of Philosophy") or in the first edition of the *Metaphysics* (1742) that would require a date of composition later than the 1720s. The case is otherwise with respect to the prefatory Dissertation and the second edition of the *Metaphysics*. In those parts of his work, it will be evident that he was responding to arguments advanced in writings published in the 1730s (in the second edition of the *Metaphysics,* 1744), and he was adapting for his own use work published in the 1740s (in the dissertation prefaced to the *Logic*).

What prompted Hutcheson to publish *A Synopsis of Metaphysics* in 1742? It appears that it was first published without his knowledge; "It was first most imperfectly and foolishly printed without my knowledge, from some loose hastily wrote papers."[47] The publisher was his former student and friend Robert Foulis. It is not known how Foulis came to be in possession of the text; Hutcheson may have given it to Foulis with a view to a later publication of a revised version. In the event, Hutcheson remained unhappy with the second edition (1744), which "tho much enlarged and altered, yet I have not leisure, either to examine the whole thoroughly or correct the Latin."[48] The second edition contained 123 duodecimo pages, compared with 89 pages in the first edition. It is possible to recognize in the alterations made in the second edition a number of notable additions.

Aristotelians, Stoics, and Eclectics

The most conspicuous new material was a chapter (Part I, chapter 5) devoted to the categories of Aristotle. We have seen that it was part of Hutch-

---

46. Hutcheson to Henry Home, ca. April 1739, in Ian Ross, "Hutcheson on Hume's *Treatise:* An Unnoticed Letter," p. 71.
47. Hutcheson to Thomas Drennan, 29 October 1743, GUL MS Gen. 1018 fol. 14.
48. *Ibid.*

eson's strategy, in his *Metaphysics* as in his *Logic,* to demonstrate that the things or entities or beings discussed by Aristotelian scholastics could be better understood as ideas brought to mind by an internal sense. In his review of the categories of Aristotle—substance, quantity, quality, and so on—Hutcheson argued again that these categories were best conceived as ideas of internal sensation. In the third edition (1749) he referred the reader to Locke for a parallel treatment of the ideas of substance and time.[49] He appears to have been enlisting the authority of Locke to reinforce an argument that ideas of substance, space, relation, and so on are real ideas that have reference to an objective reality, to things in the world. They are not, like the idea of number, ideas that can be imagined in the absence of things.

In his insistence that the categories of Aristotle are real ideas that refer to objective things external to the mind, Hutcheson may have been responding to a very different understanding of Locke's way of ideas. Edmund Law had argued, on the authority of Locke, that ideas of space, time, quantity, and quality have no real or objective existence. Like the idea of number, they may be applied to anything that may be measured, "and this very thing demonstrates that they are nothing but Ideas of pure Intellect, and have no regard to the Existence of any external Object. . . ."[50] In contrast with skeptical uses, like George Berkeley's and Edmund Law's, of the way of ideas, Hutcheson acknowledged a particular debt, in the second and third editions of his *Metaphysics,* to the work of the Scots metaphysician Andrew Baxter. Baxter had argued, following Malebranche, that the soul and its ideas are connected with the physical or objective world by divine intervention, by constant and unvarying laws of nature.[51] Hutcheson would also find in Baxter's work support for his view that the soul is an immaterial substance different from body, and that the operations of an immaterial divine providence determine the course of the physical world.[52]

49. See *A Synopsis of Metaphysics,* I, 5, pp. 101–2, nn. 3 and 4.

50. Edmund Law, *An Enquiry into the Ideas of Space, Time, Immensity and Eternity,* p. 32, and earlier, in his notes upon William King, *An Essay on the Origin of Evil,* p. 7 ff.

51. Andrew Baxter, *An Enquiry into the Nature of the Human Soul,* pp. 33–49. Vol. 2, sec. 2 of this work was a critique of Berkeley's philosophy. For discussion, see Harry M. Bracken, *The Early Reception of Berkeley's Immaterialism, 1710–1733.*

52. See *A Synopsis of Metaphysics,* I, 4, 5, pp. 92–93, n. 10; I, 5, 5, p. 109, n. 15.

Hutcheson's adaptation of the categories of Aristotle, however consistent with his general determination to locate scholastic entities in ideas of internal sensation, did not extend to Aristotelian or Peripatetic arguments for the liberty of the will. In additions made to discussions of liberty in all three parts of the *Metaphysics,* Hutcheson reinforced arguments for the Stoic theory in opposition to the Peripatetics.[53] He understood the Stoics to have maintained that the will is determined by a man's character, by the qualities of his mind, his ideas, his judgment, "and that it cannot happen otherwise."[54] The Peripatetics, in contrast, made provision for the liberty of the will; that when presented with two species of good, "on the one hand, *the right and the good,* on the other hand, the *pleasant* and the *useful,* they [minds] turn themselves of their own accord in the one direction or the other."[55] There had been no mention of the Peripatetics in the first edition of the *Metaphysics.* In the second edition, more elaborate expositions of the Stoic case invariably preceded succinct statements of the Peripatetic position. Hutcheson was at pains, nonetheless, to insist that notwithstanding the more plausible arguments of the Stoics, the Peripatetics were also men of piety. And he appears to have been eager to reconcile Stoics and Peripatetics, albeit in a manner weighted more heavily on the side of the Stoics and the determination of the will:

> In any case, however, both sides hold that God has foreseen most things from certain causes, and that he has determined in himself from the beginning that as he is always present and aware of his own omnipotence, he will rule and govern all things by constantly interposing his power, and that he has always kept in view how far and in what directions men's freedom might stray and how easily he could check it.[56]

Hutcheson's conviction that Stoics and Peripatetics might be reconciled within a metaphysics founded upon internal sensation may have been indebted to a similar project of synthesis he would have found in the writings of Henry More (1614–87), an author on whom Hutcheson conferred high

---

53. *Ibid.,* I, 4, 6, pp. 97–98; II, 2, 3, pp. 129–30; III, 3, 3, p. 171.
54. *Ibid.,* I, 4, 6, pp. 98–99; II, 2, 3, 130–31; III, 3, 3, pp. 171–72.
55. *Ibid.,* II, 2, 3, pp. 130–31.
56. *Ibid.,* III, 3, 3, p. 172.

praise, particularly in the 1740s. In his pedagogical treatment of morals, Hutcheson declared that Aristotle's theory of the virtues had been most usefully summarized by that most devout man, Henry More.[57] More thought that it was the common opinion of Aristotle and the Stoics "that to follow God or to follow Nature was the same thing as to follow Right Reason." And he took it to be Aristotle's considered response to the question where right reason was to be found "that unless a Man have within himself a Sense of things of this Nature, there is nothing to be done. . . . So that, in short, the final judgment upon this matter is all referred to inward Sense. . . ."[58] And More concluded his discussion of liberty of the will, as Hutcheson did, by referring the matter to the divine law within us, or right reason, which is to say, an "inward sense," "by which we are taught and stand bound, to prefer public Good before our private, and never to make our own pleasure or Utility to be the Measure of human Actions."[59]

There was a precedent in the ancient world for attempts, like More's and Hutcheson's, to reconcile Stoics and Peripatetics. This was the characteristic style of the Neoplatonists or "Eclectics" of the third to the sixth century. It is perhaps the most revealing part of Hutcheson's very short history of the origins of philosophy, prefaced to *A Compend of Logic,* that he concluded his narrative with a section on "the Eclectics," ancient and modern.[60] He remarked that while "the best of the ancients . . . are rightly included among the Eclectics because they were not enslaved to any master," the term is most properly applied to the Neoplatonists, including Ammonius, Plotinus, and Porphyry; he might have added to this list Simplicius and Nemesius, who are cited and praised elsewhere in his writings.[61] But Hutcheson, more remarkably, also brought under the rubric of the Eclectics

---

57. *Philosophiae Moralis Institutio Compendiaria* (Glasgow, 1745), I, 6, p. 103n. Hutcheson also appears to have been the editor of Henry More's *Divine Dialogues,* where More is celebrated in the editor's preface: see *The Correspondence and Occasional Writings of Francis Hutcheson.*

58. Henry More, *Enchiridion Ethicum: The English Translation of 1690,* I, 3, vii, p. 16.

59. *Ibid.,* III, 3, xiv, p. 190.

60. See pp. 7–8.

61. On Hutcheson's use of Simplicius, see *An Essay on the Nature and Conduct of the Passions and Affections* (1728), pp. 43n. and 125n.; on Nemesius, see *A Short Introduction to Moral Philosophy,* p. 4n., and *A Synopsis of Metaphysics,* II, 2, 3, p. 131, n. 8.

moderns "who have pointed out or entered upon a new road": in physics, Bacon and Newton; in ethics, Grotius, Cumberland, and Pufendorf; and in logic and metaphysics, Locke. Hutcheson's identification of modern natural scientists, natural jurists, and Locke as "eclectics" may have been merely derivative, like so much else in his pedagogical writings, on the work of others.[62] But Hutcheson also observed that philosophy has been improved by the efforts of those who have edited and interpreted the books of the ancients. And he reminded his readers that it was the Old Academy that was revived by Pico, Ficino, and Shaftesbury. He appears to have been signaling to his readers and students that modern philosophers, the natural scientists, the natural jurists, Locke, should be read and studied in a spirit of eclecticism, bearing in mind the ideas of philosophers (Stoic, Peripatetic, and Platonic) of the ancient world.

W. R. Scott once described Hutcheson's philosophy as "a mosaic, in being composed of separate borrowings from many sources. . . ." He described "the final result" as "an eclectic treatment of modern Philosophy, superimposed upon Ancient Eclecticism."[63] If this is an accurate description of any part of Hutcheson's philosophy, it applies with particular propriety to the texts included in this volume.

James Moore

---

62. Johann Jakob Brucker, *Historia Critica Philosophiae;* see especially vol. 2, pp. 189–462, on "the Eclectic Sect," and below, pp. 7–8, n. 16.

63. W. R. Scott, *Francis Hutcheson: His Life, Teaching and Position in the History of Philosophy,* p. 260.

A NOTE ON THE TEXT

A Compend of Logic follows the text of *Logicae Compendium* (Glasgow, 1756). A transcription of Hutcheson's "Logica" made between 1746 and 1749 by a student at the University of Glasgow (GUL MS Gen. 872) has been used to amend the published version on occasion; all such amendments have been referenced in footnotes.

A Synopsis of Metaphysics is based on the second edition, *Synopsis Metaphysicae* (Glasgow, 1744). The section "The Arguments of the Chapters" (Capitum Argumenta) was added in that edition. The subheadings listed in the "Arguments" do not include all of the subheadings entered in the text, and the wording of the subheadings in the text does not always match the wording used in the "Arguments." In this edition Hutcheson's wording in both the "Arguments" and the text, however discrepant, has been preserved. We have employed square brackets and footnotes to indicate material added to the second edition. The third edition of *Synopsis Metaphysicae* (Glasgow, 1749), published posthumously, contains numerous references to the sources of Hutcheson's arguments. These references may be helpful to the reader and are included in the notes to the text.

Abbreviations used in the notes and bibliography are GUL, Glasgow University Library; EUL, Edinburgh University Library; and GUA, Glasgow University Archives.

Finally, words added to the text to facilitate the flow of the translation have been placed between square brackets.

James Moore

Michael Silverthorne

ACKNOWLEDGMENTS

Our work on this edition of Hutcheson's Latin texts on logic and metaphysics and his inaugural lecture on the natural sociability of mankind has been assisted and enlivened by discussions with many friends and fellow scholars. The Eighteenth-Century Scottish Studies Society has provided a stimulating forum for exchanges on these subjects, and we are grateful for the hospitality extended to us on different occasions by the Institute for Advanced Studies at the University of Edinburgh and the School of Classics at the University of Exeter. The resourcefulness of the staff in the Department of Rare Books at McGill University and of the librarians of Concordia University is much appreciated.

It is also a pleasure to acknowledge the collaboration of the Department of Special Collections at the University of Glasgow and its director, David Weston. We are also much indebted to Daniel McDowell of the Chaucer Head, Presteigne, Wales, who loaned us a manuscript of Hutcheson's *Logica* for an extended period; this manuscript is now housed at the University of Glasgow.

A Compend of Logic
To which is prefixed a
Dissertation
On the
Origin of Philosophy
And Its Principal Founders and Exponents

Glasgow
At the University
Typeset by Robert and Andrew Foulis
Printers to the University
1756

Dissertation on the Origin of Philosophy and Its Principal Founders and Exponents[1]

Philosophy is the knowledge of the true and the good which men build for themselves by the powers of their own reason. Therefore we are not concerned here with the knowledge of things which has been available to men from the earliest days and which was passed down through the generations from divine revelation.

Philosophy was either barbarian or Greek. There seems to have been a considerable amount of barbarian philosophy among the Egyptians, the Chaldeans, and the Indians, but little evidence remains.[2] The study of geometry, astronomy, theology, ethics, and politics flourished among them.

The earliest authors of Greek philosophy after the poets, whose philosophy is not at all certain, were Thales of Miletus and Pythagoras, unless both of them perhaps were pupils of Pherecydes of Syros.[3] They lived at least 550 years before the birth of Christ. Pythagoras founded the Sicilian

---

1. The primary source in the ancient world for the origin of philosophy and the lives of the philosophers was written in the third century A.D. by Diogenes Laertius, *Lives of Eminent Philosophers*. This work provided material for the more comprehensive histories of ancient philosophy composed by Thomas Stanley, *The History of Philosophy: Containing the Lives, Opinions, Actions and Discourses of the Philosophers of Every Sect,* and Johann Jakob Brucker, *Historia Critica Philosophiae.* (Brucker's work was recast in English by William Enfield as *The History of Philosophy from the Earliest Times to the Beginning of the Present Century: Drawn up from Brucker's Historia Critica Philosophiae;* page references are from the 1819 edition.) Hutcheson's brief account of the origin of philosophy appears to be digested mainly from these three sources, supplemented by the preface to Henry Aldrich, *Artis Logicae Compendium:* see below, note 9 and especially note 15.

2. Brucker's *Historia,* vol. 1, bk. 1 (Enfield, pp. 43–95) was devoted to the philosophy of the Chaldeans, Indians, Egyptians, and others.

3. Diogenes Laertius, *Lives,* I, pp. 23–47, 121–29.

sect, and Thales founded the Ionian sect about the beginning of Cyrus's reign, before the return of the Jews from Babylon to their homeland.

I. The Italian Sect.[4] Pythagoras developed geometry, arithmetic, astronomy, music, ethics, and theology. He wished to be called not wise (*sophos*) but a lover of wisdom (*philosophos*). His modesty in this has been imitated by all subsequent students of wisdom. At Croton in Italy he started a school or community. He taught that there is one supreme God, who is of a nature or substance different from matter, and he believed that men's minds are also of this nature. By his teaching and example he commended the highest piety toward God and goodness toward men, as well as a temperance which would liberate men's minds from the chains of the body. This school flourished for a long time among the Italians and the Greeks. Pythagoras's successor was his son, Telauges; then Empedocles, the inventor of rhetoric; and Xenophanes; and after these, Parmenides and Leucippus. Following them came Zeno of Elea in Italy, the inventor of dialectic; Socrates was his pupil who approved the practice of arguing by questions after his example. From this school came also Democritus and Heraclitus.

II. The Ionian Sect. Thales opened a school at Miletus. Little evidence remains of him, but his successors were Anaximander, Anaximenes, Anaxagoras, and Archelaus, the last of whom is famous for his disciple Socrates.[5] They particularly cultivated geometry, astronomy and the whole of physics. The rest are more unsympathetic to religion, but the excellent Anaxagoras, who was called "the Mind," held that the whole frame and structure of the world was made by the divine mind and reason.

III. The restorer or founder of true philosophy was Socrates, born at Athens to his father Sophroniscus in the time of Darius Nothus, in the period

---

4. Diogenes Laertius, *Lives,* II, pp. 321–463. Stanley, *History,* narrates the lives and opinions of Pythagoras and other members of "the Italick Sect," pp. 346–469. Hutcheson's unusual account of Pythagoras's religious beliefs is also found in Ephraim Chambers, *Cyclopedia,* s.v. "Pythagoras."

5. Diogenes Laertius, *Lives,* I, pp. 131–49, for this succession of philosophers; also Stanley, *History,* pp. 60–73.

before Philip of Macedon in human reckoning, and four centuries before the birth of Christ. This truly divine man turned his penetrating mind away from corporeal and hidden things, which contribute little to a happy life, and gave himself completely to the cultivation of true piety and the knowledge of God, and to every virtue. Particularly conversant with ethics, politics, and economics, he taught that the minds of men are immortal and that their excellence consists in being as like to God as possible, and that after death men will be happy or miserable according as they have given themselves in this life to virtue or to vice.[6]

IV. His disciples founded various sects.[7]

1. Aristippus, who was very different from his master, held that the highest good lies in the pleasure of the body. He started the Cyrenaic school in Egypt; his daughter Arete succeeded him, and she was followed by Aristippus Metrodidaktos, and then by Antipater, Theodorus the atheist, Epitemides, and some others who made many innovations, especially Hegesias.

2. Phaedo, the founder of the Elean sect, taught that virtue is the sole good. He too had a number of successors,

3. Euclides, to whom we owe the Megarian sect, which was the most contentious of all, because it was solely dedicated to dialectic, as a result of which they are called the "wranglers" and "dialecticians."[8]

4. Antisthenes opened his school near the gates of the city, in a Gymnasium at Cynosarges, and it is because of this, and not because of their morals, that they are called Cynics.[9] His successors were Diogenes the Cynic and Crates of Thebes; everyone knows of their harsh and boorish style of life. Zeno of Citium in Cyprus was a pupil of Crates; later in life he taught in

6. Stanley, *History,* pp. 77–78, drawing upon texts of Plato, Plutarch, and Xenophon, underlines the piety of Socrates and his belief in the immortality of the soul.

7. Diogenes Laertius, *Lives,* I, pp. 195–233, provides a narrative of the lives and opinions of Aristippus, Theodorus, and Hegesias. Stanley rehearsed this account under the headings of the Cyrenaic, Megaric, and Eleatic sects in *History,* pp. 132–53.

8. "Eristici" and "elenctici."

9. Stanley, *History,* p. 277 ff.; Aldrich, *Artis Logicae Compendium,* preface, sec. 6, explains the origin of the term "cynic" in the same manner as Hutcheson.

the Stoa ("Porch") of Pisianax, and so gave the Stoics their name.[10] The
Stoics developed logic in their own way; in ethics and politics they really
followed Socrates, but with some change of terms. Notable Stoics include
Cleanthes and Chrysippus. Epicurus flourished in the time of Zeno the
Stoic, about 250 years before the birth of Christ. He started a new school;
in ethics he agreed with Aristippus, though he coined new terms to avoid
jealousy, while in physics he followed Democritus. His successors were Her-
machus, Polystratus, and others.[11]

5. Most eminent among the pupils of Socrates is Plato of Athens, a man
of altogether divine genius, who has no rivals in the cultivation of every
elegance; he founded the Old Academy.

V. The Old, the Middle, and the New Academy. Plato and Xenophon, who
were very worthy pupils of their master Socrates made outstanding ad-
vances in theology, ethics, and politics. The pupils of Plato were called
Academics from the charming park of a certain Academus in which they
used to hold their discussions. The successors of Plato were Speusippus,
Xenocrates, Polemo, Crantor, Crates, Arcesilaus (the founder of the Middle Academy, which differed from the Old Academy only in logic, that is,
over the limitations of the human understanding in discovering truth),
Lasydes, Evander, Egesinus, and Carneades, the father of the New Academy, which veered more toward the Skeptics; he was succeeded by Clito-
machus and others.[12]

VI. The Peripatetics. Outstanding among the disciples of Plato was Aristotle, who was born at Stagira, a town of Macedonia, and was given charge
of the education of Alexander the Great. Because he opened his school in

10. Stanley, *History,* p. 293 ff., and Brucker, *Historia,* II, p. 531 ff. (Enfield, I, p. 296)
treat the Stoics as successors to the Cynics. It is remarkable that no reference is made by
Hutcheson to the Stoic philosophers whom he most admired: Epictetus (in the gloss by
Simplicius) and Marcus Aurelius.
    11. Diogenes Laertius, *Lives,* II, p. 528 ff., and Stanley, *History,* pp. 533–633.
    12. Stanley, *History,* pp. 154–55, identified the same members of the Old, the Middle,
and the New Academy. This succession of names derives from Diogenes Laertius, *Lives,*
I, pp. 375–444.

the Peripatos, or covered walk, of the Lyceum, his followers are called the Peripatetics. They differed very little from Plato in ethics or theology, but were rather more distinct in metaphysics and politics. Aristotle wrote famous books over virtually the whole range of philosophy, and constructed the entire system of the art of logic with supreme skill. He was succeeded by Tyrtamus, to whom he gave the name of Theophrastus because of his godlike eloquence. *His* successors were Strato, Lyco, Aristo, Critolaus, Diodorus,[13] and others; the eleventh in succession from Aristotle was Andronicus of Rhodes, who arranged the books of the philosopher in the order in which we now have them; in his time Cicero's son was a student of Cratippus at Athens. In the period immediately following Aristotle there flourished Pyrrho, the father of the Skeptics, an assailant of all philosophy, who taught that all things are equally unknown and uncertain.[14]

VII. About 140 A.D. flourished Galen, the first of the commentators. The *floruit* of Porphyrius is 325. In 525 Boethius was born: he was the first to translate Aristotle's Logic into Latin. 614: John Philoponus the grammarian. 800: John of Damascus. 1000: Eustathius and Eustratius. 1100: Michael of Ephesus and Michael Psellus. 1200: George Pachymerus. In these same times the Arabs Alfarabius, Avicenna, and Averroes won a great reputation. Then followed the age of the Scholastics, whose thorny and uncouth philosophy retained its influence until 1453, when after the capture of Constantinople by the Turks, the literary heritage of the Greeks was brought over to the West.[15]

VIII. The Eclectics.[16] Although the best of the ancients, Pythagoras, Socrates, Plato, Aristotle, etc., are rightly included among the Eclectics because

---

13. See Stanley, *History,* pp. 269–76.

14. Hutcheson's perfunctory dismissal of Pyrrho and the Skeptics stands in marked contrast with the extensive discussion of Skeptical modes of argument, in Stanley, *History,* pp. 475–532.

15. This paragraph and its curious chronology derive from Aldrich, *Artis Logicae Compendium,* preface, secs. 9, 10, and 12.

16. There is no discussion of the Eclectics in Stanley's *History.* But Brucker wrote at length on "the Eclectic Sect" in *Historia,* II, pp. 189–462 (Enfield, II, pp. 59–101) and

they were not enslaved to any master but adopted the views that seemed to them to be closest to the truth, the term "eclectic" was especially given to those who, after the formation of the different schools, refused to join any one of them. We note Potamon of Egypt, who flourished about the time of Augustus and was imitated by the philosophers of Alexandria, though they leaned more toward the views of Plato; some of them were pagan, others Christian. [They include] from the third and fourth centuries, Ammonius, Plotinus, Clement of Alexandria, Origen, Porphyry, Iamblichus, Syrianus, and Olympiodorus. With the revival of humane letters in the West, philosophy too was improved, especially through the strenuous efforts of those who have earned the gratitude of the human race by editing and interpreting the books of the ancients. With great acclaim, however, [moderns] have pointed out or entered upon a new road: in physics, Bacon, Descartes, Kepler, Galileo, and Newton; in ethics Grotius, Cumberland, and Pufendorf (for it was the Old Academy that was revived by Mirandula, Ficino, and the Earl of Shaftesbury); and Locke in logic and metaphysics.

---

included among the Eclectics those modern philosophers to whom Hutcheson alludes in his final sentence. Eclecticism in modern philosophy meant for Brucker concentration on the facts of nature rather than on the authority of philosophical sects: *Historia,* V, pp. 4–6.

Prolegomena
The Definitions and Divisions of Logic

A faculty (*habitus*) is a more or less efficacious ability (*facultas*) to act, formed by repeated actions. Faculties are either intellectual or moral: the former strengthen and perfect the powers of the intellect, the latter the powers of the will.

There are five distinct names (they are not distinct kinds) given to our intellectual faculties: intelligence, wisdom, prudence, science, and skill, which in Greek are: *nous, sophia, phronesis, episteme, techne.*[1] Intelligence is the faculty of first principles. Wisdom is knowledge of the most excellent things. Prudence is the faculty of acting with right reason. Science is the faculty of demonstration. Skill is the faculty of producing things with right reason. Philosophy is the whole bundle of these liberal arts, and is commonly defined as "acquisition of the knowledge (*cognitio*) of human and divine things, which we pursue by the sole power of human reason." Philosophy is frequently divided into rational philosophy (or logic), natural philosophy, and moral philosophy.[2] Logic is the art which directs the mind in its acquisition of knowledge of things, and may also be called science (*scientia*).[3] Others define it as "the art of investigating and expressing truth."[4] The material object of any skill or science is the material which it

---

1. These were the names given by Aristotle to the intellectual or rational part of the soul in *Nichomachean Ethics,* bk. 6, chaps. 3–7.

2. This division of philosophy was reflected in the curriculum and in the distribution of professorships in the University of Glasgow and in other Scottish universities. See Coutts, *History of the University of Glasgow,* pp. 207–8. Hutcheson considered it "the accepted division" in antiquity; see *A Synopsis of Metaphysics,* Part I, chap. 1, p. 65.

3. Burgersdijk, *Monitio Logica,* p. 1; Aldrich, *Artis Logicae Compendium,* p. 3.

4. Le Clerc, *Logica,* p. 1; Watts, "Logick," p. 5.

treats. The formal object is the reason or purpose of treating it. The material object of logic is the intellectual operations. The formal object is to be directed to the discovery of truth. There are two natural faculties of the mind, the understanding and the will. The understanding is the faculty (*facultas*) which is concerned with getting to know the truth. The will is the faculty (*facultas*) which seeks good and avoids evil.[5]

There are three classes of operations in the intellect: (1) apprehension, (2) judgment, and (3) discourse; a twofold division into apprehension and judgment is also possible. Judgments are subdivided into noetic and dianoetic judgments. Hence logic is divided into three parts, defined by the kind of operation each is dealing with.[6]

---

5. On Hutcheson's insistence on the scholastic distinction between understanding and will, see *A Synopsis of Metaphysics,* Part II, chap. 1, p. 112 and n. 4.

6. The tripartite division of logic into apprehension, judgment, and discourse is characteristic of the logics of the seventeenth-century English Aristotelians (Robert Sanderson, Henry Aldrich), who also make it clear that these divisions of logic refer to terms, propositions, and syllogisms. The same division of the subject was employed in logics based on ideas (by Arnauld, Le Clerc, and Watts). But all of the latter also attached importance to a fourth part of logic, which they called method. Hutcheson's logic drew upon both traditions: initially upon the logic of ideas, and later, and more substantially, on the logic of the Aristotelians. His discussion of method was located, with topics and fallacies, in an appendix: see p. 54.

PART I

On Apprehension

CHAPTER I

On the Divisions of Apprehension

Apprehension is also called perception, concept, notion, intention,[1] and idea; the word which signifies it is called a term.

Apprehension is a bare representation of a thing without any opinion (*sententia*) of the mind, and is either noncomplex, for instance pen, or complex, for instance, pen in the hand.

Judgment is an act of the mind by which it forms an opinion about two ideas. The sign [of a judgment] is a proposition or expression, which is an utterance that affirms or denies something of something; it is also called predication.

Discourse is an act of the mind by which from two or more judgments a third is inferred.

1. Ideas are divided into sensations, imaginations, and pure intellections.[2]

Sensation is twofold, external and internal. External sensation is "the perception of a corporeal thing impacting the organs of the body."

---

1. Hutcheson followed John Loudon, "Logica," closely in this chapter. Loudon had written (dictated) under "Apprehension" that "first, the operations of the mind are said to be ideas or notions, perceptions, intentions." Loudon was responding (like Antoine Arnauld in *The Art of Thinking* and Nicholas Malebranche in *The Search After Truth*) to the skeptical and Epicurean logic of Pierre Gassendi, *Institutio Logicae,* for whom the first operation of the mind was "simple imagination" or "conception, apprehension, intellection, notion": p. 3 (Latin), p. 83 (English).

2. Loudon, "Logica," p. 2: "On the division of ideas into sensations, imaginations, and pure intellections."

Imagination is "the idea of a corporeal thing which is not impacting the body."

A pure intellection is "any idea which is not reached or grasped by any of the bodily senses." By intellection we not only discern things which are different from body as well as their modes, but we also attain more accurate ideas of numbers and of shapes which have several parts than those which the senses provide.[3]

The powers of bodies to excite ideas of "colors, sounds, smells, tastes, heat and cold" are called secondary qualities, or qualities which are sensible in the proper sense that we perceive each of them only by a single sense. Things which are perceived by more than one sense, by both sight and touch, for example, such as extension, figure, position, motion and rest, are primary and true qualities of bodies; hence they have the power to excite ideas of secondary qualities to which there is nothing corresponding in the bodies themselves. There are also two ideas which can be perceived both by internal and by external sense, and these are duration and number.

2. Imagination calls up a rather weak idea of a thing that had been formerly perceived by sense. And the mind can form only images whose elements have all been perceived by sense.

3. There is also an internal sense which above all furnishes pure intellections; this is called consciousness (*conscientia*) or the power of reflection. This sense affects all the actions, passions, and modes of the mind: namely, judgment, discourse, certainty, doubt, joy, sorrow, desires, aversions, love and hatred, virtues, vices. The more precise and abstract ideas of primary qualities are also attributed to pure intellections. But in truth all ideas arise from reflection or from [an] external sense.[4]

3. In opposition to the arguments of Gassendi (and Hobbes), who derived all ideas from the senses and the imagination, Arnauld, in *The Art of Thinking,* pt. 1, chap. 1, p. 32 ff., maintained that "as soon as we reflect on what occurs in the mind we recognize the difference between imagination and pure intellection." And Malebranche argued that sensation and imagination are only modifications of thought or pure intellect (*The Search After Truth,* bk. 3). John Loudon, in "Logica," included among ideas of pure intellect all ideas of spiritual things, of affirmation and negation, of truth and virtue.

4. Hutcheson's theory that ideas of pure intellect are generated by internal sensation and therefore include ideas of beauty and virtue, and other concomitant ideas, as de-

CHAPTER 2[5]

1. Ideas are either clear or obscure: a clear idea is one which "vividly affects the mind"; an obscure idea is one which affects the mind faintly.

2. Ideas may be proper [ideas] and truly depict the thing put before it or at least represent the appearance (*speciem*) which nature commonly intended; or they may be analogical [ideas] and exhibit a kind of general and imperfect impression of a thing, not as it is in itself or as it is represented in the common order of nature, but by a kind of analogy with other, very different things which are known by proper ideas. Those who have the use of sight have a proper idea of sight; a blind man has an analogous idea, but he does still have some kind of useful notion of this faculty.

3. Ideas are either simple or complex; a simple idea is a kind of uniform representation not made up of parts that are different from each other.

A complex idea is one "which is made up of dissimilar parts into which it can also be resolved."

The idea of being is the simplest [idea]; ideas of secondary qualities are also mostly simple, as well as abstract ideas of certain modes of thinking.

4. In respect of their names, ideas are either distinct or confused. A distinct idea is one "which is easily told apart from others." A confused idea is one "which is not easily told apart from others from which it is thought to be different."

But perhaps more correctly the name itself or the term which denotes the idea is said to be distinct "when a known and certain complex of ideas is bound together by a name which cannot be altered without our being aware of it"; it is confused when "that complex is not sufficiently certain, so that

---

scribed in his *Inquiry* (1725) and *Essay* (1728), constitutes the principal point of connection between his logic and his writings on aesthetics and morals. For his proposal that ideas of internal sensation should be considered ideas of reflection, as Locke understood them: see *A Synopsis of Metaphysics,* Part II, chap. 1, p. 115, n. 9.

5. The types of ideas distinguished in this chapter derive primarily from Locke, *Essay,* bk. 2, chaps. 29, 30, 31, and 32. See also Le Clerc, *Logica,* pt. 1, chaps. 9 and 10, pp. 36–43; and Loudon, "Logica," p. 27 ff.

something may at some point be added or removed [from it] without our noticing."

5. In respect of their objects, ideas are either of substances or of modes, or of substances together with their modes. A substance is "a being subsisting in itself." A mode is "a being which inheres in another [being]."

6. Ideas likewise may be real (or true), or they may be fictitious. Real ideas are "ideas which have corresponding objects," or [ideas] which arise from natural causes following the order of nature. Fictitious [ideas] are "arbitrary conjunctions of ideas not drawn from true things."

7. Ideas are either adequate or inadequate. Adequate ideas are those "which represent the whole nature of an object," or at least all of it that we want to conceive in our minds. Such are the complex or combined ideas of modes which the mind assembles in an arbitrary fashion without referring them to an external model; also ideas of modes of thinking or of states of mind. Our ideas of substances are all inadequate.

CHAPTER 3

Abstraction is "the act of the mind by which it directs itself to one or some of the ideas which are contained in a complex [idea] and ignores the rest." Abstract ideas are ideas which are denoted by names or symbols that signify several things that are similar to each other but which also have some evident differences.[6]

After the mind has observed a variety of things that give rise to various complex ideas, and has seen that they are alike in certain qualities and unlike in others, it forms a universal idea by abstracting itself from the points in which they differ, while retaining the ideas of the points in which they are alike, and by denoting them with a specific name. This is how the eighth distinction between ideas arises, that some are universal and others singular.

6. On abstraction, and on the application of knowledge by abstraction to universal ideas, see Arnauld, *The Art of Thinking,* pt. 1, chaps. 5 and 6; Locke, *Essay,* bk. 2, chap. 12, pp. 163–66; Le Clerc, *Logica,* pt. 1, chaps. 6 and 7, pp. 25–36; and Loudon, "Logica," pp. 9–11.

A singular idea is an idea "which is intended to represent one thing alone" and is denoted either by a proper noun, like Alexander the Great, or by a common noun applied to one man, for example, this man or that man.

A universal idea is an idea "which is suitable for representing several things individually" whose sign (which is a common noun) can be predicated distributively of individuals, as man [can be predicated] of Peter, Paul, etc.

Nouns which denote a collection [of things], or one thing which is an aggregate of several things, are not properly predicated of individuals and often denote singular complex ideas. Examples are the city of Rome, Alexander's army, the human race, the world.

Complex ideas are said to have comprehension, which "is a collection of all the simpler ideas which are combined in the complex," for example, in animal [are contained the ideas of] body, living, and sentient.

Universal ideas are said to have extension, or quantity, which is "a collection of objects which an idea can represent, or [objects] the word for which is predicable individually."

From what has been said about abstraction, it will be clear that the greater the extension, the less the comprehension, and *vice versa*.

CHAPTER 4[7]

A universal idea or predicable word has five species: genus, species, *differentia,* property, and accident.[8] They are defined with regard either to ideas or to terms as follows:

7. This is where chapter 4 began in Hutcheson's "Logica," p. 7. There was no chapter 4 in the published version of Hutcheson's *Logicae Compendium.*

8. These were the five predicables distinguished by Porphyry in his Isagoge or introduction to the logic of Aristotle. See Aristotle, *The Organon, or Logical Treatises of Aristotle with the Introduction of Porphyry,* vol. 2, pp. 609–33. Hutcheson's table, which describes the parallels between the predicables considered as ideas and as terms, appears to have drawn upon Arnauld, *The Art of Thinking,* pt. 1, chap. 7, pp. 52–59 (for the predicables as ideas) and Henry Aldrich, *Artis Logicae Compendium,* bk. 1, chap. 1, sec. 5, p. 5 (for the predicables considered as terms).

With respect to ideas	*With respect to terms*
1. A genus is a universal idea representing an object as a thing, which extends to other universal ideas.	1. A genus is a [word] predicable of several things which differ in kind (*specie*) in some respect (*in quid*) "or as a material part of the essence, as animal of man and brute."
2. A species is "a universal idea representing a thing, which is subordinate to a more general idea," or [an idea] which applies only to individual things.	2. A species is "a [word] predicable of several things which are numerically different in some respect (*in quid*)," or as the total essence, as man [is predicable] of Peter and Paul.

The highest genus is [the genus] "which does not have a more general genus above it," for example, being. A subaltern is one "which can be a species with respect to a more general [genus]."

The lowest species is [the species] "which covers individuals alone"; a subaltern species can be a genus.

3. A *differentia* is "a universal idea which represents a thing modified by an essential primary attribute," i.e., [an idea] which divides a genus into species, and combines with a genus to constitute a species.	3. A *differentia* is "a [word] predicable of several things that differ in species or number, in respect of some quality (*in Quale Quid*)" or as a formal part of the essence; for when it is added to a genus it completes the essence of a species and its definition.
4. A property is the "universal idea of a thing modified by an essential secondary attribute," that is, [an attribute] which is contained in the idea of the thing not formally but as a consequence; for instance, being subject to law is a property of man.	4. A property is "a [word] predicable of several things in respect of a quality necessarily" (*in Quale necessario*), that is, [an attribute] which belongs to this species, and only this species, and the whole of this species, at all times, or as bound up with its essence.
5. An accident is "the universal idea of a thing modified by a true/true mode," that is, [a mode] which may be either present or absent.	5. An accident is "a [word] predicable of several things in respect of a quality contingently" (*in Quale contingenter*).

CHAPTER 5

A genus is said to be a logical whole or universal with respect to its species which are logical parts in the division of it. On the other hand a species is said to be a metaphysical whole, with respect to its genus and its differentia, which are metaphysical parts of its essence, but is said to be a physical whole with respect to its integrating parts. For example, (1) animal is the logical whole with respect to man and the brutes; (2) man is the metaphysical whole, or formal [whole], with respect to that which is animal and rational; (3) man is the physical or integral whole with respect to body and soul. The human body is also the integral whole with respect to head, chest, abdomen, limbs, etc., which are the integrating parts.[9]

N.B. Abstract, absolute, or denominating names of true modes, as well as abstract ideas themselves, may be either genera or species when they represent objects as things, without any distinct or direct idea of the subject, for instance, justice, virtue, and their opposites; true substances regarded as appendices of other things, and their concrete and connotative names, may be *differentiae*, properties, or accidents, for example, golden, silvery, clothed, shod.

CHAPTER 6

A logical whole, or the extension of an idea, is expressed by a division, which is "the enumeration of the several things contained in the extension of a common idea or name." These are its rules:

1. "The parts should be so distinct that no single one contains within its own [extension] the extension or part of the extension of another [part]."

2. "The division should be made into the species immediately below."

---

9. In the logic of the Aristotelian scholastics, where every whole was explained by the manner in which parts participate in the whole, the tripartite division followed by Hutcheson was sometimes expressed by the terms universal (logical), essential (metaphysical), and integral (physical). See Robert Sanderson, *Logicae Artis Compendium*, I, 8, pp. 62–64; Franco Burgersdijk, *Monitio Logica* (an abstract in translation of *Institutiones Logicae*), I, 14, pp. 43–48; and Aldrich, *Artis Logicae Compendium*, I, 1, 5, p. 5.

3. "The parts should exhaust the thing divided"; or the division should be adequate.

CHAPTER 7

A metaphysical whole, or the comprehension of a complex idea, is expressed by a definition, which is "a statement which explicates the simpler ideas that are combined in a complex [idea]." There are other definitions which are improper, for instance, nominal [definition], which explicates a word, as *coelum* ("sky"), which is from [Greek] *koilon* ("hollow"). There is also accidental definition, which explicates modes, causes [and] effects. For example, man is an animal which is featherless, biped, erect, etc.; this constitutes a description. [And] there is physical definition, which explicates natural parts; for instance, man is an animal consisting of an organic body and a soul endowed with reason.

The rules [of definition] are:

1. "Definitions should be short."

2. "They should be clear."

3. "They should be adequate," so that they may be reciprocating, i.e., so that the definition and the thing defined may be mutually predicated of each other distributively.

4. "Avoid metaphors."

5. "They should consist of the nearest genus and the proper *differentia*."[10]

Categories or predicaments are "a series of ideas or terms arranged by degrees (*gradatim*) under the same highest genus." Different authorities give different categories. For Aristotle there are ten: substance, quantity, quality, relation, action, passion, place, time, position, and state.[11] He means that every predication or affirmation may be reduced to one of these. If we explain one, the rest will be understood.

---

10. See Sanderson, *Logicae Artis Compendium,* I, 17, pp. 59–60.
11. See Aristotle, *Organon,* II, pp. 636–39, and *A Synopsis of Metaphysics,* Part I, chap. 5, pp. 101–10, for an extended discussion of Aristotle's categories.

These are the substances:[12]

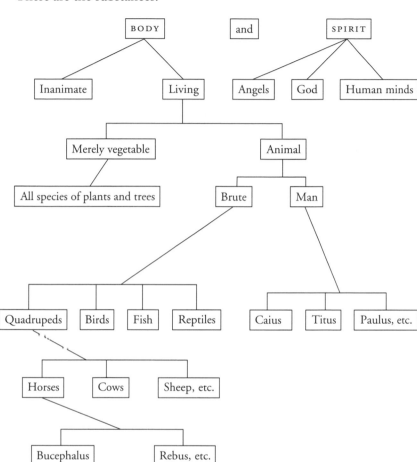

Hence also that of which something is affirmed or denied in any category should be called a subject.

CHAPTER 8

A term is "a name which signifies an idea or a thing, and which can be the subject or predicate of a proposition"; hence it is called a predicable (*categorema*).

12. This illustration of the various forms of substance is "the tree of Porphyry" (*Arbor Porphyriana*): see Aldrich, *Artis Logicae Compendium,* II, 1, 2, p. 36.

Other components of terms are jointly predicable (*syncategoremata*), such as all, no. Some are mixed, such as always, i.e., in all time; no one, i.e., no man; [he] runs, [he] is running.[13]

An intention of signifying, or the understanding (*acceptio*) of a word, is called a *suppositio*. When it stands for an idea or a thing, it is called a formal *suppositio;* when it stands for the uttered word itself, it is called a material *suppositio.*

An example of the former is saying, Man is an animal; an example of the latter is, Man is a monosyllable. In a formal *suppositio,* the name is sometimes of the first intention, or of personal supposition, that is, in a normal act of understanding (*acceptio*): as in the phrase, Man is an animal. Otherwise it is of the second intention, or of simple *suppositio* for the idea or the term, that is, when a term of art (*aliquid artificiale*) is used of the same thing, for example, Man is a species.[14]

The divisions of terms into universal and singular, abstract and concrete, are evident from the divisions of ideas.

A transcendent term is one which belongs to every real thing, such as being, thing, one, something. A supertranscendent term is one which also belongs to fictions, such as imaginable, possible. All other terms are non-transcendental.

Every term where "not" is absent is finite; where the particle "not" is present, it is infinite, as in not-man, not-learned. "Not" is said to be *infinitans.* Finite and infinite [terms] together comprehend every being disjunctively: every being is either learned or not-learned, and so on; they exhaust the whole range of being.

A univocal term is "predicable of several things individually according to the same idea," as animal [is predicable] of man and of beast.

An equivocal term is "predicable of several things individually according to different ideas," like *Gallus.* "Where there is some underlying reason for it or affinity of meaning," a term is said to be analogous or deliberately equivocal, as [when] healthy [is predicated] of animal and of food, or Al-

---

13. See Aldrich, *Artis Logicae Compendium,* I, 1, 3, pp. 3–4.
14. See Sanderson, *Logicae Artis Compendium,* II, 2, pp. 75–82.

exander of a man and of a picture. When there is no reason, it is said to be equivocal by chance, like *Gallus* or (in English) *canon.* [15]

CHAPTER 9

Compatible terms may be predicated of one and the same thing at the same time, like *strong* and *pious;* they are often disparate.

Conflicting or opposed terms [are those] which "cannot be predicated of each other, nor of the same thing, in the same respect, and at the same time." This opposition of terms is noncomplex; the opposition of propositions, on the other hand, is said to be complex. [16]

There are four species of noncomplex opposition: contrary, contradictory, relatively opposed, and privatively opposed. Disparates do not conflict (*pugnant*), for they are "terms denoting ideas in which there is very little or nothing in common, beyond the vague idea of being or of mode," as in *brave* and *tall* or *sweet* and *white.*

Contraries are "true opposed qualities," such as *pain* and *pleasure.*

Contradictories are "a word and its negation," such as *learned* and *not-learned* or *man* and *not-man.*

Relatively opposed are relative terms, such as *father* and *son.*

Privatively opposed are "a quality and its absence in a subject which has the capacity for it," as in *sighted* and *blind* in the case of an animal.

Negatively opposed are "a quality and its absence in any kind of subject," as in *sighted* and *nonsighted,* which are also contradictories.

15. See Sanderson, *Logicae Artis Compendium,* I, 8, pp. 26–27, and Aldrich, *Artis Logicae Compendium,* I, 1, 3, p. 4.

16. See Sanderson, *Logicae Artis Compendium,* I, 15, pp. 51–54.

On the Noetic Judgment and the Proposition

CHAPTER I

A judgment is "an action of the mind by which it gives a verdict on two ideas in comparison with each other." That is, a verdict is given that either the ideas represent the same object, or a certain relation or connection exists between their objects.[1]

A noetic judgment is "when a verdict is given about ideas which are being directly compared with each other."

A dianoetic judgment is "a verdict of the mind about two ideas, by means of comparison of both with a third."[2]

A proposition is "a statement which expresses a noetic judgment." There are three parts to it: subject, predicate, and copula.

The subject is "that about which something is affirmed or denied." The predicate is "that which is affirmed or denied." The copula is the logical verb (*verbum*), *is* or *is-not*.

N.B. Subjects and predicates are distinguished not by their position but by the sequence of speech. These three parts are always present, either explicitly or suppressed and implied: for example, curro ["I-run"] = *ego sum currens* ["I am running"].

---

1. Compare Carmichael, "A Short Introduction to Logic," in *Natural Rights,* p. 298, who had employed the same language in his definition of judgment.

2. The distinction between noetic and dianoetic judgments was made by Loudon, "Compendium Logicae," p. 51. Carmichael, "Short Introduction," p. 304, made a similar distinction between immediate judgment, in which two ideas are compared, and mediate judgment, which requires the intervention of a third idea.

CHAPTER 2

In respect of their internal form or quality, propositions, like judgments, are either affirmative or negative.[3]

In respect of their content, propositions are either true or false. Every [proposition] is either true or false; no [proposition] is both true and false; and there are no [propositions] which change from true to false, if we look at the judgment itself and not at the words. Those which seem to be both true and false are double or denote two judgments. Those which seem to change are likewise double; this is obvious from the nature of the word, which is "a word which implies time." Hence, when the same words are uttered at different times, they sometimes give rise to quite different propositions.

Logical truth is "the agreement (*convenientia*) of the signs with the things signified." Moral truth is "the agreement of the signs with the sense of the mind"; it belongs to the ethical forum.

With regard to quantity, propositions are universal, particular, singular, or indefinite.

1. A universal proposition is "when the subject is a universal term in its whole extension," or is distributed.

2. A particular proposition is one "whose common subject is restricted to a part of its extension," or is not distributed.

The marks of distribution or universality are *all, no, each,* etc. Notes of particularity are *someone, a certain, not every,* etc.

3. A singular proposition is one "whose subject is singular or individual," i.e., [a subject] which, not having a divisible extension, is understood of the whole; the same rules apply to singulars as to universals.

---

3. In this chapter, Hutcheson followed Loudon's classification of noetic judgments or propositions, set out in "Compendium Logicae." He did not reiterate Loudon's illustrations, which were designed to reinforce Presbyterian orthodoxy: for instance, as an example of an affirmative proposition, "a sincerely pious life leads to beatitude"; of a negative proposition, "a disgraceful life does not lead to beatitude" (pp. 18–19).

4. An indefinite proposition is "when a common subject is not modified by any mark of quantity." In the sense of the speaker, however, it is always either universal or particular. For example, *men are animals* is universal; *men are learned* is particular; it depends whether the content is necessary or contingent.

We need only look at two of these kinds, namely universal and particular, because the others come under the same rules.

From the different combinations of quality and quantity, four classes of propositions arise, which are indicated by well-known symbols.

A asserts, E denies, and both generally.
I asserts, O denies, but both particularly.[4]

In respect of substance, propositions are either categorical or hypothetical. A categorical [proposition] "indicates something absolutely." A hypothetical proposition "indicates something subject to a condition."

The [following] divisions show the responses to the most frequent questions about propositions.

What [proposition]? Categorical or hypothetical. What sort of [proposition]? Negative or affirmative. What quantity of [proposition]? Universal, particular, indefinite, singular.

CHAPTER 3

Axioms about the quantity of terms:

1. "In every affirmative proposition the predicate is taken particularly," and it is not also required that it be true.

---

4. The symbols (A, E, I, O) employed to denote the four classes of propositions are described by James Clow, "A System of Logic," as "a Distich invented by the Schoolmen," p. 140. See also W. and M. Kneale, *The Development of Logic,* p. 56: "the vowels by which the four types have been distinguished since the Middle Ages [formed] no part of Aristotle's work." These symbols were widely used by logicians in the early modern period to illustrate the four figures of the syllogism. See Part III, chap. 5, p. 37.

2. "In a negative proposition the predicate is taken universally" or is distributed, for a negation is understood to be false if any part of the predicate may be truly affirmed of the subject.

3. The quantity of subjects is understood from the signs prefixed [to them]. Hence in A, the subject is universal, and the predicate is particular. In E, both are universal. In I, both are particular. In O, the subject is particular, and the predicate is universal.

Only those propositions are said to be universal in which the subject is distributed, and a predicate is affirmed or denied of the individual things which are covered by the common word. This is not the case when the predicate is [made up] of several [things] collectively: thus, *All men are mortal* is universal, but not the following: All men form one state; all the apostles were twelve.

Propositions about kinds of individuals are in a certain sense universal; e.g., Every animal was in Noah's ark, or, the Gospel has been preached to men of all nations.

Here it is said that certain individuals of each kind were in the ark or have heard the Gospel, but these things are not predicated separately of every individual or of each individual in the kinds.

CHAPTER 4

These are the axioms about universals:

1. "Whatever is affirmed of a distributed subject (that is, [of a subject] universally taken) may be affirmed of all the inferiors which are contained in its extension."

2. "Whatever is denied of a distributed subject can equally be denied of all its inferiors." These two in combination are the *dictum de omni et nullo;* on this depend both subalternation and the force of the syllogism, which we shall discuss later.[5]

---

5. The *dictum de omni et nullo* (the saying concerning all and none) derives via scholastic logicians from Aristotle, "The Prior Analytics," I, 1, 7, analyzed in *Organon,* II,

CHAPTER 5

Some propositions are simple, others complex; simple [propositions] "denote one single judgment"; complex [propositions] "denote more than one judgment."

Among complex propositions, the modal propositions are preeminent [which are] "when something is both predicated and the mode of its connection with the subject is made clear." There are four modes: the necessary, the impossible, the possible, and the contingent.[6] But generally modal [propositions] are simple [propositions], or signify a single judgment of a speaker. For they are ambiguous. Sometimes they merely affirm or deny the statement itself more emphatically, as in saying, "God most certainly exists" or "Certainly no man is immortal." Sometimes the proposition itself, which is called the statement, is the subject, and the mode is predicated of it, as in saying, "the Divine existence is necessary," or "God is, is a necessary proposition"; and similarly with the other modals.

In the same way it is shown that the four kinds [of modal propositions], which might appear from their names to be complex, are simple, namely: (1) conditional [propositions]; (2) disjunctive [propositions]; (3) negative copulative [propositions]; and (4) relative [propositions].

In a conditional or hypothetical [proposition] there are two parts, the antecedent and the consequent: for example, if God exists, the world is governed by providence. Neither of these is asserted; it is merely asserted that they are connected. Hence this [proposition] also is equally true: If there were no God, there would be no providence.

In disjunctive [propositions] the whole subject is said to be included in two connected predicates; for example, *it is either day or night* means the same as *all time is included in daytime and nighttime.*[7]

In negative copulative [propositions] it is denied that both the predicates

---

p. 649. It was used by Hutcheson to explain subalternation, II, 7, p. 29, and the reduction of syllogisms, III, 6, p. 41.

6. See Sanderson, *Logicae Artis Compendium,* II, 8, p. 103 ff.

7. See Sanderson, *Logicae Artis Compendium,* II, 10, pp. 112–16; Arnauld, *The Art of Thinking,* II, 9, pp. 128–34.

are compatible with the subject at the same time: it is not both day and night; i.e., no time is both daytime and nighttime.

In relative [propositions] the terms may be complex, but the judgment is single, namely, that the reasons (*rationes*) are equal or unequal.

The true complex propositions therefore are (1) copulative, (2) causal, (3) adversative, (4) exclusive, (5) inceptive, and (6) desitive;[8] and they are easy to learn.

CHAPTER 6

Some propositions or judgments are abstract, "in which from the comparison of ideas itself, there is seen or shown to be a relationship apart from any consideration of time"; hence they are said to be eternal and unalterable truths.

Other propositions are absolute; they assert that a thing is, was or will be at a certain time, or ascribe a common accident to it as existing at a certain time.

Abstract affirmative propositions, in which ideas are not only viewed in themselves but are related to objects, are all hypothetical and merely predicate attributes on the hypothesis that the thing exists. An absolute conclusion can only be deduced from absolute premisses, and abstract conclusions from abstract [premisses].

Other propositions are [self-]evident; here, by a power natural to the mind, "a certain relation or connection is perceived among the terms in themselves." Nor is there any other criterion of truth.[9] Other [propositions] are probable, when connection of that kind is not certain. And others are manifestly false.

---

8. These terms are explained in Arnauld, *The Art of Thinking*, II, 10, pp. 134–42: "Sentences stating that something commences are *inceptives;* those stating that something ceases are *desistives.*"

9. Carmichael, "A Short Introduction to Logic," chap. 2, sec. 7, in *Natural Rights,* pp. 302–3, provides a more ample discussion of *abstract, absolute hypothetical,* and *intuitive* propositions.

CHAPTER 7

The relative states (*affectiones*) of propositions are subalternation, conversion, and opposition.

1. Subalternation is "the deduction of a particular proposition from a universal [proposition]"; the former is called the subalternating [proposition], the latter the subalternated; for example, Every man is an animal, therefore, Some man is an animal. This is clear from the *dictum de omni.* "But from a particular to a universal [proposition] there is no inference."

2. Conversion is "the transposition of the subject into the place of the predicate." The given proposition is called the convertend, and the derived proposition the converse. And since every relation, likeness, or equality is mutual, the consequence will be valid provided that the same terms are used in the converse with the same extension and with the same temporal relation (*ratio*).

Conversion is threefold. It is either (i) *simpliciter,* "when the same quantity of propositions is kept". no A is B and no B is A; or (ii) it is *per accidens,* "when the convertend is universal and the converse is particular": as in, all A is B, some B is A; or (iii) by contraposition, "when the negations [of the terms] are put in the place of the terms and are transposed": as in, Every man is an animal, therefore, that which is not-animal is not-man.[10]

Universal negative and particular affirmative [propositions] are converted *simpliciter.* Universal affirmative [propositions], as well as [universal] negative [propositions], may be converted *per accidens;* and it is only in this way that [universal] affirmative [propositions] can [be converted], because their predicates are particular.

Universal affirmative [propositions] and particular negative [propositions] [can be converted] by contraposition: Some man is not European, therefore, some not-European is not a not-man, i.e., is a man.

---

10. On subalternation and conversion of propositions, see Sanderson, *Logicae Artis Compendium,* II, 7, pp. 100–103, and Aldrich, *Artis Logicae Compendium,* I, 2, pp. 10–12.

E and I are converted *simpliciter,* E or A *per accidens,*
A and O *per contra;* that's all there is to conversion.[11]

The value of these [conversions] lies in proving the validity of syllogisms, and in perfecting them.

3. Opposition of propositions is said to be complex. Opposed propositions are "two propositions which affirm and deny the same predicate about the same subject, in accordance with the same thing, in the same manner, at the same time."

There are three kinds of opposed [propositions], namely, contradictory, contrary, and subcontrary. Subaltern [propositions] do not conflict.

Contradictory [propositions] are those "of which one is universal, the other particular, one is affirmative, the other negative"; or which are opposed in quantity and quality, as, A and O, E and I.

Contrary [propositions] are "two universal [propositions], one affirmative, the other negative," which conflict in quality, not in quantity, like A and E.

Subcontrary [propositions] are "two particular [propositions], one affirmative, the other negative"; they too are in conflict by quality alone, like I and O. Since they are often both true at the same time, namely when they have contingent content, they are not truly opposed.

The rules of opposition are: (1) "of contradictories, one is always true, the other false"; this is the major opposition. (2) "Contraries are never at the same time true, but are sometimes both false at the same time," i.e., with contingent content. (3) "Subcontrary [propositions] are never false at the same time." If it is false that some man is learned, it will not be false that some man is not learned, since the contradictory of the former is true.[12]

---

11. The Latin is a mnemonic in two hexameter verses: "FEcɪ simpliciter convertitur, Ev A per accid./Ast O per contra; sic fit conversio tota." See Aldrich, *Artis Logicae Compendium,* I, 2, 5, p. 12, for a slightly modified form of these verses.

12. On contradictory, contrary, and subcontrary propositions, see Sanderson, *Logicae Artis Compendium,* I, 15, pp. 51–54, and Arnauld, *The Art of Thinking,* II, 4, pp. 113–14.

PART III

On Discourse

CHAPTER I

When the relation or connection of two ideas or terms cannot be directly perceived, the relation between them will often be able to be seen by a comparison of both of them with some third or middle [idea or term] or with several middle [ideas or terms] which are clearly connected with each other. This mental process is dianoetic judgment or discourse.

When there is only one middle, we are said to have a syllogism; when there are several middles connected with each other, by which the comparison of the terms is made, it is a sorites, or complex form of reasoning.[1] First, therefore, we must deal with the simple and categorical syllogism, for the other more complex forms may be reduced to syllogisms.

A syllogism is "discourse in which a third proposition is inferred from two propositions rightly arranged."

Before a proof is given by means of a syllogism, there is a question or problem of showing the relationship between two terms. These terms are called the Extremes; they are the Major term and the Minor term. The Major term is "the predicate of the question" or of the conclusion, and the Minor term is "the subject of the question." The Middle Term is that which is compared with both of the extreme terms in the premissed propositions.

Irrespective of the content of the syllogism, there are these three terms: the Major, the Minor, and the Middle Terms. Taking account of the content, there are three propositions: the Major Proposition, the Minor Prop-

---

1. See Part III, chap. 7, p. 43.

osition (these are also called the Premisses), and the Conclusion. They are distinguished not by their order but by their nature.

1. The major proposition "is that in which the major term is compared with the middle term" and is called the proposition par excellence.

2. The minor proposition is that "in which the minor term is compared with the middle term" and is called the assumption or subsumption.

3. The conclusion is that "in which the extremes are compared with each other," and the middle term never appears here.

CHAPTER 2

The whole force of the syllogism may be explained from the following axioms.[2]

Axiom 1. "Those things which agree with a single third thing agree with each other."

2. "Those of which one agrees and the other does not agree with one and the same third thing, do not agree with each other."

3. "Those which agree in no third thing, do not agree with each other."

4. "Those which do not disagree with any third thing, do not disagree with each other." From these [axioms] the general rules of syllogisms are deduced. The first three are about the quality of propositions.

Rule 1. If one of the premisses is negative, the conclusion will be negative (by axiom 2).

Rule 2. If both the premisses are affirmative, the conclusion will be affirmative (axiom 1).

Rule 3. From two negative [premisses] nothing follows because those which agree with each other and those which disagree with each other may both be different from a third.

Two [rules] on the Quantity of Terms:

2. See Aldrich, *Artis Logicae Compendium,* III, 2, p. 4.

Rule 4. The middle must be distributed once, or taken universally; for a common term often contains two or more species which are mutually opposed to each other, and from which predication may be made according to different parts of its own extension; therefore terms do not truly agree with a third term, unless one at least agrees with the whole of the middle.

Rule 5. No term may be taken more universally in the conclusion than it was in the premisses, because an inference from particular to universal is not valid.

On the Quantity of Propositions:

Rule 6. "If one of the premisses is particular, the conclusion will be particular." For (i) suppose the conclusion is affirmative: therefore (by rule 1) both premisses are affirmative; but no term is distributed in a particular [premiss]; therefore (by rule 4) the middle term has to be distributed in the other one; it is therefore the subject of a universal affirmative; therefore the other extreme is also taken particularly, since it is the predicate of an affirmative, ergo, the conclusion will be particular (by rule 5). (ii): Suppose the conclusion is negative: therefore, its predicate is distributed; hence (by rules 5 and 4) both the major term and the middle term have to be distributed in the premisses, but (rule 3) when one premiss is negative, the other is affirmative. If one [premiss] is particular, only these two terms can be distributed; when one premiss is affirmative, the other should be particular. Therefore the minor extreme, the subject of the conclusion, is not distributed in the premisses; therefore (by rule 5) it is not distributed in the conclusion.

Rule 7. "From two particulars nothing follows," at least in our normal way of speaking, according to which the predicate of a negative is taken to be distributed. For (i) if the conclusion is affirmative and both premisses are affirmative, no term in the premisses is distributed (contrary to rule 4). (ii) Suppose the conclusion is negative; therefore some predicate is distributed, but the predicate is distributed only in particular premisses; it will therefore be invalid (contrary to rule 4 or 5).

Rules 1 and 7 are thus reduced to one rule. The conclusion follows the weaker side, i.e., the negative or particular. All the rules are contained in these verses:[3]

---

3. Aldrich, *Artis Logicae Compendium,* cites this mnemonic in the same form at III, 3, p. 16.

You must distribute the middle, and there should be no fourth term.
Both premisses should not be both negative and particular.
The conclusion should follow the weaker side;
And it may not be distributed or negative, except when a premiss is.[4]

In a curious and unusual manner of speaking, a certain negative conclusion may be reached, with the predicate undistributed, as in this example:

Certain Frenchmen are learned,
Certain Englishmen are not learned,
Therefore,
Certain Englishmen are not certain Frenchmen.

CHAPTER 3

A figure of a syllogism is "the proper arrangement of the middle in the premisses"; there are only four figures.

1. That in which the middle is the subject of the major and the predicate of the minor.

2. That in which the middle is the predicate of both.

3. That in which the middle is the subject of both.

4. That in which the middle is the predicate of the major and the subject of the minor.

In the first [the middle is] sub[ject and] pre[dicate]; in the second [it is] twice a pre[dicate]; in the third [it is] twice a sub[ject]; and in the fourth [it is] pre[dicate and] sub[ject].

The mood of the syllogism is "the correct determination of the propositions according to quantity and quality."

Sixty-four arrangements are possible of the four letters A, E, I, O; of these, fifty-two are excluded by the general rules. There remain, therefore, twelve concluding modes of which not all lead to a conclusion in every figure because of the nature of the figure; and some are not useful at all.

4. This paragraph was a footnote in Hutcheson's text.

CHAPTER 4

The special rules of the figures are as follows.

1. i. In figure 1 the minor [premiss] must be affirmative; if it were negative, the conclusion would be negative (by rule 1), and its predicate would be distributed. But the major would be affirmative (by rule 3), and its predicate would not be distributed; hence there would be a fallacy (contrary to rule 5).

ii. The major [premiss] must be universal. For the minor is affirmative (from the former rule), and therefore its predicate is particular, namely the middle term. It must therefore (by rule 4) be distributed in the major of which it is the subject. These things will be more easily made clear by the schema below, where the letters denote distributed terms.[5]

Here are examples of fallacies.

Example 1. M = b: Example 2. $m \begin{cases} = b \\ > B \end{cases}$

$\qquad\qquad$ D > M $\qquad\qquad\qquad\qquad$ D = m

Therefore D > B[6] $\qquad\qquad$ Therefore D[7]

N.B. Capital letters denote distributed terms; lowercase letters particular terms.

---

5. The letters used in this chapter to denote distributed terms are not found in the mss. of Hutcheson's "Logica," nor were they employed by Aldrich. James Clow, in his lectures on Hutcheson's logic, "A System of Logic," p. 179, offered the following clarification of the symbols used by Hutcheson:

> In the following Scheme, which Dr. Hutcheson, in the Compend, used to exemplify the Rules of the Figures, where the Capital Letters signify that the terms are taken Universally, and the small ones that they are taken Particularly, B or b represents the Major Term, D or d the Minor and M or m the Middle term. {=} is the Sign of an Affirmative Proposition, and {>} of a Negative one.

6. "Contrary to Rule 5th": Clow, p. 179.
7. "Contrary to Rule 4th": Clow, p. 179.

2. Rules of the second figure:

i. One of the premisses must be negative. For since the middle term is predicated of both, it would be distributed in neither if both were affirmative (contrary to rule 4).

ii. The major must be universal. For the conclusion is negative, and its predicate is distributed. It must therefore (by rule 5) be distributed in the major of which it is the subject.

$$B = m \qquad\qquad\qquad b = m$$
$$D - m \quad \text{against 4} \qquad D > M \quad \text{against 5}$$
$$D = B \qquad\qquad\qquad D > B$$

3. Rules of the third figure:

i. The minor must be affirmative, for the same reason as in the previous figure.

ii. The conclusion must be particular. For since the minor is affirmative, its predicate, the minor term, is not distributed; therefore (by rule 5) it is not distributed in the conclusion of which it is the subject.

Examples of fallacies:

$$M \left. \begin{cases} = b \\ > B \end{cases} \right.$$

$$\left. \begin{matrix} M = b \\ M > D \\ D > B \end{matrix} \right\} \text{against 5} \qquad\qquad \frac{M = d}{} \left. \begin{matrix} \\ \\ \\ \end{matrix} \right\} \text{against 5}$$

$$D \left. \begin{cases} > B \\ = b \end{cases} \right.$$

4. Rules of the fourth figure:

i. "If the major is affirmative, the minor must be universal"; otherwise it will contravene rule 4.

ii. If the conclusion is negative, the major must be universal; otherwise it will contravene 5.

iii. If the minor is affirmative, the conclusion must be particular, for the same reason as in the third figure.[8]

$$
\left.\begin{array}{l}
\text{I}:\text{B}=\text{M} \\[2pt]
\hline
\text{m}>\text{D} \\[2pt]
:\,=\text{d} \\[2pt]
\text{ergo}
\end{array}\right\} \text{contra 4.}
\qquad
\left.\begin{array}{l}
>\text{M} \\[2pt]
\text{b} \\[2pt]
\;=\text{m} \\[2pt]
\hline
\;=\text{d} \\[2pt]
\text{M} \\[2pt]
\;>\text{D} \\[2pt]
\hline
\text{D}>\text{B}
\end{array}\right\} \text{contra 5.}
\qquad
\left.\begin{array}{l}
>\text{M} \\[2pt]
\text{B} \\[2pt]
\;=\text{m} \\[2pt]
\text{M}=\text{d} \\[2pt]
\hline
\;>\text{B} \\[2pt]
\text{D} \\[2pt]
\;=\text{b}
\end{array}\right\} \text{contra 5.}
$$

CHAPTER 5

The concluding modes in the four figures are six.

1. AAA, EAE, AII, EIO, *AAI, *EAO.

2. EAE, AEE, EIO, AOO, *EAO, *AEO.

3. AAI, EAO, IAI, AII, OAO, EIO.

4. AAI, AEE, IAI, EAO, EIO, *AEO.[9]

Thus there are two [modes] in the first [figure], two likewise in the second, and one in the fourth, which are useless and have no names, because they make a particular inference where the valid conclusion would be universal.

The named modes are contained in these verses:

Barbara, Celarent, Darii, and Ferio are of the First;
Cesare, Camestres, Festino, Baroko are of the Second;
The Third claims Darapti and Felapton,
And includes Disamis, Datisi, Bocardo, Ferison.
Bramantip, Camenes, Dimaris, Fresapo, Fresison,

8. Clow also identified in his lectures the modes of the four figures which are excluded by an application of the rules and those modes which remain valid: "A System of Logic," pp. 179–83. Those modes of the four figures which remain valid or useful are summarized by Hutcheson in the first paragraph of chap. 5.

9. Hutcheson considered the five modes marked by asterisks to be redundant. They are represented as subaltern modes in the figures that follow.

Are of the Fourth. But the five which arise from the five universal [modes]
Are unnamed, and have no use in good reasoning.

Here are examples of the modes according to the vowels which are contained in the words [of the mnemonic], A, E, I, O.

FIGURE 1

Bar	all A is b
bA	all c is a: therefore
rA	all c is b.

CE	no A is B
lA	all C is a
rEnt	no C is B.

DA	all A is b
rI	some C is a
I	some C is b.

FEr	no A is b
rI	some c is a
O	some c is not b.

Unnamed	
A	all A is b
A	all C is A
I	some c is b.
	(This is Subaltern 1, Barbara.)

E	no A is B
A	all C is A
O	some C is not B.
	(Subaltern 2, Celarent)

FIGURE 2

CE	no B is A
sA	all C is a
rE	no C is B.

CA	all B is a
mEs	no C is A
trEs	no c is B.
fEs	no B is A
tI	some c is a
nO	some c is not B.
bA	all B is A
rOk	some c is not A
O	some c is not B.
E	no B is A
A	all C is a
O	some C is not b.
	(Subaltern Cesare)
A	all B is a
E	no C is A
O	some c is not B.
	(Subaltern Camestres)

FIGURE 3

dA	all A is B
rAp	all A is C
tI	some C is b.
fE	no A is B
lAp	all A is C
tOn	some c is not B.
dI	some a is b
sA	all A is c
mI	some c is b.
dA	all A is b
tI	some a is c
sI	some c is b.

bO	some a is not B
kAr	all A is C
dO	some C is not B.

fE	no A is B
rI	some a is c
sOn	some c is not B.

FIGURE 4

brA	all B is a
mAn	all A is c
tIp	some c is a.

cA	all B is a
mE	no A is C
nEs	no C is B.

dI	some b is a
mA	all A is C
rIs	some c is B.

fE	no B is A
sA	all A is C
pO	some C is not B.

frE	no B is A
sI	some a is C
sOn	some c is not B.

A	all B is A
E	no A is C
O	some C is not B.
	(Subaltern Camenes)

CHAPTER 6

From axioms 1 and 2 (p. 32) the force of the inference in all of these modes will be clear, since both of the extremes are compared with the middle, and one of them with the distributed middle; and either both agree with it, or one only does not agree.

The Aristotelians neatly demonstrate the force of the inference, and perfect the syllogisms, by means of reduction, since the validity of all [the syllogisms] in figure 1 is evident from the *dictum de omni et nullo* (see p. 26); they also give, in their technical language, the rules of conversion and opposition, by means of which all the other modes can be reduced to the four modes of the first figure, which Aristotle calls the perfect [modes].[10]

There are two kinds of reduction, ostensive and *ad absurdum*. The initial letters in each of the modes (B, C, D, and F) indicate the modes of the first figure to which the modes of the other [figures] are to be reduced, i.e., those of which the initial letter is the same.[11] S and P following a vowel show that that proposition is to be converted, S *simpliciter,* P *per accidens.* M shows that the propositions are to be transposed, K that the reduction is made *per impossibile,* of which more later. When this is done, the conclusion reached will be either the same as in reducing Cesare, Festino, etc., or [a conclusion] which implies the same conclusion, or the contradictory to the conceded premiss. The validity of an ostensive reduction is known from the rules of conversion and subalternation.

Reduction to the impossible is as follows. If it is denied that a given conclusion follows from true premises, let the contradictory of the conclusion be substituted for the premiss whose symbol includes a K, like the major in Bokardo and the minor in Baroko; these premisses will then show in Barbara the truth of the contradictory of the premiss which was

---

10. See Sanderson, *Logicae Artis Compendium,* III, 5, pp. 132–37, and Aldrich, *Artis Logicae Compendium,* I, 3, pp. 20–21. The reader may find it helpful to compare Hutcheson's presentation with the more elaborate commentary on Aldrich's logic provided in John Huyshe, *A Treatise on Logic, on the Basis of Aldrich, with Illustrative Notes.*

11. Thus C in Cesare indicates that it may be reduced to Celarent, Ferison to Ferio, and so on.

claimed to be true. If therefore the given premises had been true, the conclusion would also have been true; for if it was not, its contradictory would have been true, and if that had been true, it will show (in Barbara) that the other premiss is false, contrary to the hypothesis.

Ba	all B is a	Bar	all B is a
rok	some C is not A	ba	all C is b
o	some C is not B	ra	all C is a
	if not.		

For these rules of syllogisms to hold, we have to look carefully for the true subjects and predicates of the propositions, which are sometimes not at all obvious to beginners; and then we have to determine whether they are really affirmative or negative as they are used in the argument. For in complex [propositions], sometimes one part is negative, the other is affirmative, and occasionally it is the negative part (the less obvious part) which is chiefly in point. For example,

God alone is free from error   (From the negative minor reasoning this seems
No council is God   to be in 2, but it is really in 1 [Barbara].)

Therefore

Everything different from God may err,
Every council is different from God.

Likewise,

Holy Scripture is to be believed,   (This seems to be in 2 but is
Mathematical proof is not Holy Scripture.   in 1 with a negative minor.)

All Holy Scripture is worthy of belief,
Mathematical proof is not Holy Scripture.

And the *dictum de omni et nullo* is so useful in proving a true argument and detecting a false one, that by its help any intelligent person may be able to see both true syllogistic force and its fallacious semblance, according to whether one of the premisses contains the conclusion or not, even before applying the special rules of syllogisms.

CHAPTER 7

With regard to the remaining forms of argument, it is evident that they are imperfect syllogisms or may be reduced to imperfect syllogisms.

1. The enthymeme[12] or rhetorical syllogism is "when one of the premises is unspoken because it is quite obvious"; it is for this reason that an enthymematic judgment has full syllogistic force.

2. Induction is "an inference from various examples," of which the chief use is in physics, in politics, and in household matters. It does not generate the highest credit or exclude all fears of the contrary, unless it is clear that there are absolutely no contrary examples.

3. An epicheirema[13] is "a complex syllogism in which a confirmation is attached to one or both of the premises."

4. Sorites is "discourse which contains several syllogisms which are connected with each other," or where there are several middle terms which are connected with each other or with the extremes in several propositions of which if even one is negative, the conclusion will be negative, and if two are negative or any middle term is not distributed at least once, there will be no inference.

5. A dilemma is "a kind of epicheirema, where in making a division, that which is shown about the individual parts in the premises is concluded of the whole."

6. A hypothetical syllogism is "one in which one of the premises is hypothetical"; when the minor is hypothetical, so also is the conclusion; these also serve to prove the inference in an enthymeme. More frequent are those in which the major is hypothetical, for example:

---

12. Literally, something retained in the mind: where the syllogism is reduced from three propositions to two, an antecedent and consequent, the implicit premise must be made explicit for the argument to be tested by the figures and modes outlined above.

13. Literally, to move one's hand to a thing and thereby confirm it or to make an inference from common experience.

Major: If this [is], that will be	Or, If this [is], that will be,
Minor: But this [is] (*con.*),	But not that, therefore not this
therefore also that.	either.

But since a more general predicate follows from any of the corresponding kinds (for example, If it is a man, if it is a horse, etc., it will also be an animal), but from a general predicate, no one particular species will follow (for from the fact that it is an animal, it does not follow that it will be a horse or an ass), it is evident that hypothetical syllogisms rightly proceed (1) from the positing of an antecedent to the positing of a consequent, or (2) from the removal of a consequent to the removal of an antecedent.

1) If Titius is a man, he is also an animal,	2) If it were a bird, it would fly,
But he is a man, therefore he is an animal.	But it does not fly, therefore it is not a bird.

It is a fallacious inference from the removal of an antecedent, or the positing of a consequent:

If Titius is a horse, he is an animal,	Or, But he is an animal,
He is not a horse, therefore he is not an animal.	Therefore he is a horse.

The positing of a negative will be a negation, and the removal of it an affirmation.

Hypothetical [syllogisms] are reduced to categorical [syllogisms] by this general method: "every case which posits that Titius is a man, posits that he is an animal; but every case, or some case, posits that he is a man; therefore, etc." But often it may be more easily and briefly done when there is either the same subject or the same predicate to the antecedent and the consequent; for example:

If man is an animal, he has sensation,
But every man is an animal, therefore he has sensation.

Every animal has sensation.
Every man is an animal; therefore,
Every man has sensation.

If every animal has sensation, every man has sensation;
But every animal has sensation; therefore,
Every man has sensation.

Every man is an animal.   ⎤ (by transposition of
Every animal has sensation, ⎬ the premises it
Every man has sensation.   ⎦ concludes in Barbara)

7. Disjunctive syllogisms are "those in which the major is disjunctive, [whether] affirmative or negative." Either it is day, or it is night; but it is not day, therefore it is night. Or, it is not both night and day, but it is day; therefore it is not night. The force of the inference is obvious enough, when by positing an affirmative disjunctive major, an affirmative conclusion is drawn from a negative minor; or from a copulative negative major and an affirmative minor, the conclusion is negative. For in the former case the syllogism will be reduced to Barbara.

All time different from daytime is night;
But this time is different from daytime.
Therefore . . .

In the other case.
No daytime is night,
But this time is day.
Therefore . . .

There is no inference from an affirmative minor, in the former, or from a negative [minor] in the latter.

CHAPTER 8

As far as content is concerned, syllogisms are either certain or probable depending on their premises.

A demonstration is "an argument duly reaching a conclusion from certain premises," and it is either ostensive, or leading to absurdity; the latter is the case when the contradictory of a proposition is shown to be false, from which it will be clear that it is itself true. The former is either *a priori,* or *of a cause,*[14] "when an effect is shown from a known cause." But there are causes of being and causes of knowing. The former are prior by nature and *per se;* the latter [are prior] in being known and in relation to us. Demonstrations drawn from both kinds of causes are called *a priori,* but especially those which are drawn from things prior by nature.[15]

"The discipline which relies on demonstrations" is science. The general rules of science are

1. "All terms must be accurately defined," nor is their meaning ever to be altered.

2. "Certain and evident axioms are to be posited."

3. "One must proceed from the better known to the less known by demonstrations step by step," and premisses which go beyond axioms and propositions previously demonstrated are not to be admitted.

Demonstrations only deal with abstract propositions, especially in geometry and arithmetic.

There is no single principle of human knowledge which you may rightly say is prior to the rest. There are many evident principles apart from the most general axioms. Nor will any syllogism carry full credence unless both terms of the conclusion are found connected with the middle term in evident propositions. In demonstration, therefore, through several syllogisms which are connected in a continuous series, the number of evident propositions will exceed the number of middle terms by one.

In absolute propositions, and in those which are chiefly useful in life, there is another way of knowing which has its own proper evidence, albeit different from demonstrative [evidence]. Absolute propositions asserting that things exist are known (1) by consciousness, (2) by sense, (3) by reasoning, or by an observed link with existing things, or (4) by testimony. Other experiential truths about the powers and qualities of things are

14. Hutcheson writes this in Greek (*tou dioti*); the terminology goes back to Aristotle, "Analytica Posteriora," I, 13, 3: *Organon,* vol. 2, p. 669.
15. See Sanderson, *Logicae Artis Compendium,* III, 5, p. 132, and Aldrich, *Artis Logicae Compendium,* I, 5, p. 32.

chiefly learned by experience, and by a varied acquaintance with life, and by induction; and whenever any example is similar, it should, other things being equal, be included with the larger rather than the smaller number. For rarely can men see any connection among the actual powers and qualities of things.

There are innumerable degrees of likelihood, from the slightest probability to full and stable assent; from the judicious appreciation [of their degrees] grave men are more likely to earn a reputation for prudence and wisdom than from cleverness in the sciences.

"Assent given to arguments which are probable but do not achieve the highest likelihood" is called opinion. Where either of the premises is uncertain, there is only a probable conclusion; hence in a long chain of arguments, the result will be a very weak assent.

Arguments which create belief are either artificial and involve the use of reasoning, or inartificial, from testimony. "In recent [writers][16] assent resting on testimony is belief (*par excellence*)." Belief is either divine or human, depending on whether the assent rests on the testimony of God or of men.

Divine belief will be a fully firm assent when it is clearly established that God has revealed something, since a superior nature cannot deceive or be deceived.

Human belief too, although often hazardous, may sometimes attain full certainty, when it is clear that the witnesses could not have been deceived, and could not have intended to deceive others, so that neither their knowledge nor their reliability nor their truthfulness is in doubt.

Sometimes the knowledge of witnesses will be evident from the nature of the matter in hand; and their reliability will be established if they have not been induced to give testimony about the question in hand by any reward or other inducements; even more so when they testify to their own peril or loss, and could not expect to persuade others, if they themselves knew that the thing was otherwise.

If testimony is not liable to any suspicion of fraud or ignorance, belief may be given (1) to facts which cannot be known in any other way; (2) also

16. For example, Locke, *Essay,* IV, XV, and XVI, pp. 654–68.

to things totally different from what we have previously observed, if indeed there are no internal arguments that prevent belief; (3) and third, even to things that are strange and contrary to all our experience or observation, provided the testimony deals with material and circumstances that are different and remote from our own affairs.

Appendix on Topics, Fallacies, and Method

CHAPTER I

On Topics

The doctrine of topics, which should not perhaps be ignored by orators, who often have to marshal a large array of arguments to create or confirm belief, is not so useful for logicians, whose art aims chiefly at developing or teaching sciences in which nothing further needs to be added to any valid argument.[1] In any case, topics are "certain general heads of arguments, or the names of the *genera* in which they are found." Each science or art has its own topics, together with the actual [art] of teaching them. Only the broadest *genera* need to be treated by the logician.

I. The topics of grammar are drawn either from the meanings of words or from etymological connections; critics have further [topics], which are the rules of interpretation.

II. The topics of logic are:

1. From definition: what the definition agrees with, that also the thing defined agrees with, and *vice versa*. What the definition does not agree with, neither does the thing defined [agree with], and *vice versa*.

---

1. Hutcheson's examination of "topics" (treated at length by Aristotle: see *Organon*, II, pp. 357–540) appears rather to have been an abridgment of the treatment of this subject in Arnauld, *The Art of Thinking*, pt. 3, chap. 18, pp. 240–46, where topics taken from grammar, logic, and metaphysics were summarized. Hutcheson's presentation added a fourth and a fifth set of topics, taken from ethics and physics.

2. From division (which are also the topics from the genus): (i) A logical part being posited, i.e., a species, the whole too is posited, i.e., the genus, but not the other way about: He is a man, therefore also an animal. (ii) Another topic is the *dictum de omni et nullo*. (iii) What may be predicated of individual parts, is true of the whole, if something is not collectively negatived; or negation of parts affects the totality or whole number.[2]

3. From genus and species: (i) when the species is posited, the genus is posited, and (ii) when the genus is removed, the species is removed; but neither will hold vice versa.

4. From differentia and property: (i) With whatever either one of these agrees under the same nearest genus, the species also agrees, and *vice versa*. (ii) Anything of which either one is denied, the species is also denied of it.

5. From accident: when an accident is posited, a substance is posited, but not *vice versa*.

6. From things which are opposed, whether complexly or incomplexly. The rules given above are so many topics.

III. Metaphysical topics:

1. From the whole and the part: when a physical whole is posited, all the combined parts [of it] are posited, and when these are posited and combined, the whole is posited.

2. The part is less than the whole both in quantity and dignity. Topics here may include those from definition, genus and species, depending upon different understandings (*acceptio*) of the whole. Metaphysical topics also include all the axioms about efficient causes.

IV. Ethical topics are nearly all ends, especially ultimate ends, but there are also the different species of the fitting and the good; and when we learn these from the topics, we also learn the virtues, duties, natural laws, and different degrees of goodness and badness. Arguments are also drawn from

2. The numbers assigned topics 3, 4, 5, and 6 follow "Logica," pp. 45–46. In the 1756 edition, these topics were numbered 4, 5, 6, 7; there was no number 3.

men's appetites and from natural desires to demonstrate laws and to dissect questions of fact, since all plans of action derive from these. The axioms are as follows:

(1) The more that dispositions, intentions, and habits of mind contribute to human advantage, the better they are. And (2) the more they facilitate the assaults of evil, so much the worse they are. (3) Things which are commended by men's higher desires, which are more proper to man, and which exercise the faculties which are proper to man, are better than those which we share with the beasts. (4) All things gentler and kindlier are, other things being equal, more worthy of a good man, all contrary things are unworthy, and so on.

In questions of fact we should chiefly look at the Cassian query: "Who benefits?"[3] These are the axioms: (1) No one is gratuitously either bad or deceitful. (2) No one deliberately acts against the obvious advantage of himself and his own, except in hope of a greater advantage or from a specially strong sense of duty. (3) No sane man, however evil, attempts to deceive, when he has no reason to expect that his deceit will succeed. (4) No sane man is mistaken in things which are exposed to a long and full scrutiny by his senses.

V. The topics of physics are also "from ends," for the perfect work whether of nature or of art which is that which is most suited to the ends it sets itself. We make best progress in the knowledge of things by combining experiments and geometrical reasoning.

CHAPTER 2

On Fallacies and Sophisms

I. The causes of errors lie either in the will or in the understanding, though the understanding is also to some extent influenced by defects of the will.

---

3. *Cui bono?* "For whose good?" "Who benefits?" This is the question which L. Cassius Longinus (consul, 127 B.C.) used to ask when sitting as a judge. The main source is Cicero, *Pro Sexto Roscio Amerino* 30 (84), in vol. 6, *The Speeches*.

[Errors] of the [will] are haste or rashness, bad passions and emotions. For where there is no sincere zeal to know the truth and a love of goodness, a man will soon tire of careful and painstaking inquiry; he will turn his mind to other pursuits or pleasures, content with an immediate appearance of truth, however deceptive. Where there is party zeal or pride or indolence, men will remain stuck in their childhood prejudices or in the opinions favored by the sect to which they have attached themselves, and assail with senseless passion all those who hold contrary opinions, however innocent those opinions may be and truer than their own. When a man anticipates honor or riches from a vigorous defense of his sect, oil is poured on the flames; and the arrogance of a proud person is deeply wounded if anyone who disagrees with him assumes he has deeper insight, and appears to be accusing him of ignorance or low intelligence.

Men are also too quick to take up beliefs which contribute to their own advantage or pleasure; arguments in the other direction are either ignored or weighed on an unequal balance.

II. The causes of the errors which afflict the understanding are slowness of mind (which however can be quite well remedied by hard work) and the deceptive appearances of things. Deceptive appearances are either axioms or principles, rashly picked up and not always true, or terms which are confused, or of indeterminate meaning, and frequently altered without our knowledge. These are the sources of fallacious arguments or sophisms.

Paralogisms openly err in the form itself. Sophisms seem to retain legitimate form, but contain either false or ambiguous propositions or conceal a fault of form under a misleading veil of words.

III. The Aristotelians count thirteen classes of sophisms, six in diction and seven outside of diction.[4] Of sophisms in language, the first and second are equivocations in words, or ambiguities in expression or speech. Casual equivocations do not even deceive children, but confused terms may deceive even the learned: this is the great value of definitions.

---

4. Aristotle, "The Sophistical Elenchi," in *Organon,* II, pp. 540–608; Sanderson, *Logicae Artis Compendium,* III, 28, pp. 206–10, and III, 29, pp. 210–16.

The third and fourth [linguistic sophisms] proceed from a divided sense to a compound sense, or from a compound sense to a divided [sense]. Thus it would be wrong to infer that the wicked are approved by God, or that God delights in them while their wickedness persists, [simply] because they please him when their character changes, or that the blind can see or the deaf hear, because they can do so when cured.

The fifth and sixth are sophisms of nuance, or figurative expression, which will not deceive anyone unless he is very careless.

IV. The seven fallacies outside of diction are these:

1. From the accident to the thing itself. Thus the Epicureans badly argued that God has a form because neither virtue nor reason is seen without form; it is also incorrect to condemn all use of wine and all civil power because serious evils arise from their abuse.

2. From the qualified statement to the simple statement. Thus it would be wrong to infer that reasoning, discourse, and restraint of emotions should be ascribed to God because they are perfections and virtues; or to argue that because these things cannot be ascribed to God, therefore there is not in God every virtue and perfection. Riches do harm to the wicked; therefore they are simply bad in their kind.

3. *Ignoratio elenchi* occurs when one believes that a dispute can be resolved by proving something about which both sides agree. Thus, they will say that all the pagans will perish for ever, because no one can be saved except through Christ, when what needed to be proved was that no one could be saved through Christ who did not know him. Thus some men attempt to show that taking up arms against tyrants is always wicked, because it is illicit to resist a legitimate ruler.

4. Not causes for cause: for example, nature everywhere abhors a vacuum; therefore water in pumps will rise to any height you please. Seditions and factions are more frequent in free states; therefore liberty must be proscribed. Greed and many other evils arise from private property; therefore it is desirable to have community of property. Any free man will make mistakes in using his own judgment; therefore it is not to be permitted.

5. The fallacy of the consequent. Examples of this even include mistakes by quite learned people: bodies projected directly upward fall straight back to the place from which they were projected; therefore the earth does not move: and a thousand others.

6. *Petitio principii,* when what has to be proved is assumed as given. For example, the following "proof" of the Ptolemaic system: the center of the universe is the point to which all things are borne by their own weight; but all things that we see are borne toward the earth; therefore, etc.

7. The fallacy of more than one question, of which examples are afforded by questions about exclusive, inceptive, and desitive[5] propositions.

CHAPTER 3

On Method and Logical Practice

I.[6] One method is the way of discovery, which is also called the analytic [method]; the other is the way of teaching, and is the synthetic [method]. Both may be either professional and academic, or public and popular.

The analytic [method], beginning from consideration of singular or more complex [things], or from effects or from a proposed end, proceeds to general, simple [things], to causes, means, and origins. The synthetic [method] proceeds in the opposite order, from the latter to the former.

Principles of knowledge are included among causes, as well as what are properly called causes of being.

The synthetic [method] first proposes definitions, then postulates and axioms, and simpler and easier propositions; and when these have been proved, it proceeds by way of them to more complex and difficult [propositions], following the rules of demonstration given above. Writers of geometry afford examples of both methods.

5. See Part II, chap. 5, p. 28, n. 8.
6. The divisions of this chapter (I, II, III) derive from "Logica," pp. 54–58. In the published text (1756) only Section II was marked.

II. Logical practice consists in the treatment of themes.[7]

A theme is anything that can be put forward for the understanding to grasp. It is either simple, or a term of some kind; or it is complex, that is, a proposition or statement which has to be confirmed or explained.

In treating a simple theme, (1) we must first explain the origin of a complex word or term and its different meanings and particularly the sense which we want, then (2) its essential attributes, whether primary or secondary, and its more prominent accidents. (3) We must also discuss their origin and end and their causes, if the subject allows it, and (4) the relations existing between it and other things. (5) It is to be divided into its parts, either logical or physical, if there are any.

III. The treatment of a complex theme is either solo or social.[8] The solo treatment consists either of exegesis or of analysis. There is exegesis of the proposition or illustration of its effect, and there is confirmation. There is analysis of the exegesis or the resolution into its parts of a longer piece which someone else has written, and its explication.

There are three chief parts of exegesis: (1) *paraskeue* or preparation, which explains the terms of the question, settles its status, and puts forward the major opinions of the learned. (2) There is *kataskeue*, or confirmation, which chooses the true view and confirms it by the best arguments, rebuts counterarguments, and cites the testimonies of learned men. (3) And finally there is *anaskeue*, which dissolves objections and either claims for the speaker's side, or modestly refutes, the testimonies of famous men which seem to oppose it. Sometimes we should preface it all with a *proparaskeue* about the importance and occasion of the question; and sometimes there is an *episkeue* attached, which gives a summing-up, together with useful corollaries. But above all the rules, we should listen to the poet's [advice]:

7. Hutcheson's treatment of themes and of the rules for considering a simple theme rehearse the observations made on this subject by Gershom Carmichael, "A Short Introduction to Logic," chap. 4, sec. 2, in *Natural Rights*, pp. 309–11.

8. Hutcheson's remarks on the solo treatment of a complex theme again reflect Carmichael's observations in "A Short Introduction to Logic," chap. 4, sec. 3, *Natural Rights*, pp. 311–12.

Take material, you who write, equal to your powers; and ponder for a long time what your shoulders can bear and what they refuse to bear: if a man has chosen his subject effectively, eloquence will not desert him nor lucid order fail him.[9]

It is the function of an analysis to demonstrate in a given piece all these parts of *exegesis* and to explain them, or at least to reveal the true sense of the writer. One must therefore look at: (1) Who is speaking? (2) what about? (3) with what purpose and intention? (4) to whom? And (5) on what occasion? Finally, accounts should be given of the antecedents and consequents.

In treating a complex theme with a companion, or in disputation, the rules to be observed are easy and well known, and swiftly learned by practice.[10]

THE END

---

9. From Horace, *Ars Poetica*, ll. 38–41, in *Satires, Epistles, and Ars Poetica*, p. 452.
10. See Carmichael, "A Short Introduction to Logic," chap. 4, sec. 4, in *Natural Rights*, pp. 312–15.

A

Synopsis

of

Metaphysics

Comprehending

ONTOLOGY and PNEUMATOLOGY

Second enlarged edition

A.D. 1744

THE ARGUMENTS
OF THE CHAPTERS

Part I. On Being and the Common Attributes of Things

Part II. On the Human Mind

Part III On God

On Being and the Common Attributes of Things

CHAPTER I

On Being (*De Ente*)

In antiquity the accepted division of *philosophy* was into *natural* philosophy, which contained *all the speculative sciences* about both corporeal and incorporeal things; *moral* philosophy, i.e., *ethical* and *political* philosophy; and *logical* philosophy, which included both *logic* and *rhetoric*.

What metaphysics is

The Aristotelians[1] shifted all inquiry about the *most general attributes of things* and about *God* and the *soul,* from the territory of *physics* to that of *metaphysics;* they called metaphysics "the science of *being* in abstraction from matter"; and they meant it to contain the whole of the doctrine of the most common attributes, of the more general divisions of being, and of God and of the human mind.

Ontology and pneumatology

A different method has won favor among some more recent [writers]:[2] they define *ontology,* as they call it, as *the science of being and of the most common*

---

1. "The Aristotelians": see above, Hutcheson's account of the Peripatetics, the Scholastics, and the Eclectics, in "Dissertation on the Origin of Philosophy," pp. 6–8, and discussion in the introduction, pp. xxiii–xxvii.

2. Gerard de Vries, *Determinationes Ontologicae* (*Outlines of Ontology*) in *De Natura*

65

attributes of things (which is inadequate). They follow it up with *pneumatology,* which is *the doctrine of God and of the human mind,* and with *physics,* which is *the science of body.* In presenting a short summary of these [sciences], we proceed from the more general to the less general.[3]

I.

How beings are known

Although our minds cannot make contact with anything without the intervention of some *idea,* whether proper or analogical, since it is not things themselves but ideas or perceptions which are presented directly to the mind, nevertheless we are compelled by nature itself to relate most of our ideas to external things as their images or representations.[4] We retain the *memory of a past sensation* with complete certainty that it previously existed, and that we are able at will to recall a kind of faint idea of it, when the *sensation* itself no longer remains. This is very good evidence that certain ideas are representations of other things. In addition, every man has a *consciousness of himself,* or a certain sense which does not allow him to doubt that he remains the same today as he was yesterday, however much his thoughts may be changed or for some time intermitted; and he has no hesitation in ascribing to himself previous sensations, judgments, and feelings of which he retains the memory.[5] This is also the source of the notion or intellection (*informatio*) of a true thing which is different from any idea at

---

Dei et Humanae Mentis (*On the Nature of God and the Human Mind*). Jean Le Clerc, *Ontologia; sive de Ente in Genere* (*Ontology; or, On Being in General*). (This work was dedicated to John Locke.)

3. In the first edition, *Metaphysicae Synopsis* (1742), the three preceding paragraphs were located in a prolegomena.

4. It will be evident in what follows that in Hutcheson's exposition of being, the various entities and categories of being are understood (as they were by Locke and Le Clerc) as ideas. In the ontology of de Vries, by contrast, being is predicated directly of objects or things. Hutcheson was also concerned, as some followers of Locke were not, to relate ideas to objects or real existences. See also Part I, chap. 3, sec. 4, n. 11, pp. 84–85.

5. In his letter to William Mace, 6 September 1727, Hutcheson had elaborated a similar theory of the self. See *A Synopsis of Metaphysics,* II, 3, 3, pp. 140–41.

all. We are likewise impelled by nature for a similar reason to relate certain impressions which we have received by sight or touch, to things which are wholly external, of which they are images. All of this shows that *things* are *real,* different from ideas, and subject to them; and they are usually called *objects of ideas.*

Now, since things are known by the intervention of ideas, and *words* are attached to ideas to perform their function in speaking, we must be careful in all our philosophy not to attribute to external things or to *objects* of ideas those things that belong only to ideas or to words. The carelessness of the *scholastics* in this matter has caused endless confusion in metaphysics.

2.

Being (Ens), *essence, and existence are related*

The general and abstract idea of being is utterly simple and rejects all definition; and since it is involved in every other idea, it may be *univocally* predicated of the *objects* of all other [ideas]. The object therefore of every affirmative true proposition is *something* which truly *is* or *exists,* at the time to which the proposition relates. *Essence* and *existence* are words related to being; and *in the abstract* signify much the same, so far as they refer to objects, as the actual term *being.* No *essence* can be understood in things themselves which does not *exist;* nor is *existence* something in things themselves which is added to *essence.* Since the natures or essences of things seem to be represented to us by our ideas, particularly by our complex ideas which contain the more evident attributes (*sensible qualities, powers, and relations*), we call these complex ideas *essences;* and the ones which belong to ideas alone, we often rashly ascribe to things. And since the mind itself often forms ideas of this kind, without the prompting of an external thing, from simple ideas which it had previously received, although it knows well enough that no object corresponds to them at that point in time, some have fondly imagined that *certain essences, and eternal ones at that, have been without existence;* and if at any time a thing emerges which is similar to such an idea, then they suppose that *existence* supervening on an *essence* is forming a true thing or a real being. Hence they have said that *essence* and *existence* are *principia essendi* or constitutive of a being (*entis*). But [the truth is that] anything which has a real *essence* has *existence* at the same time in the same sense in which it has *essence* or in which it is a *being* or a *thing* (*aliquid*).

What essence is; what existence is

These words do not mean at all the same thing.[6] For *essence* denotes *the primary attributes of things,* such as are normally contained in complex ideas, even when there is no object. *The notion of existence is always simple,* and one which is necessarily suggested to the mind by every sensation as well as by that consciousness of itself as existing which accompanies every thought. It is also suggested by sensations which, at the prompting of nature, seem to portray external things as existing; for no sentient being doubts that he feels or that he exists; and the force of nature itself prevents most men from doubting the existence of external bodies. These general and abstract notions of essence and existence are simple; the idea of a singular or less general essence is often complex, but in the case of existence it is always absolutely simple; it includes only a vague reference to some portion of time; and all notion of essence is abstracted from it.

[Four indications of existence

Things are perceived to exist either by an *internal* sense, by which means each man knows that he exists; or by an *external* sense, which by the force of nature sufficiently confirms to every man that other things also exist; or by *reasoning* from effects, causes, or concomitants known by sense; or, finally, by *testimony.*

---

6. De Vries, in contrast, maintained that existence and essence should not be distinguished: "And like being and essence, so too existence and essence are equivalent terms. So existence is wrongly thought to be something different from the essence of being. . . ." *Determinationes Ontologicae,* chap. 3, sec. 6, p. 105.

What are the essences of things

Although the inner natures or essences of things are hidden from us, they do arouse various ideas in us by a fixed law of nature, and among these certain primary ideas which we see are necessarily connected with each other and belong to the thing presented (*rei objectae*), we call the essence of the thing. Of these attributes no one is prior or posterior to another in the thing itself; but in our knowing of them it is often different, and varies according to the method of investigation. Hence there may be several *definitions* of one and the same thing, depending upon which of its attributes the others are derived from. Some definitions, however, are much more appropriate than others.

3.

Actuality and potentiality

In no matter do the scholastics misuse words more than in their doctrine of *actuality* and *potentiality;* to these words they attach a whole host of things in a very confused manner.[7] *Physical actuality,* which is the power of acting, is either *primary* or *secondary: primary actuality* is the power of acting, while *secondary actuality* is the action itself. *Active,* or actualizing (*actuosa*), *physical potentiality* is primary actuality itself, while *passive potentiality* is *the capacity to be acted upon,* or that natural mutability of a thing by which it is subject to the force of an actualizing nature, and can be variously altered by it.

Metaphysical actuality is *the actual existence of a thing,* and sometimes any quality which perfects it, particularly its powers of acting. The *potentiality* which corresponds to this is called *the possibility of a nonexistent thing,* or the state of an existing thing which is so subject to some actualizing nature that it may be changed in various different ways. God therefore,

7. The multiple meanings ascribed to "actuality" and "potentiality" by scholastic philosophers were reviewed by Francisco Suarez in *Disputationes Metaphysicae* (1597, 1st edition; cited from 1963 reprint). Vol. 2: Disputatio XLIII: "De Potentia et Actu," pp. 633–63.

primary being, creator, and governor of all other things and not subject to change, is called *pure actuality;* and all other things are said to have been *in potentiality* from the beginning; and they became *real,* or true, *beings* when *actuality* supervened upon potentiality. But even in this state there remains something *potential,* because they may be altered in various ways or destroyed by the power of God. There is nothing in all this confused language except that primary being is eternal, without beginning, absolute and immutable in every perfection, and subject to nothing. The ideas of all other things could have been formed before they existed; and though they do exist, yet they may be changed by the power of God. It would be very wrong to conclude from this that *actuality* and *potentiality* are principles of being.][8]

4.

No idea more general than being

They altogether abuse words who imagine that there is any idea more general than being. What they call an *imaginable [thing]* is a real notion, for which there happens to be no object. In whatever sense you speak of an *imaginable* or a *something,* in the same sense you would speak of a *real being,* whether you are speaking of ideas or of things subject [to them]. Nor is there anything intermediate between *being* and *mere nothing.* Things suggested are *relations, possibles, impossibles, external denominations, privations, negations,* and *beings of reason.*[9]

Relations

Relations are *certain notions,* arising from *the thought of two things,* which have no object other than the things being compared and their properties and actions; the contemplation of all of which suggests the notion of a relation or link between them. The things compared are called *terms,* of

8. The four paragraphs between brackets were added in 1744.
9. The list of suggested things that are supposed to stand between being and nothing is found in de Vries, *Determinationes Ontologicae,* chap. 4, pp. 106–11.

which one is the *subject* or *relatum,* the other the *correlate.* The reason for comparing them, which is perhaps some action of one or the other of them or a quality or property which they both share, is said to be the *ground.* Relations are real ideas, whose objects consist of various absolutely real things external to the mind; not, however, something different from the *ground* and the *terms.*

Possibles

Possibles are *terms or complex ideas whose parts are consistent with each other.* When there is no object, they are said to be *purely possible.* They are real ideas which have no object.

Impossibles

Impossibles are *complex terms whose parts separately denote ideas so contrary one to another that they cannot be combined.* They are real words which separately signify real ideas, and nothing more.

External denominations

External denominations are *passively signifying adjectival expressions which represent a real action or quality in some thing which is being referred to in an oblique and confused manner;* in the Latin language, however, they are not joined with a substantive noun of the actual agent or of the possessor of the quality.

Negations and privations

Negations and *privations* are *words that denote the sentiment or notion of a speaker that a certain thing does not have a certain real quality.* If [the quality] is natural to a thing of this kind, the word indicating that it is absent is called a *privation;* otherwise, it is called a *negation.* Of neither is there any real action, property, or predicate.

Entities of reason

Entities of reason are either *ideas of which there is no object,* which are said to be subjectively *beings of reason;* or *complex terms whose parts conflict with each other,* though *the parts themselves are objectively beings of reason.* All of these are either real ideas, or at least real expressions; there are no objects corresponding to them.

5.

The root of possibility

In the celebrated question whether the *root* or cause *of possibility* lies intrinsically in things or comes to them from outside,[10] the question may be this: "Where is the power which can make an object appropriate to any idea whatsoever?" This is certainly to be found only in God. Or the question may be: "By what criterion do we know that an object can be made [which is] consistent with this term but not with that one?" This criterion is to be sought in the terms themselves. If their parts agree with each other, they are *possible,* since there is every power in God. If not, they are *impossible,* or rather the terms signify nothing. It is pointless to ask whether there might be a thing that would be subject to such a term, since terms have meaning only by the intervention of an idea, and there is no complex idea subject to such a term.

It is hardly within our judgment to say for sure what things can happen and what cannot, for in the weakness of our intellect, we may be unaware of those contradictions between highly complex terms which would not be hidden from one who had a fuller knowledge of things. But when a contradiction is sufficiently obvious, we rightly declare a term to be *impossible.*

10. De Vries had defined intrinsic possibility as "whatever can be conceived without contradiction"; he defined extrinsic possibility as "whatever can be produced by the power of some cause." *Determinationes Ontologicae,* chap. 4, secs. 11, 12, and 13, p. 108. Hutcheson restates the question in terms of relations between objects and ideas, and between ideas and terms.

6.

[All ideas are relative except the idea of being

Of the idea of being we say that it alone is completely absolute. All others, whether of substances or modes or attributes of any kind, involve in themselves, whether distinctly and clearly, or confusedly and obscurely, some link or relation of their object to other things. This will be immediately obvious to anyone who thinks about one or two individual [ideas].][11]

11. Section 6 was added in 1744.

CHAPTER 2

On the Axioms of Metaphysics

I.

What an axiom is

Metaphysical axioms are defined as *the most general propositions, self-evident and unchangeable.* Not every proposition which is self-evident is unchangeable; nor is every unchangeable proposition self-evident.

In what sense they are innate

The ancients spoke of these axioms as innate in the sense that it is natural for men to understand them, since we have such a power of reason in us as will lead almost all men to a knowledge of them.[1] Some recent writers,[2] however, speak of axioms as innate only if they have been known and recognized from the moment that the mind was born. In this sense these axioms are not innate; their most general terms arise in the mind at a very late stage, only after it has made many comparisons of individual ideas and abstractions from qualities, distinguishing one from another. And the fact

---

1. Aristotle, *Metaphysics,* 997 a7, 1005 b33. The notion that axioms should be considered innate derives not from Aristotle but from Neoplatonist commentators on his work, remarked above, introduction, pp. xxvi–xxvii and "Dissertation on the Origin of Philosophy," pp. 7–8. De Vries, *Determinationes Ontologicae,* chap. 2, sec. 3, p. 102: "Axioms are commonly called innate truths because they so shine out with their own light that . . . the mind of every man rushes into agreement with them of its own accord."

2. Locke, *Essay,* bk. 1, chap. 2, sec. 4, p. 49. Jean Le Clerc, *Pneumatologia seu de Spiritibus,* chap. 5, sec. 22, p. 102: "Metaphysical axioms are said to be eternal truths, . . . [and] innumerable men, either idiots or barbarians, declaim that these are innate ideas, as if they were but to no avail."

that all men readily agree to these axioms does not prove that they have been known from the start or impressed on the mind from the start. For all will assent to any proposition, including a singular proposition, which concerns any sensible object presented to it, when there is an obvious connection or opposition between subject and predicate; yet these authors say that singular and sensible ideas are not innate.

2.

[No principle is the first of all

There is no absolutely first principle of human cognition. For there are very many axioms, as well as a large number of less general propositions, which are known of themselves; and in every demonstration or series of syllogisms, each extreme term has to be found once in some proposition which is self-evident; otherwise it will not be licit to draw a conclusion.

Some men have wasted a great deal of effort in elaborating a criterion of truth, since there is no criterion to be found other than the faculty of reason itself or the power of understanding which is native to the mind.

Self-evident assertions, as well as proven truths, are said to be eternal and immutable, because whenever any mind turns to consider them, it will see the connection or contradiction between subjects and predicates which is asserted in the proposition. We do not need to seek any other cause of this connection than that which formed the ideas themselves, since in certain ideas other ideas are necessarily implied by their own nature, so that they cannot be fully and distinctly thought without them. Hence the truth of such propositions cannot be altered even by the power of God, since the subject cannot be conceived or thought without immediately including the predicate.]3,4

---

3. De Vries, *Determinationes Ontologicae,* chap. 2, sec. 4, p. 102: "Hence they are called both immediate propositions and common notions; in fact they are also eternal and immutable truths, seeing that not even by divine power can they by any other means be other than they are."

4. The three paragraphs enclosed in brackets were added in 1744.

3.

[*Axioms*] *indubitable*

It is not credible that anyone can seriously doubt these axioms. If anyone doubted about everything, he would certainly be always at a stand. Nor would the assertion *I think* (although it is the first of all absolute propositions) help to elicit any other proposition in anyone who had doubts about axioms, not even to prove the very fact that *he himself exists*. Much less will this absolute proposition establish abstract conclusions. For abstract conclusions arise from abstract propositions alone, and absolute conclusions from absolute propositions.

[*They are not viewed in God*[5]

However much there may be a common agreement of all men about the truth of these axioms, as well as about all demonstrated truths, among those who understand demonstrations, it must not be imagined that all men view this unique truth in some common nature, as if it were a kind of *mode* inherent to it. For the fact is that when several men have ideas that are very similar to each other but not the same, they will also see similar connections and relationships between them. The only permissible conclusion is that all men have been equipped with a similar power of reason.][6]

Axioms of little use

They are equally in error who think axioms so important that they believe them to be necessary or very useful in every act of knowing.[7] For singular and less general propositions become known first even without the help of

---

5. Malebranche, *The Search After Truth,* bk. 3, pt. 2, chap. 6, p. 234: "our view is that we see God when we see eternal truths."

6. This paragraph was added in 1744.

7. Le Clerc made extensive use of axioms in his ontology: for example, concerning existence (chap. 6); concerning wholes and parts (chap. 7); concerning causes (chap. 10). In the preface, p. 3, he proposed that he would show "how all our ideas lead to undoubted axioms."

axioms, though by their help truths previously ascertained are more easily explained to others.

[All axioms are known of themselves once the mind directs itself to see them. Their credit does not come from *induction;* no credit resting on that ground would be very strong, but their credit we see is very strong.][8]

4.

Two [axioms] which are quite useful

Among metaphysical axioms that are especially useful are two which are completely true when we are speaking of objects, not of ideas: *every being exists,* and *a real quality or property or action is to be attributed only to a being.* With their help we avoid a perennial confusion of metaphysics, when things which are proper to ideas or words are ascribed to things external to the mind. We would often avoid the temptation to make this mistake, if in metaphysics we gave ourselves the instruction that "every adjectival term needs its substantive," even though this is not the case in Latin grammar.

From these axioms this corollary follows: "All abstract, affirmative propositions are hypothetical when they concern things, not ideas," where the *existence* of the object is understood as an antecedent condition without which they are not true.

[Other axioms are sometimes collected here in vain. "It is impossible for the same thing to be and not to be; everything is or is not; the whole is greater than its parts; things which agree with a third thing agree with each other." And many others like them, of which some have no use; others are not relevant for common life. But afterward[9] some axioms will be proposed which are not useless.][10]

8. This paragraph was added in 1744.

9. This note was added in 1749: "See Chapter 4, Section 5 [p. 91]: on causes. Wolff, in his *Ontology,* has recently given an account of axioms and their usefulness, with a diligence that will appear unclear to some." Hutcheson had ordered the "Logica," "Psychologia," and "Cosmologia" of Christian Wolff during his term as quaestor for the library of the University of Glasgow, 1732 to 1734. The "Ontologia" or "Philosophia Prima sive Ontologia" was ordered for Glasgow University Library in 1736, GUA 26624.

10. This paragraph was added in the third edition.

CHAPTER 3

On the Properties of Being

I.

The most common attributes of being are certain ideas involved and implicated in the very notion of being, which are interchangeable with being itself, and may be predicated of all its constituents.

There are commonly reckoned to be three attributes of being: *unity, truth,* and *goodness;* some add to these a connection with *space* and *time,* or the *where* and the *when.*[1]

Unity, identity, difference

Unity is either *specific* or *numerical:* the former should rather be called *similarity,* the latter *identity. Numerical identity,* which is sufficiently obvious, refuses to be defined. And the doctrine of the scholastics about unity has no use except to rectify their own errors about universal natures. They speak of unity as a property "by which a being is undivided in itself and divided from every other thing." This means only that no thing is several things in itself.[2] No question can be raised about identity unless two ideas occur which are different in some way, when at the very least some thing has been observed at different times or in different places. Any parts of *space* and *time* are obviously different from any other parts of *space* and *time,* though

---

1. In this chapter, Hutcheson was following the order of topics addressed by de Vries, *Determinationes Ontologicae,* chaps. 6, 8, 9, and 10.

2. See de Vries, *Determinationes Ontologicae,* chap. 6, sec. 5, p. 113: "Since it has been shown that identity is intimately linked with unity, there does not seem to be any reason why we should not say that One and the Same are one and the same."

all are very similar. When ideas of things are different or dissimilar, we know most plainly that the things which arouse those ideas are different.

[*Identity*] *of minds* [*and*] *of ideas*

Questions arise about *identity* in the case either of the mind itself or of ideas, or of physical things. A man is conscious that his mind remains the same by a kind of *internal perception* which is totally *certain* but *inexpressible;* by this he also knows that his mind is wholly different from any other mind. But of another mind observed at different times we merely infer that it is the same mind by arguments that are *probable* but do nevertheless sometimes approximate to certainty. When a perfectly similar idea, judgment, sensation, or state of mind is recalled at different times, these recollections are different in some way simply because of the difference of time, so that they can scarcely be said to be the same as the earlier ones to which they are very similar. However, this difference is rarely so great as that between bodies which occupy different positions at the same time, or from completely similar motions of the same body repeated at different times. However similar physical bodies may be, a real difference between them will become apparent if they occupy different locations at the same time; without this criterion, there will be no completely convincing evidence, but we will be left to decide which bodies are similar and which dissimilar with the help of the ideas which they arouse.

[*The principle of individuation*

So much for the signs by which we distinguish identity or difference. If it is asked why a thing is one, which is the question of the *principle of individuation* in a thing, the only answer that can be given is the actual existing nature of the thing. For whatever cause made or created any thing whatsoever also made it one or individual in the sense intended by the metaphysicians. But there are several kinds of such unity.][3]

3. This paragraph was added in 1744.

[*Identity of*] *physical bodies*

A physical thing is often said to be one and the same because we judge that all the parts of its matter remain the same; this is called *unity of substance.* But organic bodies and some artifacts, when men are not concerned with the identity of their *material,* are said to remain the same so long as their fabric remains much the same, or when an artificial mechanism continues to be useful for the same purposes, even though its material changes every day, as new parts take the place of former parts. We see this happening in every living body and in all things that grow from the earth.

2.

Truth for logicians and moralists

For *logicians* and *moralists truth* means something useful and deserving to be known; for *metaphysicians* it is nothing other than the fact that *each thing is such as the all-knowing God judges it to be, or that it truly is the very thing that it is. Logical truth is the agreement of a proposition with things themselves. Ethical truth is the agreement of a proposition with the sentiment of the mind.*

[*Metaphysical truth*

In some noted authors[4] *metaphysical truth* means the same as the constancy of nature, its stability, or a kind of metaphorical solidity and grandeur. In this sense that which is infinite is also the truest. Finite things are less true; at least their truth is confined within narrow limits beyond which they have no truth. From the notion of each true quality the mind easily ascends to grasp the highest degree of [that quality], which is comprehensible in a kind of general and obscure notion; and it is a small step from there to believing that a nature endowed with that supreme and absolute perfection exists. As

---

4. Ralph Cudworth, *The True Intellectual System of the Universe;* Samuel Clarke, *A Demonstration of the Being and Attributes of God;* Andrew Baxter, *Enquiry.* See also Part I, chap. 4, n. 2, p. 87.

far as concerns duration and extension, the mind can hardly if at all refrain from believing, without any process of reasoning, that there exists a some-thing which is boundless and eternal.][5]

3.

Goodness or perfection

The only sense in which all things might be said to be *good* is that we believe that God has formed all things by his excellent design for the most noble ends which each thing may most appropriately serve, or that no thing is lacking its own essential attributes which metaphysicians call its *perfec-tions*.[6] Why this is called *goodness* or what it contributes to a knowledge of things no one can easily say. [*Physical perfection*] Those things are said to have *physical goodness, which make and keep any sentient nature happy, and give it pleasure without harm.* Likewise living things and things endowed with sense are said to be *perfect in virtue of themselves,* since they have the qualities and faculties to make or keep themselves happy. Some kinds of such things are more perfect than others, in that they have more senses and higher faculties to experience pleasures. When none of those which are normally found in such a thing is lacking, the thing is said to possess *per-fection of parts;* the greater they are, the more it excels in *perfection of degrees.* [*Moral goodness*] Taking others into account, things which are endowed with life, sense, and powers of reason, are judged to be *morally good when they have the ability and, above all, the constant will or character which renders them able and willing to serve the happiness of others.* For all men strive to attain this power for themselves; they praise such a character in others; ev-eryone would discover through his internal sense, as he surveyed his acts,

5. This paragraph was added in 1744.
6. De Vries, *Determinationes Ontologicae,* chap. 8, sec. 11, p. 119. "So that we may reason more clearly about goodness, we must recognize that what is properly called [goodness] is in fact multiple; namely, metaphysical or transcendental, physical or nat-ural, or, finally, ethical or moral."

intentions, and decisions, that such [a character] would be the happiest for himself.[7]

Absolute and qualified perfections

There are many species of living things, endowed with different senses, which take pleasure from very different things, and therefore the same powers cannot be regarded as perfections in every kind of thing. Those which are useful and pleasing to one species would be useless and deadly for another. Things which would give one species the highest happiness that it is capable of possessing, another species cannot allow; or if it did allow them, they would afford the very lowest pleasure. Hence has arisen the chief distinction between perfections, that *some will make any nature endowed with them happy, and include no imperfection,* whereas *others can be of benefit only to lower natures, as they involve an imperfection and offer a remedy or mitigation of it.* These are called *relative perfections,* or *perfections in a qualified sense,* whereas the former are said to be *pure* and *absolute perfections.*[8]

4.

May space and time be predicated of all things?

Among the commonest attributes of being some of the most learned men[9] include *certain necessary connections with space and time,* which they insist are real things if we may trust our ideas at all: they seem to have real attributes: in both cases their own proper extension or quantity extends to infinity; in both cases their parts are immutable; and although they allow

7. The distinctive character of Hutcheson's idea of moral goodness, as expressed in these sentences, may be contrasted with the definition proposed by de Vries, *Determinationes Ontologicae,* chap. 8, sec. 3, p. 119: "Ethical goodness consists in the conformity of a rational being with the law of nature or with the practical dictates of right reason. The privation of such is usually called sin. But we will have to discuss this in practical or moral philosophy."

8. Hutcheson was again following de Vries, *Determinationes Ontologicae,* chap. 8, sec. 18, p. 121.

9. The learned men whom Hutcheson had in mind are specified in the following note.

things which are distinct from themselves to coexist with them and penetrate them, they are not penetrable by any things which have the same parts
as themselves. There is a mutual relation or connection between all *space*
and *time,* since every *time* is the same in every *space;* and every *space* seems
to remain the same in every *time,* since virtually everything is connected
with some part of *both.* They are the means by which we distinguish the
truest difference between things which are very similar, since *both* have
completely distinct parts. Neither motion nor the speed of motion can be
understood without both of them. Long duration, more than anything,
makes every pleasure or pain significant for the happiness or misery of life.
Neither the physical world nor any physical property can be understood
without *both of them.* Without *time* there can be no properties or activities
of the human mind, albeit they seem to be quite unconnected with *space.*
No part of *either* can exist without the rest, or perish if the rest remain.
But whether they are things in themselves made by God, in order that he
might make the physical world and successive things, or whether they are
infinite modes of the infinite God, it is not easy to determine for certain.
Although the first view is so obscure that it exceeds the reach of the mind,
it seems closer to the truth, because *both* [space and time] consist of parts
which are truly different. All things known to us and all their properties
seem to persist in *time;* a kind of perception of *time* accompanies every
perception or feeling of which the mind is aware. Only bodies and their
properties seem to exist in *space,* not the properties which seem appropriate
to spirits. Hence we quite easily conceive that there was once no extended
space before God had made the physical world; but we can scarcely, if at
all, conceive that *duration* or *time* had a beginning or will have an end.[10]
And we are totally ignorant what connection the divine nature has with
either.

10. The following note was added in the third edition (1749): "On this question,
consult [John] Locke, *An Essay Concerning Human Understanding;* Henry More, *Enchiridion Metaphysicum;* [Ralph] Cudworth, *The True Intellectual System of the Universe;*
Samuel Clarke, in his letters to Leibniz, all famous and learned men, and other well-
known writers."

[*An opinion different from the former*[11]

Some ancient philosophers[12] seem to have believed that both *space* and *time* were notions that are absolutely necessary to us, but to which nothing external corresponds any more than to ideas of *numbers*. They took the view that *space* is an abstract idea of physical magnitude, reached by the subtraction of all the other properties of body. Likewise *time* is a similarly abstracted idea of the continuation or succession which we have observed in the movements of the mind or in a series of thoughts. And furthermore [they argued] a certain size or quantity and parts and relations are ascribed to *numbers* as well as to space and time, albeit all agree that *number* does not exist apart from things numbered, outside of any mind. However, we will by no means settle the problem by this method. No one, necessarily, imagines number extending beyond every one of the things numbered, and indeed as something which would survive in the absence of any numbered things. No one [imagines] number [as] implicated of itself in the true qualities of external objects. Neither can the position of things or their motion, or succession of thoughts or the so-called *coexistence* of other things with space and time, be understood, unless something real outside the mind corresponds to these ideas.

But however much these two things are believed to be real, there seems to be no reason why they are believed to be attributes of one thing more than of any other thing that is both extended and enduring. And we cannot therefore properly infer that both things are uncreated and eternal on the

---

11. In the following paragraphs, Hutcheson was responding to the more skeptical position taken by Edmund Law, *An Enquiry into the Ideas of Space, Time, Immensity and Eternity.* Law argued, against Samuel Clarke, and in a manner that he took to be consistent with Locke, that ideas of space and time are abstract ideas, that they have no real or objective existence. He declared of the idea of space, "that it can hardly be any fix'd determinate Object in Nature . . . but rather one of *Entia Rationis,* or an Ideal Image arbitrarily set up in the Mind. . . ." p. 4. See also Part I, chap. 5, sec. 2, n. 5, p. 102.

12. Among ancient philosophers who denied the reality of space and time, the most notable was no doubt Zeno of Elea. Edmund Law referred his readers to Pierre Bayle's *Dictionary* article "Zeno," Remarks E and F, for a demonstration of "the impossibility of Motion . . . on the supposition of a real Space or Extension infinitely divisible." *An Enquiry into the Ideas of Space, Time, Immensity and Eternity,* p. 67, note B; Bayle, *A General Dictionary, Historical and Critical.*

ground that the mind can remove neither by thinking, since no more can those who enjoy sight remove colors from corporeal nature, and yet nothing external in the things themselves corresponds to these ideas. There is a great difference between a kind of necessary tendency of the mind to represent certain things to itself, and a sure conclusion of reason that they truly are so. There is no place in philosophy where the weakness of human intelligence is more evident in understanding things which we use virtually all the time and which occur in everybody's speech, than in this very topic of space and time.

Permanent and successive time

The schoolmen seem to be talking in empty phrases, without advancing knowledge, when they divide *time (τὸ Quando)*[13] into *permanent,* or *simultaneous,* and *successive,* ascribing the former to God alone; as also when they divide *space (τὸ Ubi)*[14] into *circumscriptive,* which is appropriate to bodies, *definitive,* which is appropriate to created spirits, and *repletive,* which they ascribe to God alone, who fills all places by his essence without any extension.[15] All this seems to be beyond the power and reach of our understanding.

There are learned men[16] who confidently maintain that it is to be taken as a necessary axiom in philosophy, that *what is nowhere (nullibi) is not,* and also that *nothing can act where it is not by means of its essence.* But they should ask themselves whether *being somewhere (τὸ alicubi esse)* means the same as either *being diffused throughout space,* which belongs only to the

---

13. "Time" is a translation of τὸ *Quando,* which is a Latinization of Aristotle's category τὸ ποτε; Latin has no definite article.

14. "Space" is a translation of τὸ *Ubi,* which is a Latinization of Aristotle's category τὸ πού.

15. See de Vries, *Determinationes Ontologicae,* chap. 9, secs. 4, 6, and 7, p. 122, on the division of space into circumscriptive, definitive, and repletive; and chap. 10, secs. 3 and 5, p. 123, on the division of time into permanent and successive.

16. Edmund Law, in *An Enquiry into the Ideas of Space, Time, Immensity and Eternity,* chap. 1, and earlier in the notes to his translation of William King, *An Essay on the Origin of Evil,* n. 13, pp. 31–34. In both places, Law was expanding upon the arguments of Leibniz in his exchange with Clarke, in "A collection of papers which passed between the late learned Mr. Leibniz and Dr. Clarke."

infinite, or *being diffused through a part of space,* which will be appropriate only to things with figure and extension; and whether both do not presuppose a thing composed of parts however combined. They should also ask whether either one of these is appropriate to the qualities or actions of the mind, which are judgment, reasoning, love, hatred, desire, joy, and sorrow. They should also wonder whether they are not being deceived by the wrappings of words, in that they are happy to avoid employing the nouns *time* and extended *space* by making use of the adverbs *where, anywhere,* and *when.*][17]

---

17. The four paragraphs between brackets were added in 1744.

CHAPTER 4

On the Principal Divisions of Being

I.

Dependence and independence of being; the latter is supreme perfection

The first division of being is into *dependent* or created being and *independent* being, which has been made or created from nothing.[1] *Independent* things seem to imply perfection, *absolute* things absolute perfection, and *relative* things a relative perfection. Indeed, independence which is absolute and full of perfections seems to imply infinity,[2] since it is not intelligible that an absolutely primary thing whose nature has not been limited or circumscribed by any prior thing at its discretion should possess any one finite perfection rather than another, or be restricted to perfections of one kind so as not to possess the others. That therefore has supreme perfection which is absolutely primary, and all other things take their origin from it.

[Some learned men therefore do not seem to have correctly expressed their view of independence, in implying that any perfection or attribute of a primary nature could have been the cause or reason why that nature exists, since a primary nature cannot have a cause or ground of *being* (*essendi*),

---

1. De Vries had also made independence and dependence the first division of being: *Determinationes Ontologicae,* chap. 11.

2. Samuel Clarke argued that an independent being must also be an infinite being, "for else it would be impossible there should be any Infinite at all, unless an Effect could be more perfect than its Cause." *A Demonstration of the Being and Attributes of God,* p. 87. See also Ralph Cudworth, *The True Intellectual System of the Universe,* p. 649: "To assert an *Infinite Being* is nothing else but to assert a Being *Absolutely Perfect,* . . . *God,* and *Infinite* and *Absolutely Perfect* being but different names for One and the same thing."

as they term it. Nor in a nature which we have represented as not yet in existence can we suppose there is any attribute or internal *necessity* which brings this about or requires that the thing itself should exist.][3]

The sign of dependence

Metaphysicians therefore conclude that *every nature is dependent to which any mode, from a certain range of modes, is wholly necessary, if it is equally capable of all such modes.* For if it were supposed that it was independent, it would have had, on this hypothesis, some one mode before any action or choice of any cause whatsoever; this one mode therefore would be more connected with the nature or essence of that thing, above all other such modes; and therefore it would not be equally capable of other such modes, nor would it equally admit any of them at all. Every body (*corpus*) necessarily has some space, some figure, and some state of either motion or rest; it cannot exist without such properties. However, it is indifferent to all [particular] places, and is equally capable of all figures, and of every movement or rest. The thing therefore is dependent and made to be.

2.

Necessary and contingent being

Related to the former is another division of being into *necessary* and *contingent,* or rather *voluntary,* being. *Necessary being* is *that which does not depend on a will;* the term is the opposite of *voluntary* or *discretionary being.*

[Internal and external necessity

One [kind of] necessity is *internal necessity,* also called *antecedent necessity.* It exists in the very nature of a thing; for example, there is a necessity of connection between the terms of a self-evident or proven abstract propo-

---

3. This paragraph was added in the second edition (1744). The "learned men" in question appear to be "Spinoza and his Followers," as discussed by Clarke, *A Demonstration of the Being and Attributes of God,* p. 122 ff.

sition. It is also called absolute necessity, since it remains the same in every time and place. The other [kind] is *external necessity*, a *subsequent* or *hypothetical* necessity which necessarily follows upon something else which has been previously posited, or a hypothesis.][4] A *perception* is said to be *necessary* if it presents itself to us, whether we will or no; a *voluntary* [perception], on the other hand, is one which we can change, obstruct, or stop. *Judgment* is *necessary;* this is either *because the nature of the object is such that it cannot be changed for any reason so as to render the judgment untrue*, or *because the connection or conflict between the terms in the stated proposition is such as to ensure that the proposition will always be true.* This necessity of abstract propositions remains the same in every time and place; and the arguments by which it is shown are called causes, i.e., *causes of knowledge* (an analogical use of the word "cause"). The *necessity of being (essendi)*, as a result of which *beings (entia)* are said to be necessary, denotes an *existence which does not depend on a will;* if entities do not depend on a human will, they are called necessary entities *so far as men are concerned.* If existence does not depend on any will at all, it is said to be *absolute necessity,* since the thing is said to have existed of itself from eternity, and to be so constant and perfect that it does not perish of its own accord and cannot be destroyed by any other force. The same necessity is also called *intrinsic* and is distinct from the necessity which originates externally and on the basis of a hypothesis, since things are only necessary [either] because they depend on the immutable will of God or necessarily follow from other things pre-

---

4. The sentences between brackets were added in 1744. Samuel Clarke had described the necessity of God as "Antecedent . . . to our supposition of its Being"; that is, it would be self-contradictory to deny the existence of a necessarily existent being: *A Demonstration of the Being and Attributes of God,* p. 28. It was argued against Clarke that the necessity he contended for was more properly considered a consequent or subsequent necessity to be inferred from the order of the creation. "A Dissertation upon the Argument a Priori for Proving the Existence of a First Cause" [by Daniel Waterland] appended to Edmund Law, *An Enquiry into the Ideas of Space, Time, Immensity and Eternity:* "Dissertation," pp. 51–52, 56, and Law, chap. 5, "Of Self-Existence and Necessary Existence," pp. 148–49. Hutcheson was never persuaded of the cogency of Clarke's arguments from intrinsic or antecedent necessity, as the remainder of this paragraph attests. Hutcheson told William Leechman that he had written a letter [no longer extant] to Clarke, ca. 1717, to express his doubts on this subject. See William Leechman, "Account of the Life and Character of the Author," prefaced to *A System of Moral Philosophy,* pp. iv–vi.

viously posited. From the absolute necessity of a thing it can only be inferred that it is eternal in itself; its other attributes or perfections do not seem to be able to be derived from this, except by confusing the necessity of judgment with the necessity of the thing itself. Nor should it be said that any attribute of a thing precedes the subject itself or is the ground of its being.

3.

[*Simple and multiple being*

Beings are divided into *simple* and *multiple beings. Souls* or *spirits* are *simpler beings,* and we discuss them elsewhere.[5] Of these the *simplest* is a [*soul* or *spirit*] which is not only without any parts but has all its virtues so necessarily connected with its nature that nothing adventitious can befall it, nothing new occur to it. *Multiple* [*beings*] are either *composite,* when their parts are joined in a kind of natural bond or union like animal and vegetable bodies, or *merely multiple,* like a heap, or a corporeal mass endowed with mere power of cohesion, which is distinguished by this alone from a being by aggregation, though that too has its own metaphysical unity.][6]

4.

Finite and infinite [*being*]

There is another *division* of being, into *finite* and *infinite.*[7] *Finite* is self-explanatory from the name. *Infinite* is "that which is greater than everything finite," or "that which rejects all relationship with finite things." All things perceived by the senses appear to be *finite.* We acquire the notion of *infinity* not only from the fact that in certain things, namely numbers, sizes, and

5. See Part II, chap. 3: "Whether spirit is a different thing from body."
6. Section 3 was added in 1744.
7. See de Vries, *Determinationes Ontologicae,* chap. 15 ("Infinite, Finite, Indefinite"), pp. 144–46. In the first edition of Hutcheson's metaphysics (1742), these two paragraphs, on finite and infinite, followed the discussion of causation (sec. 5 below) as it does in de Vries's work.

time, the mind can always go on, and sees that in adding new parts, in extending or amplifying an idea, or in dividing a quantity where it is impossible to arrive at portions which are absolutely the smallest, its progress cannot be arrested; some call this *potential infinity.* But [we acquire the notion of infinity] above all [from the fact] that in contemplating space the mind sees that no bounds can be anywhere conceived beyond which it cannot reach, and because it is quite certain that there has always been something without a beginning, and that past duration has been infinite. This notion of infinity we transfer to things that are quite different, namely power, wisdom, and goodness, for we want these things to be as great as they absolutely can be.

Difficult questions about infinite things

There are many fierce disputes about *infinite things.* These are the points that seem most likely. *There can hardly be more than one thing of the same kind which is infinite in every way. There cannot be an infinite [thing] which is greater than an[other] infinite [thing] in the respect in which it is infinite. Infinite things, as they are infinite, cannot be multiplied; nor can they have any finite relation to finite parts, though things that are infinite in one respect and finite in another, if there are any such, may be multiplied and divided.* If anyone chooses to spend time on these questions, which wholly exceed the powers of our minds, he will receive just one reward: he will be made more aware of his own limitations and any intellectual arrogance he may have will be diminished.

5.

There is another division of *being,* into *cause* and *thing caused.* The idea of *power, force, efficacy, action, causality* is simple; it arises when we see from the proximity of certain things, and from their motion or their effect on other things, that new sensations instantly follow in ourselves, and new motions or changes of form in those other things.[8] Moreover, we find from

8. Hutcheson explained causation in terms of ideas; like Locke, *Essay,* bk. 2, chap.

our awareness of our own intentions that our ideas are changed in different ways in our minds by our own efforts, and movements are aroused in our bodily members. And in these events we not only see that the desired change follows, but also perceive our minds exercising some sort of actual *initiative* (*energia*). The notion of *action* or *efficiency,* therefore, which should clearly be counted among the simpler [ideas], denotes something quite different from the fact that one thing or an alteration in a thing follows another thing, or that this thing preceded that thing in time, or has normally preceded it, even though this is quite often the only indication of efficiency that we have. And then, since the physical properties which affect the senses are known, namely, the forces of inertia, weight, mobility, and figure, we may infer from the force and nature of these qualities what changes in other things or in themselves bodies which have these qualities may effect by their own motion or impact. [But since the nature of the causes is not perspicuous to us, our knowledge of efficiency is also exiguous, and we more often make inferences by use and wont than by sure reasoning as to what effects are to be expected from any given cause or from what cause a given effect springs. Such is the ignorance of men in this matter that although we are quite aware that we are doing something in changing our thoughts and desires and appetites, yet all the rest of our human efficacy is uncertain, even in the movement and control of our own bodies; of this elsewhere.][9]

[As for the forces or attractions attributed to other bodies which seem to give rise to gravity, cohesion of parts, elasticity, and other such things, whether they are necessarily in bodies of themselves or can coexist with the inertia of matter, or whether, on the other hand, they are caused by the continuous power of a nature which is far different and incorporeal in a fixed order in accordance with certain laws, the most learned men are at variance on the question of *how* it occurs, as also in the matter of the continuation of a motion already begun and its communication after a collision

---

26, and Le Clerc, *Ontologia,* chap. 9. De Vries, *Determinationes Ontologicae,* chap. 12, in contrast, explained causation in terms of things.

9. The sentences between brackets were added in 1744. In the 1749 edition, a note was added to "of this elsewhere": "See Part II, Chapter IV, Section 1," p. 145 below. See also sec. 6 of this chapter, pp. 96–99.

of bodies.[10] The arguments which show that more than anything else one must invoke a certain power and design of nature which is far from corporeal are based on the fact that we have seen time and again that we have been able to formulate innumerable laws of nature, of the most diverse and different kinds, and understand them without any contradiction, like those laws which we see affording the highest degree of security and usefulness to all things.][11]

Logical causes, moral causes, etc.

We will say nothing here of *logical* causes, which are said to be causes of *knowing,* such as the premisses of conclusions, or of *metaphysical* causes, which are not truly distinguished from effects, such as attributes which are easily enough known and from which others seem to arise. Those are called *moral* causes which have done or omitted, according to their own wills or states of mind, things from which some good or evil could be foreseen as likely to arise either of its own accord and from its own nature or by the intervention of other causes of any kind whatsoever, which they have aroused or failed to restrain.[12] *Denials* therefore and *privations,* as well as real things, have their own moral causes.

Material causes and formal causes improper

Those *causes* which are called *material causes, formal causes,* and *final causes* have received the name [of cause] by a transference of meaning; only an *efficient* cause is properly called a *cause.* A *material* cause achieves nothing,

---

10. Hutcheson's note (1749): "On this matter, consult Malebranche and certain Newtonians." Baxter, *Enquiry,* reviews the opinions of various Newtonians on the subject in secs. 1 and 2.

11. This paragraph was added in 1744.

12. Compare Le Clerc, *Ontologia,* chap. 9, sec. 5, for many distinct ideas of causality: physical, moral, logical (between parts and whole), principal and instrumental, *per se* and accidental, and so on.

whereas a *real cause* effects something either by itself or as a result. A *formal cause* effects nothing, but is itself effected.[13]

Final causes

An *end* is *a certain pleasing and desired thing, in the hope of obtaining which an agent is prompted to act;* it may be pleasure perhaps or things which afford pleasure. Pleasure effects nothing by itself, but expectation of it moves a man, so that he wants to do those things which seem likely to produce pleasure.

Therefore when a man acts in view of an end, the end had previously been known to him and desired; innate in him is *self-love* (*philautia,* or an appetite for his own happiness), or a certain kindly feeling toward others. Further, when a man desires an end *for its own sake,* the thing desired has become pleasing to him because he has a certain sense which is prior to all reasoning; for there is no place for reasoning about *ultimate ends,* but only about aids or *means* as they are called. And if anyone desires something *for the sake of another,* again some feeling toward him for whose sake he desires it has necessarily preceded [the desire]. A *final end* is *whatever is sought for its own sake.* Hence every man has many ultimate ends, among which indeed a struggle or process of comparison may occur, with a view to discovering which one makes the greater contribution to a happy life. In this struggle there is little room for reasoning, since the question is rather to be settled either by a sense, external or internal,[14] which instructs one as to what things afford the greatest pleasure, or by experience of things, which reveals what are the more constant and lasting pleasures.

Axioms about efficient causes

Here are the common axioms about *efficient causes,* which are either quite true or close to the truth. 1. *Every cause is a true or existing thing.* 2. *Every cause is prior to its own effect, if not in time at least in nature. That is, in order*

---

13. De Vries, *Determinationes Ontologicae,* chap. 12, sec. 22, p. 128, also dismisses material and formal causes as "outside the realm of physics." Also Le Clerc, *Ontologia:* see chap. 9, p. 36.

14. See Part II, chap. 2, n. 5, and the introduction, pp. xv and xxvi.

for it to exist, the existence of the thing effected is not required; but the latter is unable to exist if the cause does not exist. For a thing which is endowed with effective force does not depend on its effect, even though it gets to be called a cause because of the effect. 3. *No thing is a cause of itself.* 4. *Nor are several things mutually causes of each other; or, in causes there is no circle.* 5. *As soon as a cause acts, its true effect exists without any interval of time, though not the whole system of effects which perhaps it was set to bring about by a long chain of actions.* 6. *There is no true perfection in a created thing, which the cause itself did not possess, if not in a similar manner yet in a superior or at least an equal manner.* 7. *Any cause will effect nothing at all, if it is not determined by its own character or nature, or by its present disposition in the given circumstances, to ensure above everything that it does this now rather than not do it, but remains indifferent to both directions.* These [axioms] seem to carry assent without any reasoning.

Concerning effects

From these [axioms] metaphysicians infer: 1. *That the continued duration, as well as the first existence, of a made or created thing is to be attributed to the power of the efficient cause, whether this requires continued action on the part of the cause or whether such constancy of nature, or perfection, has been granted to the created thing from the start as may last for the necessary time.* 2. *No effect, at least no effect which depends on human power, lasts longer than while the cause operates.* This will not seem strange to anyone who has studied human efficacy. Human efficacy consists wholly of variously altering one's own thoughts and feelings and initiating or directing movements in one's own body. But the motion which we excite in our bodies is often continued without any effort on our part; and the force which we have impressed on contiguous bodies by means of our limbs seems to continue without our will and without our efficacy.

No infinite series of causes

The arguments which show that *there cannot be an infinite series of causes without a first and independent cause* are very similar, namely, that every term in that series is dependent and effected; therefore the whole series has been effected, even though there may be nothing outside the series on which the whole series depends or by which it is effected; and that it is true of each part of the series that it has been determined by the efficacy of some cause to exist rather than not exist; therefore it will be true of the whole series that it has been determined to exist by the efficacy of another. To these can be added [the argument] that each term in that series, apart from the last, is both cause and caused; and for each term there is one act of effecting and one thing effected; but if a final term is added, the things effected will be more than were the effecting actions; which is absurd. Since, however, arguments equal to and very similar to these (namely the argument which infers that what is true of any part of an infinite is true also of the whole infinite) can be adduced to overturn an infinity of *space* and *time,* it does not seem safe or necessary in such a grave question as *the existence of God* to rely on these arguments alone; for we find everywhere throughout this whole universe traces of so great a power and intelligence, which lead to a certain nature that is supremely excellent, the most wise and most powerful creator of the world. And there cannot be any suspicion that this superior nature sprang from a prior cause, much less that there has been an infinite series of things of that kind, since every cause in that series would have to be regarded as at least equal in virtue to the creator of the world. Anyone, therefore, who, believing that the world has been created, takes refuge in such a series of causes in order not to acknowledge the one eternal God, since it is not credible that things of such great power and virtue should have perished while their works still remain, verily, he will substitute innumerable gods in place of the one God.

6.

Rational causes, necessary causes, and contingent causes

There is a well-known division of *causes* into *rational, necessary,* and *contingent.* Neither *contingency,* however, nor *chance* or *fortune,* denotes a true efficacious nature; these words are used when effects result either from natural causes in such a way that we cannot foresee them, or from free causes when there is no obvious incentive which would certainly direct the cause in one direction or the other, and no indication from which a spectator could predict the choice. Therefore all contingent things are effected either by necessary or by free causes. Furthermore, necessary causes which seem to act without design or will should be regarded as instruments which perform a function rather than as *acting,* and when they do seem to be acting or impelling, they themselves are also acted upon or impelled. Only deliberately acting things, therefore, seem to have a real power within themselves, or truly to effect anything.

What is liberty?

There is a difficult question about the *liberty of deliberately operating causes:* do they have within themselves *the power to twist and turn, so that they can set themselves to will a thing or its contrary equally,* which is called the *liberty of contrariety* (as if one were to say that he can desire and pursue either that which seems to him pleasant or that which appears harmful and annoying), or *do they have at least the power to set themselves to act or not to act, to will or not to will,* which is the *liberty of contradiction.*[15] It was the opinion of the Stoics[16] that our *desires* and *aversions* are excited by the images of *good* and *evil* which appear to the mind, together with the *character* and *qualities* of the mind itself, in accordance with a certain constant law of our nature, and further, that the character of the mind itself is set by the earliest fabric of [its] nature and then by education and morals. They also held, therefore, that *judgments* and *opinions* are always formed from the *sagacity, caution,* or *diligence* which the mind possesses at that time on the basis of the indications of good and evil which things themselves display; and *volitions* and *actions* emerge from the *calm* or *violent* passions of the mind. And all these *necessary antecedents of actions* were set and foreseen by God himself. [By *free causes* therefore they mean *those which can do what they will and abstain from what they reject, however much they may actually have been im-*

15. The distinction between liberty of contrariety and liberty of contradiction was made by scholastic moralists: Eustache, *Ethica sive Summa Moralis Disciplinae,* p. 12; Carmichael, *Natural Rights,* p. 24.

16. On the ideas of the Stoics concerning the necessity of human actions, see the introduction, p. xxv, and below: II, 2, 3, pp. 129–31, and III, 3, 3, p. 171.

pelled to will or to reject. For they take the view that the power of directing oneself, which some imagine to be determined neither by the character of the agent nor by the appearance of good and evil nor by the judgment of the agent, is absurd and useless, and properly does not occur except when incentives are offered which are equal in both directions, which rarely happens; and even in this case the inclination of the self in either direction would have no quality of virtue or vice. And if anyone were to make use of this power to act against what seems to him to be the prevailing incentive, his action would be stupid if not wicked. On this whole question each one will best judge who examines himself to see whether or not in every deliberate intention to act (for few would maintain that when we are blindly carried away by a passionate emotion, we are free in this sense) he has before him some prospect of obtaining a good or repulsing an evil, by which his mind was moved to will. Similarly, in things which are completely equal, let him see whether or not he chooses one thing over the rest because it was the first that occurred to him, or because he has attached a feigned and imaginary image of good to the direction which he chooses. On this question the Stoics argue that *nothing* arises *without a cause;* and if anything were indeed effected by a cause which was indifferent and capable of going in either direction, and were not inclined to one direction or the other, either by its own character and nature or by the circumstances assumed to surround it, such a decision would not amount to a cause.

Others, however, respond[17] that such is the nature of *rational causes* that they can move in any direction, that they are themselves the cause of their inclining or turning, and that this characteristic is theirs by nature. They concede that they nearly always follow their own judgments in some way but that there are two particular appearances that move the will, namely, [the appearance] of right (*honestum*) and duty, or of the pleasant and the

---

17. Peripatetic moralists were critical of Stoic determinism, insisting upon the ability of reason or rational causes to direct the will to beatitude or lasting happiness. Eustache, *Ethica,* p. 55ff; Burgersdijk, *Idea Philosophiae tum Moralis tum Naturalis,* Oxford, 1654, pp. 37–38, 52–54. See the introduction, p. xxv, and Part II, chap. 2, n. 8, pp. 130–31.

useful, and that it is in their own power to incline and turn themselves to either of these.][18]

7.

Beings are divided into substances and accidents

Finally, *beings* are divided into *substances* and *modes* or *accidents,* and not without reason. The first notion of *substance,* a quite simple notion, arises for each man from the fact that he is aware of *himself as persisting,* even though his thoughts, sensations, and feelings are constantly changing, and that he cannot imagine himself other than he has always been, despite these mental variations. Similarly, we perceive by sight and touch that bodies take on new colors and new shapes and quietly change their motions, while their quantity or extension, mass, weight, and solidity remain constant. Thus we call *the thing that, despite its change of properties, remains itself, a substance;* and *the changeable properties* we call *accidents.*

What are the truest modes

The *principal modes* which truly add something to their substances seem to be *the power of moving,* that is, *motions* and *figures* in *corporeal things,* and in *our minds* the *operations or passions of perceiving, understanding, and willing.* [19]

[*Corporeal substances and thinking substances*

Substances are either *extended* or *thinking;* there are perhaps several kinds of both which are fundamentally different from each other. If there is any

---

18. The sentences that appear between brackets were added in 1744. In the 1749 edition, there is a note: "See Part II, Chapters 2 and 3 [pp. 126–44] and Part III, Chapter 3, Section 3 [pp. 171–72]. Read the chapter of Locke cited above, 'On Power,' and other frequently encountered writers."

19. The following note appears in the 1749 edition: "See the letters of Samuel Clarke against Dodwell, and his defenders, on the difference between thinking thing and body."

reality in *space,* it is different from every body; and among bodies themselves there have perhaps been from the beginning certain notable differences which are hidden from us. Likewise the kinds of thinking things which are widely different from each other are perhaps innumerable, of which some are far more highly endowed with senses and powers and fitted to lead their lives in quite contrary ways: from the feeblest souls of immobile shellfish, not to speak of plants, to the highest orders of angels and God himself. And though we call them all by the common name of *spirit* or *soul,* we should not rush to the judgment that they are all alike in nature and differ only in degree.][20]

Body, magnitude and extended things are the concern of physics and mathematics, spirits of pneumatology.

20. This paragraph was added in 1744.

On the Categories and the General Properties of Being

I.

We shall survey the chief general properties of beings by going briefly through the ten categories that Archytas[2] is said to have first discovered and Aristotle certainly confirmed, whatever the division of things may actually be. The ten categories are: *substance, quantity, quality, relation, action, passion, place, time, position, and state.*

Substance

Substance is a *thing subsisting in itself,* and which does not inhere in another thing as modes or *accidents* do, which are much better known than substances themselves. For the nature of substances is unknown, except that we draw from our own selves a sort of dim idea of a thing bereft of its *qualities.*[3] The other things said about substances in the scholastics are not useful. Here are the definitions of the technical terms.

Subsistence is the *completeness* of a *substance* and is lacking in parts of a natural thing which have been separated from the rest of it. A *subsistent* is defined as an underlying subject (*suppositum*) or individual nature (*hypostasis*). A person is a *suppositum* endowed with reason.

1. This chapter was added in 1744.
2. Archytas, a Pythagorean who influenced Plato, is credited with the authorship of a work on categories by Simplicius in his commentaries on the categories of Aristotle. See Simplicius, *On Aristotle's "Categories 1–4,"* p. 18.
3. In the third edition (1749) this note was added: "See the Essay of Locke, cited above, on ideas of substances." (Locke, *Essay,* II, chaps. 23–24.)

2.

The kinds of quantity

Quantity is an ambiguous word; and the various kinds of quantities cannot be defined because they are represented by simple ideas. These [are] the simple kinds [of quantity]. [First,] *magnitude,* which is appropriate to body or space. [*Magnitude is threefold.*] It is itself threefold: *linear, surface,* and *solid;* of all three, there is a real nature and a distinct knowledge, though the first two are never found apart from the last.

Time

The second kind of quantity is *time,* whose space or extension is completely different from the previous kind, and is called *diuturnity* or *duration;* it accompanies the actions and passions of the mind and all the motions of which the mind is conscious. For every thought carries with it a sense of a certain time, and every man is as conscious of that as he is aware of himself thinking. Hence it discerns order and sequence among the various operations of the understanding or the will; and it knows which things come first and which come after, and whether it has spent a long or a little time on a thing. Things are said to *coexist* with this series of thoughts, because they occupy the same portion of time. This *coexistence,* therefore, of time by no means fully describes the notion, since a third something has to be clearly recognized which equally measures both the sequence of thought and other things or events. And the notion of time should not necessarily be related to motion, even though we find in movements convenient measures of it.[4] A good deal has been said about this before.[5]

4. In the third edition (1749) there is the following note: "See Locke, as above, on the modes of time." (Locke, *Essay,* II, chaps. 14–15.)

5. The subject of time was examined in Part I, chap. 3, sec. 4, pp. 82–86, where Hutcheson argued that space and time are indeed ideas as Locke contended, not properties inherent in objects. But Hutcheson also held that we would be incapable of understanding things, their position and motion, "unless something real outside the mind corresponds to those ideas." See the introduction for Hutcheson's response to Edmund Law, p. xxiv, who considered it a consequence of Locke's way of ideas that space and time had no real existence.

True quantities uncertain

Here we mention in passing that we cannot know by any sure indicator whether the true quantities of magnitudes and times equal, surpass or are surpassed by our ideas of them. It will, however, be readily agreed that the same relation among them is preserved in our ideas. It is bodies that excite the first ideas of figures; but the mind itself can variously compound them and can perfect and complete them more than the figures that are found anywhere in bodies themselves. Physics and geometry tell us that these two classes of quantities are infinitely divisible, and by their help so too are movements, angles (*inclinationes*), and ratios (*rationes*).

Number

The third kind of quantity, which is widely different from the other kinds, is found in *numbers*. Though our first notions of numbers are aroused by the bodies perceived by our senses, yet all things can equally be numbered, including some that are very different from bodies. In fact, ideas of numbers can be absolutely perfect without ideas of bodies at all. Ideas of numbers or their relations (*rationes*) are not therefore to be necessarily related to magnitudes, since things which are superior in number are often inferior in magnitude, and things which have no magnitude at all can be compared with each other by means of number.[6] Indeed, numerical relations, when they can be used, are the most convenient measures of other relations, because they are easier to handle.[7]

---

6. In his letter to William Mace, 6 September 1727, Hutcheson observed that "Numbers are the clearest ideas we have, and their relations are the most distinct, but often have nothing to do with wholes or parts, and are alike applicable to heterogeneous or homogeneous qualities" (*European Magazine,* September 1788, p. 159).

7. In the third edition (1749) there is a note: "Here we should note in passing the doctrine of the man who is by far the best and most intelligent: Isaac Barrow (Barovius), *Lectures on Mathematics* (*Lectiones Mathematicae*)." It may be significant that it was Barrow's attempt to apply geometry to optics that prompted Berkeley's extended critique of "optic axes" in *An Essay Towards a New Theory of Vision,* a theory which was in turn countered by Hutcheson in his letter to William Mace, 6 September 1727: see the introduction, p. xiv and n. 19.

There is no number outside the mind separate from the actual things numbered, and nothing corresponds to the idea of [number] except the things numbered. The power of numbering is most useful, however, in measuring things themselves and their relations (*rationes*). These three kinds of quantity can achieve nothing by themselves in the absence of bodies, and space and time are not liable to any alteration. Time and space indeed seem to most people to be actually infinite, and clearly number can be increased without end. We cannot, however, understand an infinite number, because the concept of multiplicity (*multitudo*) is defined by number itself.

Other quantities

There are other notions of quantities in a variety of different things. The quantity which is attributed to motion or moving forces may be related to space and time. A wholly different quantity is ascribed to powers and qualities, e.g., to sharpness of mind and intelligence, the movements and drives of the will, love, hate, virtue, vice, joy, sorrow, and the sensible qualities themselves; but they are rarely counted as quantities.

3.

Two kinds of qualities: motion and thought

There are several types of *quality* (which also refuses to be defined), and they are different from each other. The most important of those which are really in things are *strength, power, active habits, talents,* and *propensities,* all of which are primarily qualities of minds. As for the sensible qualities which are called *sensitive,* which are perceived by one sense alone, they are senses or states or modifications of the mind itself, although external things often seem to be endowed with them or affected by them. Figure, motion, rest, and position are accessible by several senses (the last pertains to the ninth category). There are, therefore, only two kinds of true qualities or accidents: *thoughts* and *propensities* (*propensiones*) on the one hand, which belong to spirits, and on the other hand, *motion, rest,* and *figure,* which belong to bodies.

Rest and figure

Some learned men[8] doubt whether *rest* is something real, distinct from the inertia by which bodies keep their state or motion by means of a force which is real but perhaps not their own or is derived originally from elsewhere. Likewise some[9] hold that *figure* is the mere denomination of a mass which is derived from the relation of its parts to certain parts of space, and that the parts themselves do not otherwise change when the figure changes. And indeed figure by itself can effect nothing, although a certain configuration of a solid physical mass offers no resistance to gravity and other forces imposed upon it, while solid masses in other shapes do. Hence logs may be split by impacted wedges but cannot be split by objects of other shapes, and spheres and cylinders will roll when a cube would stay still.

Gravity, cohesion, etc.

It is also disputed whether gravity itself, elasticity, cohesion, and some other things of that sort are powers of bodies themselves and essentially involved in physical nature; or whether on the other hand they are powers which are continuously exerted on them by a superior nature in accordance with fixed laws or at least implanted by it in the beginning.[10] The latter is more likely;

---

8. In this reference to "learned men" and in the two following references, Hutcheson appears to have had in mind certain physicists whose writings served as introductions to the philosophy of Newton at Scottish universities and dissenting academies: W. J. 's Gravesande, *Mathematical Elements of Natural Philosophy; or, An Introduction to Sir Isaac Newton's Philosophy*, and Henry Pemberton, *A View of Sir Isaac Newton's Philosophy*. On the idea of rest or inertia, see 's Gravesande, bk. 1, chap. 2, pp. 4–5, and Pemberton, p. 28: "The real and absolute motion of any body is not visible to us: for we are ourselves in constant motion along with the earth on which we dwell; insomuch that we perceive bodies to move so far only as their motion is different from our own. When a body appears to us to lie at rest, in reality it only continues the motion it has received, without putting forth any power to change that motion." Francis Hutcheson is listed as one of the subscribers to the Dublin edition of Pemberton's work.

9. On the idea of figure, see 's Gravesande, bk. 1, chap. 2, p. 5, and bk. 1, chap. 14, pp. 43–44, on the application of the idea of figure to wedges and cylinders.

10. Andrew Baxter, in *Enquiry*, sec. 1, note K, pp. 33–49, appealed to the authority of the same Newtonians against Newton himself, who had proposed that "a subtle elastic

the reason is that, although innumerable laws or systems (*rationes*) could seemingly be devised, we see that only one is in fact in force, even though it is not a bit more necessary in its own nature than the others. The only qualities, therefore, which clearly add something real to their substances are thoughts and motions; about the rest there is no agreement among the learned.

Quality appropriate to the subject

It is certain of every true quality that the quality of one thing cannot at the same time be a quality of another thing, even though the latter may have a quality of its own which is very like the other. Qualities appropriate to physical mass are divided and diffused through the parts of a body, so that each part has its own portion of a divided quality. If, therefore, there are any individual qualities, they inhere in a simple and individual thing.

4.

Relation

There are many disputes among the scholastics about *relations*. We will briefly expound the more useful points.

When we look at two or more things which are not completely different from each other, and a property is apparent which is common to both or all of them, a *relative* idea arises which exhibits the connection or relationship between them. In every relation three things (or virtually three) exist: a *related thing* or *subject,* a *correlate* or *term,* and a *ground.*[11] The first two are the things compared; the last is the property in which they are compared or the action which affords a reason for comparison. Thus the relations among magnitudes of the same kind are defined in terms of *magnitude*

---

fluid . . . might be the cause of gravity and the cause of many other phenomena" (cited by Baxter, p. 34). Baxter was determined to vindicate "the universality of Providence, or the immediate presence of God . . . in all the operations of nature," p. 39, a project endorsed by Hutcheson. See above, Part I, chap. 5, p. 92, and below, this chapter, n. 14; Part II, chap. 4, p. 145; and Part III, chap. 5, p. 180.

11. See chap. 1, sec. 4, p. 70 on relations.

itself, the relations among times in terms of *duration,* and among numbers in terms of *how many.* Bodies and spirits may be compared with each other with respect to any other properties or qualities whatsoever. There are innumerable names for relations, according as the related things are similar, dissimilar, equal, greater, smaller, double, triple, etc., and swifter, slower, longer, shorter, more, less, tighter, looser, heavier, lighter, and we could add six hundred others. Moral relations are principally grounded in the actions, duties, agreements, and injuries of the related subjects.

Relation not an external thing

Apart from the related things themselves and the cause of comparison or ground, which is sometimes no different from the nature or essence of the related things, there is nothing more in the things themselves which corresponds to a relative idea; otherwise there would be innumerable other things attached to just about every thing. For there is no part of matter which does not bear some relation to every other part, no spirit which will not be found to be either similar or dissimilar, equal or unequal, to every other. Whenever, therefore, a relation is ascribed to things themselves, reference is always being made, albeit vaguely and obscurely, to a relative idea which either is or may be in a mind.[12]

Ideas of relations not useless

Relative ideas are not, however, for this reason artificial or useless. For not any and every relative idea arises at random from the known properties of related things, but only the idea which corresponds to the natures and properties of both. And when one of the related things and its relationship to the other are both known, knowledge of the other itself will also be gained.

---

12. In the course of his argument against Samuel Clarke's theory that moral distinctions are grounded in the relations of things, Hutcheson affirmed that "Relations are not real Qualities inherent in external Natures, but only Ideas necessarily accompanying our Perception of two objects and comparing them." *Illustrations on the Moral Sense,* sec. 2, p. 156.

For in all inquiries we are chiefly asking what things lead to other things? what things will help us to carry out our intentions? what things are more fit or suitable to which, for the purpose of being useful to us? All the sciences, therefore, are concerned with investigating connections (*rationes*) and relations.

The clearest relations are those of numbers

The relations of numbers are clearer and more distinct than all others. And in investigating relations no one can desire anything further than to reduce them to relations of numbers. Hence it is surprising that certain learned men[13] have taken the position that almost all knowledge of connections (*rationes*) has been taken from the connections (*rationes*) of magnitudes and should be reduced to them, and that there is no relationship among numbers, except so far as they exhibit certain degrees of magnitude which are equal to each other. To the contrary, things which are smaller in number are often greater in magnitude, and relations of numbers may obtain between things which are devoid of all magnitude. We grant that measurements of time and motion in particular have to be drawn from magnitudes, yet the connections between them are most easily measured by numbers when this is possible. But both kinds of measurement are almost wholly rejected not only by the so-called secondary sensible qualities, but also by almost all the properties of spirits.

Every relation is mutual and reciprocal, and [there is] the same foundation in the things themselves when the relation is converted, even though it will have a very different or contrary name.

13. The reference may be to Berkeley, who had argued that mathematicians were in error when they substituted calculations based on fluxions or infinitesimals for magnitudes or quantities; he described fluxions as "the ghosts of departed quantities" (*The Analyst* [1734], sec. 35; *Works,* vol. 4, p. 89). Hutcheson was impatient to have this work answered: see letter to Colin Maclaurin, 21 April 1737, in which Berkeley is described as "a man bursting almost with vanity long ago," Aberdeen University Library MS 206/11.

5.

Action and passion

Action and *passion* are *related,* and the relation between them is obvious: they are not two different things distinct from the actual objects of which the one acts and the other is acted upon. For a single thing supervenes, namely, the action as a result of which the state of the passive thing changes. We have previously explained,[14] so far as we could, the simple notion of *power and action.*

One last point remains, which we touched upon before, about any action attributed to bodies: the bodies themselves which are said to act are also acted upon, or are moved at that time by another force, equally with the things which they impact. [*Laws of Nature*] And since a corporeal nature can neither understand a law properly so called nor obey it of its own accord, everything which is said to happen *by the law of nature* (as some learned men believe)[15] is brought about in a determinate order and uniform manner in response to specific surrounding conditions by the first cause of all things, which sustains all things by its own continuous force as it permeates them all; the qualities, motions, contacts, and collisions of matter merely afford it the occasion. The inertia which is thought to be always necessary to matter does not seem to be consistent with certain actions which are attributed to matter. But no mortal man has adequate knowledge and expertise in these things.

6.

The remaining categories

We have discussed the main points about *space, time,* and *position* in chapter 3.[16] Concerning *state* we need say no more than that the powers of

---

14. In the third edition (1749), there is the following note: "See above, Chapter IV, Section 5," pp. 92–93.

15. In the third edition (1749): "namely Malebranche, Baxter and some Newtonians."

16. See above, pp. 78–86.

neither body nor mind are located in this category. It includes only those things which are substances in themselves but are normally found in union and combination with other things.

THE END OF ONTOLOGY

PART II

On the Human Mind

CHAPTER I

On the Powers of the Mind, and First
on the Understanding

I.

The definition of pneumatology

The *science of spirits* is called *pneumatics* by modern writers; among the ancients it was a part of *metaphysics* or of *physics.*[1] But as we have no certain knowledge of any spirits other than human minds and the good God almighty, when we rely on the resources of our own reason alone, they will necessarily be the principal subjects of our discussion. And since we must progress from things that we know in order to bring more obscure things to light, without regard to the dignity of the things themselves, pneumatics rightly begins from knowledge of the human mind.

Spirit is substance which thinks or can think

Spirit, soul, mind denote the same nature, whatever it may be, *which thinks or can think, and which is conscious of its own actions.*[2] It is likely that there

---

1. On the study of pneumatology in Scottish universities in the early eighteenth century, see the introduction, p. xxii.
2. In the first edition (1742), the text continued after this sentence with a discussion

is a very large number of such natures, various orders of them, in fact, equipped with various powers: most of them much inferior to human minds with which they have very little in common, but many also perhaps which are superior. Though all of them are called by the same name of spirit or soul, they are almost a whole world, as they say, different from each other. We must first give some account of the powers of minds before determining anything about their nature. It is quite obvious that the human soul is distinct from the gross body which is accessible to the external senses, since no one has said that thought, prudence, arts, or virtues are located in flesh or bones, or in the veins or gross humors.

2.

The twofold power of minds: understanding and willing

Since no one has yet shown whether there is any power in the mind which causes the body to grow and flourish and be nurtured by the food it takes in, we shall ignore the *auxetic* and *threptic* force of the soul which the ancients so often mentioned.[3] The other powers of the mind we might reasonably reduce to two, namely, the faculty of *understanding* and the faculty of *willing,* which are concerned respectively with knowing things and with rendering life happy.[4]

The *senses* report to the *understanding,* which is those powers or that

---

of spirit and the ways in which spirit differs from body. This order of presentation followed de Vries, *Determinationes Pneumatologicae,* sec. 1, in *De Natura Dei et Humanae Mentis.* In the second edition of *A Synopsis of Metaphysics* (1744) this discussion has been moved to chap. 3, pp. 138–44.

3. The *auxetic* and *threptic* powers of the soul are Aristotle's terms for the powers responsible for the "growth" and "nourishment" of all living things. See Aristotle, *On the Soul,* II, 4, especially 415 a23, p. 85 in the Hett translation.

4. De Vries, *Determinationes Pneumatologicae,* sec. 2, chap. 6. Locke thought that the distinction of the faculties into understanding and willing had "misled many into a confused notion of so many distinct agents in us." *Essay,* II, 21, 6, p. 237. In contrast to Locke, Hutcheson liked to remind his critics of the importance of the distinction between the understanding and the will: *An Essay on the Nature and Conduct of the Passions and Affections* (1742), pp. 30–31n., and *Illustrations upon the Moral Sense* (1742), pp. 219–22.

ordering of the soul by which, at the prompting of certain things, it immediately receives certain ideas, which are not alterable at its discretion, but which a certain superior nature, the parent and creator of the soul, seems to have formed; and he has so structured the mind that it refers certain sensations to external things, as images which depict their nature or qualities.

Sensations and their causes

Learned men have adopted different opinions about the cause and origin of ideas. None of them can affirm anything beyond this one single point: that ideas arise in the mind from a certain contact with things, according to certain laws which become known by practice and attention; nor can they be referred to any other cause than divine power. We must also credit divine power with the fact that certain external sensations and other ideas are similar to external things.[5]

3.

Sensations are either direct and antecedent or reflexive and subsequent[6]

One [kind of] *sensation* is *primary* and *direct, when a certain appearance (species) is first presented to the mind,* and the other is *reflexive* and *subsequent sensation, when a certain new appearance (species) occurs to a mind as it attends to things which it has previously perceived.* We must first discuss direct sensation.

---

5. Malebranche, *The Search After Truth,* pp. 46–47, and Locke, "An Examination of Malebranche's Opinion," secs. 10–16.

6. De Vries, *Determinationes Pneumatologicae,* II, 2, does not speak of sensation but of *apprehensio,* which he defines as *nuda perceptio.* Hutcheson's distinction between direct sensation and reflexive sensation follows Locke, *Essay,* II, 20–24.

External sensation

The *sensations* which arise in the mind as the result of a certain motion excited in the body or impressed upon it are said to be *external* and are commonly reduced to five kinds. However, if instead of distinguishing perceptions, we were to make a division of the senses, there would be more than five.

Sensible qualities, secondary or primary

There is an important distinction between *sensible qualities:* some affect only one sense, others more than one. Of the former kind are *colors, sounds, tastes, smells, heat* and *cold;* of the latter, *duration, number, extension, figure, motion* and *rest,* which may be perceived by more than one sense, and indeed some of them are perceived by an internal sense. Qualities of the former kind would properly be called *sensible,* qualities of the latter kind rather *states [of mind] (affectiones) that accompany sensation.* [We judge that the ideas of these [qualities] and of the relations which hold between them are representations of external things, under the guidance of nature; hence they are classified as *intellectual ideas,* because in them the powers of reason are exercised with the greatest profit and pleasure.][7]

[Sensible qualities] either pleasing or painful or neutral

Some sensible qualities are pleasant, some painful, others neutral or indifferent. In the case of some sensible qualities, mild sensations are pleasing, intense sensations painful. But these sensations depict or represent neither external objects nor actual motions excited in the body itself; however, without the sense of colors or any tactile quality, all bodies would be totally hidden from us, as well as their positions, figures, motions, and sizes. There are also the other sensations properly so called, which are sure signs or indications of things or movements which can help or harm the body; we are warned by a sense of pain to avoid those which do us harm, but are stim-

---

7. This sentence was added in 1744.

ulated by a pleasing sense to pursue those which can help. *Not without design, I think, not without the power of the gods.*[8]

Ideas accompanying every sensation, duration and number

Certain sensations of concomitant ideas do or may accompany absolutely every perception of the mind; such are the notions of *duration* and *number.* For any perception of the mind and any action of which the mind itself is aware carries a portion of duration with it; several of these succeeding each other in a certain series also suggest to the mind some longer space of time. In the same way, it is not only things perceived by external sense which may be *numbered,* but also those which are perceived by the internal sense or by reflection, as it is called.[9]

Others are perceptible by sight and by touch

Extension, figure, motion and rest are perceived by two senses, that is, by sight and by touch. Certain writers call these, rather well, the *primary properties* (*affectiones*) of bodies, because under the guidance of nature we believe them to be present just as they are seen in things themselves,[10] and physicists tell us that the whole power of bodies to excite sensible ideas depends on one or other of them.[11] They speak of sensible qualities, however, as merely secondary *properties* (*affectiones*) or *qualities:* there is nothing like them in external things, though these things, by a fixed law of nature, have a certain power of exciting these ideas in us, [a power] which they get from their primary qualities.

---

8. Virgil, *Aeneid,* bk. 5, 56, in vol. 1, p. 476: Aeneas reflects that it is not without design that he has been driven by a storm to land in the very place where his father died. Hutcheson makes evocative use of the beginning of book 5 of the *Aeneid* in his inaugural lecture. See p. 191.

9. Locke used the term "internal sense" on occasion (for example, *Essay,* II, 1, 4, p. 105), as Hutcheson recalled in *An Essay on the Nature and Conduct of the Passions and Affections,* preface, p. xi. But Locke preferred to use the term "reflection" for those ideas "the mind gets by reflecting on its own operations," *Essay,* p. 105.

10. Locke, *Essay,* II, 8, 9, p. 135.

11. Robert Boyle, *Origin of Forms and Qualities,* pp. 18–19.

Whether this perception of primary qualities be called an action or a passive process of the mind, the only cause which seems able to be suggested for the similarity or congruence between ideas of this kind and things themselves is God himself, who by a fixed law of nature ensures that the notions of things which are aroused in the presence of objects are similar to the things themselves, or at least depict their physical appearances, if not their true qualities.

[God himself seems to have made the forms or elements of all ideas, without our own minds contributing anything at this point. But once ideas have been admitted, the mind can ring the changes upon them, and vigorously exercise its powers in doing so. It can either retain ideas or dismiss them, pay attention to them or turn to others; it can divide concrete ideas by *abstracting,* or join simple ideas and compound them. It can in a certain manner enlarge ideas or diminish them, compare them with each other and learn their relations. In all these [activities] no less than in willed motions and appetites, the mind is conscious to itself of truly doing something.

From the pleasing senses which are called *pleasures* arises our first acquaintance with *good,* from painful senses our first acquaintance with *evil.* And those things which serve to procure the former and avert the latter are called *useful,* and their opposites are called *useless* or *harmful.* When the sublimer senses come into play, they introduce notions of superior goods and graver ills. From these we understand what a happy life is and what is a miserable life, and they must necessarily be attributed to certain natural senses.

Appearances which are perceived by *taste, smell,* and *touch* are closely related to specific parts of the body; they indicate what directly helps or harms the body, and have an immediate effect. By *sight* and *hearing* we acquire some knowledge of distant things, and sometimes of far superior pleasures; in fact, sight and hearing are very useful in our learning about things and developing understanding. All these senses, then, have been usefully given by nature either to protect our bodies or to preserve the human race or for the purpose of living a good and pleasant life, as will be more evident in the case of the nobler senses soon to be expounded.][12]

12. The last three paragraphs were added in the second edition, 1744.

4.

Internal senses or consciousness (conscientia)

The other power of perception is a certain *internal sense,* or *consciousness, by means of which everything that takes place in the mind is known.* [13] Each man knows his own sensations, judgments, reflections, volitions, desires, and intentions; they cannot be concealed from the mind in which they are. By this power of the mind each man knows himself and has a perception of himself and can direct his attention to himself and his own actions. Hence there may be full knowledge of spirits and bodies alike; the inner nature of both are unknown, [but] the properties (*affectiones*) are known.

Ideas of modes of thinking are abstract ideas like many others

It cannot be denied that we have general ideas of these modes of thinking, and that they are abstracted from the properties which distinguish individual ideas. For wherever a similarity is seen between different things, or several things are included in one class, or designated by any common word or symbol, one part of a complex idea comes before the mind, and the rest of it is left out.

5.

Reflexive or subsequent sensations

Now it remains for us to discuss *subsequent and reflexive sensation,* or *those appearances of things or that sense which occurs to the mind when it is directed toward things previously perceived.* We call them sensations because these

---

13. *A Short Introduction to Moral Philosophy,* p. 6: "Internal senses are those powers or determinations of the mind by which it perceives or is conscious of itself, . . . this power some celebrated writers call *consciousness* or *reflection.*"

ideas or perceptions arise by a fixed law of nature, not at our discretion. There are many kinds of them, and we will deal with them briefly.[14]

Novelty, grandeur, similarity, and certain harmonies of sounds are pleasing to them

Some of the things which affect an external sense and would seem to be neutral to it are pleasing, or in some cases unpleasing, to a kind of reflexive sense, when the mind pays attention not only to its external sensations but also to the ideas which accompany them, and is also moved by a kind of impression that is different from the pleasing external sensations. In the first place, *novelty* is pleasing to the mind because we have a kind of natural impulse to know things, or a desire for knowledge. Likewise the *grandeur* of anything we see is pleasing. And a certain *similarity* among several things is also pleasing, when *difference* and *variety* are also present. Most pleasing are the combination and harmony of certain sounds, when not only are the higher and lower sounds themselves enjoyed, but also the lengths of the notes and the various other devices so familiar to music lovers.

And all imitation

Virtually all imitation is pleasing, whether in works of art in the classical sense—painting, sculpture, and engraving—or in movement and rhythmical speech.

And knowledge of things

A sense of great happiness accompanies *learning* and *knowledge*.

---

14. For a parallel discussion of reflex or subsequent sensations, see *A Short Introduction to Moral Philosophy*, p. 12 ff.

And skilled crafts

It gives great pleasure to look at things which have been cleverly and skill-fully made to fill a certain need, even for those who do not expect to get any use from them.

The common sense, and sympathy of affections

We must include among these *reflexive senses* the sense which is called *common.* This sense takes joy from the happiness of another man's good fortune and sorrow from his adversity, so long as there is no animosity, re-sentment, enmity, or abhorrence of disgraceful behavior. By the wonderful fabric of our nature also, most of the emotions and passions of other men excite similar feelings in us by a kind of *sympathetic influence.*

The sense of the fitting and the good

Of all these reflexive senses the most notable is the sense of the *fitting* and the *good,* which passes judgment as from the bench on all the things men do, on all our pleasures of body or mind, on our opinions, sentiments, actions, prayers, intentions, and feelings, determining in each case what is fine, fitting and good, and what is the measure in each. Almost all the plea-sures which we have in common with the animals seem to this sense to be vile and shameful. But resolutions to act that display a nobler character, that intimate powers of mind and reason, that give evidence of a kindly disposition, and especially those which reveal a constant and steady will to do good and to deserve well of others, move all hearts by their very good-ness; and for the man who possesses them, when he calls them to mind, they are glorious and full of joy.

This power is innate, gratuitous, and at hand

That this power is innate to the mind and that a man does not approve either his own or others' actions because of any advantage they have or pleasure they bring him is clear from the fact that each man thinks his own duties toward others are more virtuous the more they are associated with risk of loss to himself, and the less they are intended for his own advantage, honor, or reputation; and from the fact that we praise the good actions of other men which we read of or hear about, even from earlier centuries, as much as we praise present actions that are good, and even approve virtue, loyalty, and patriotism in an enemy, though it does us harm ourselves. In approving these services in which a man has done something for another from friendship, faith, or courage, we cannot expect that either honor, pleasure, advantage, or reward will accrue to us. Even men who scarcely believed in rewards after death still thought it was *sweet and fitting* at times *to die for their country,*[15] and they believe that even their enemies should praise their death.[16]

Related to this is that sense of *praise* and *honor* when a man sees that his intentions and his actions are approved by the verdict of other men; the opposite of this is that very painful *sense of blame* if one's actions and intentions are condemned by others. Men are still moved by both of these feelings even when they do not expect any further benefit from other people's approval or disadvantage from their censure. Even dying men are anxious about their posthumous fame, no less than those who look forward to a long life.

The sense of humor

By the aid of these senses, then, some of the things that happen to us appear delightful, fitting, glorious, and honorable to us, while others seem vile and contemptible, and we may discern yet another reflexive sense: a sense of things that are *ridiculous* or apt to cause laughter, that is, when a thing arouses contrary sensations at one and the same time. In the case of men's intentions and actions, bad behavior that does not cause grievous sorrow or death gives rise to laughter, because there is some dignity in the very name of man because we have a certain opinion of his prudence and intelligence, whereas bad behavior that leads to serious pain or death rather

---

15. This is a quotation from Horace, *Odes,* 3, 2, 13, p. 144, in *Odes and Epodes.*
16. Hutcheson's note (1749): "these things are more fully proved in the ethics."

excites pity. In the case of other things, we are moved to laughter by those which exhibit some splendid spectacle at the same time as a contradictory image of something cheap, lowly, and contemptible. This sense is very beneficial, whether in increasing the pleasure of conversation or in correcting men's morals.

6.

Memory, the power of reasoning, imagination[17]

From these powers of perception, the mind acquires for itself all the furniture of ideas that the faculty of judging and reasoning makes use of, and it preserves them by means of *memory.* For there is a power in the mind which can recall a weaker image or notion of any sensation; this is true of every action, judgment, will, and motion of the mind. [This faculty is called the *imagination* when it has to do with ideas of bodies. There is a similar power involved with all other ideas, which can ring the changes on them. However, there is no imagination or notion whose simpler elements the mind has not previously taken in by some external or internal sense. The mind is able to store and keep such notions, so that oftentimes it can recall them a long time afterward.[18]

Although both memory and imagination depend to some extent on body in the present state of the soul, nevertheless both powers seem to be within the mind itself, because it often recalls of its own accord ideas it once received, including those which have nothing in common with the body or with external sense. Indeed, images once invoked also run through the fancy of their own accord in some strange fashion, whether because they are connected in some wonderful way with certain previous images, and we must speak of this later, or for some other obscure reason. The Cartesian doctrine of some kind of *animal spirits,* readily passing through

17. Hutcheson's note (1749): "memory and imagination."
18. Hutcheson's note (1749): "On the origin of all ideas, as on the conclusions of reason, read Locke's oft-cited book on Human Understanding."

interconnected and open passages of the brain, has altogether too much of the note of fiction.[19]

We must give a word of warning about the external sense and the imagination, lest being too familiar with them, we judge things that belong to neither of them as untrue or unreliable. To the contrary, those things that are truest and contribute most to a happy or a wretched life are in no way subject to these faculties.][20]

Natural associations of ideas

We must not ignore that other capacity of the mind, which is so important in our lives, of storing up associations between ideas which have once impressed it, so that when anything subsequently suggests one idea, it also triggers the others which are associated with it. To this capacity we owe facility in speech and, indeed, almost all our memory of things past.

7.

All good is distinguished from evil by a certain sense; useful things are also perceived by reason

The mind is supplied with a variety of images of good and bad things through the senses and by reasoning. *Those which are pleasing in themselves to any of the senses* are called *good; those which arouse a distressing sense* are *bad;* and they are ultimate in their own kind, and to be sought or avoided for themselves. The reasonings we bring to bear here are not primarily concerned with ultimate goods or evils themselves, but with the means or aids which we make use of in pursuing ultimate goods or rejecting evils. Since the importance of any good to a happy life depends at the same time on the value of the pleasing sensation or the *intensity* and *duration* of the pleasure, there will be room for a kind of simple reasoning, or rather recollec-

---

19. Malebranche described the influence of animal spirits upon the imagination and memory in *The Search After Truth,* bk. 2, pp. 87 ff. and 106 ff.
20. The three paragraphs between brackets were added in the second edition (1744).

tion, in comparing ultimate ends with each other so that we may make a comparison of the values or degrees of different sensations. We train our capacity to judge the duration of goods through our use and experience of things. We should take the same approach to making discriminations between evils.

Some pleasures accompany passions for passing things; others accompany actions

Some pleasant and painful sensations accompany passions; others accompany actions, though in both cases the sensation itself may be called a passion. [*The happier [pleasures] are those which accompany actions.*] But although all happiness lies in some sensation, it is still rightly said that the happiness of every nature that is born to act lies in action, since the pleasures that accompany certain human actions are much superior, much more worthy and enduring, than those which can arise from any passion or physical impulse. For some sensations are vastly superior to others. Not all natures that are truly happy are also equally happy. For those which are endowed with few senses or with senses which are capable only of the lighter pleasures will draw the greatest happiness of which they are capable from things that will never satisfy the [longing for] a happy life of a superior nature, equipped by nature with a nobler sense.

8.

Habit, a quality which perfects an innate power

Another wonderful capacity in both mind and body is that if an action is frequently repeated, it will become easy to do it thereafter. This is called *habit,* and by habit a man's native powers can be wonderfully developed; and it does not seem that the whole power of habit resides in *memory.* In oft-repeated sensations, the pleasure or pain gradually diminishes; but if pleasant things ever cease, one misses them dreadfully, simply because one had frequent enjoyment of them before.

9.

Relative ideas: when several things have a property in common

When the mind compares ideas which have been received by internal or external sense, a new idea arises which is called a *relative* idea; it exhibits the relation or connection between the things compared, so long as they are not completely different. If between the things compared there is nothing common to both, or no similar quality or property in both, there will be no relation or connection between them.[21]

Judgments, some abstract, others absolute

Judgment, which is called the second operation of the understanding, can hardly be totally distinct from perception. For an *absolute judgment* may be said to be *the complex perception of a thing existing at a certain time,* which is prompted either directly by means of the senses or by the intervention of reason, when one discerns the connection of the thing which is the subject of the judgment with the things which sense shows to exist. *Abstract judgments* are *perceptions of relations which exist between things observed;* or, if anyone thinks that judgments are distinct actions of the mind, which nevertheless originate in these perceptions, the act of judging is represented by a simple idea which cannot be defined.

How our judgments are in our own power

We will not linger over this other question, as to whether a judgment is a passion of the mind rather than an action.[22] The mind seems to be active in the process of cognition, in careful attention, in comparison of ideas with each other, and in its desires and intentions to act. Almost everyone would agree that we do not judge that a thing is this way or that way because we wanted so to judge. The only way, therefore, in which our judgments

21. Hutcheson's note (1749): "see Part I, Chapter V, Section 4," pp. 106–8.
22. See de Vries, *Determinationes Pneumatologicae,* II, III, 21.

are in our power or follow the behest of our will, is that it is within our power to direct our attention to either side [of an argument] and to carefully examine both. And since a sane man soberly directs his mind by particular arguments and understands them, he cannot withhold his assent; or, if the arguments which he understands are only probable, he will perceive, even against his own will, that the side to which they point is probably or likely to be true. There is therefore a greater freedom involved in apprehensions, which we can vary at will, than in judgments. But since against most arguments which are only probable, the presumption or suspicion remains that there may be other more likely arguments on the other side, it is within our power to withhold the full assent of our minds to this conclusion, even though it seems more likely, and to abstain from acting, until we have also examined the arguments which point in the other direction. There are countless degrees of likeliness, and some approach very close to full certainty and seem to offer full and perfect credit.

CHAPTER 2

On the Will

I.

What the will is

As soon as an image of good or evil is presented to the mind, another faculty of the soul comes into action, which is distinct from every sense and is called the *will;* it seeks (*appetens*) every kind of pleasant sensation and all actions, events, or external things which seem likely to arouse them, and shuns and rejects everything contrary to them. [Innate in every man is a constant desire (*appetitio*) for happiness, which never fails to display itself, when opportunity offers, in pursuing (*appetendo*) things that seem to make for a happy life and in spurning things that do not. There is, however, no innate notion of the supreme good, or of an aggregation of all goods, to which we may refer all our intentions. What it would be correct to say is that the mind, so long as it maintains a calm and provident motion, is formed to seek every good thing in itself and to shun every evil; and when several things come before it which it cannot have all at the same time, it turns to those which seem greater and more excellent. The same should also be said of warding off evils. Hence we must often reject pleasures which it is not possible to enjoy without the loss of greater and more lasting [pleasures], or which are followed by more serious pains. And likewise pains must sometimes be borne, if that is the only way we can obtain greater pleasures or avoid more serious pains.]¹

---

1. The sentences between brackets were added in 1744.

The two meanings of desiring

Just as we include among the operations of the understanding not only sensations which are *perceived by the body* and are common to us with the brute animals, but also the nobler powers of perception which are proper to man and which convey the notion of superior goods, so also man's *desire* (*appetitus*) is twofold. One desire we share with the dumb animals. It is called *sensual* [*desire*] and directs us toward pleasure by a kind of blind instinct; it is driven by a quite violent emotion of the mind to obtain certain sensual goods and avoid sensual ills. The other is a calm emotion which calls in the counsel of reason and pursues things that are judged, in the light of all the circumstances, to be superior, and are seized by a nobler sense. It is called *rational* [*desire*], or *will* in the proper sense.[2] We will first give an account of this desire; it is common to us with every creature endowed with reason.

2.

Rational desire

Such a desire or aversion arises spontaneously when an image of good or evil is presented and considered in all its circumstances, without a prior decision or command of the will. A desire or aversion is very often followed closely by a kind of deliberation about all the arguments and considerations in favor of getting the thing we want or of avoiding the thing we dislike. After these arguments and considerations have been explored, there follows an *intention* (*propositum*) or *determination* (*consilium*) to do those things that seem most likely to achieve the end. The first desire or aversion the scholastics call *simple wanting;* the intention to act, after the agent, so far

---

2. The distinction between sensual desire and rational desire was a commonplace in the writing of scholastic moralists: for example, in Eustache, *Ethica,* I, pp. 10–11, and Heereboord, *Collegium Logicum Pneumaticae,* I, 8, p. 43. Hutcheson insisted upon it in later editions of *An Essay on the Nature and Conduct of the Passions and Affections* (1742), sec. 2, p. 32n., and *Illustrations upon the Moral Sense* (1742), sec. 1, p. 214, against his rationalist critics, who would reduce all actions, desires, and volitions to exercises of the intellect or understanding.

as his intelligence and diligence allows, has weighed everything that precedes, accompanies, or seems likely to follow the action, they call *efficacious volition.*[3]

How mixed things are desired

Just as we seek by nature every good which is worthy in itself and shun every evil, so when good things are mingled with ills, the will inclines to those which seem more numerous and more excellent. Thus there is a certain deliberation about ends themselves, or about things which seem good or evil in themselves and which are called *objective ends,* though there is no deliberation about the *ultimate end,* the *formal end* as they call it, or about happiness itself and the rejection of misery.[4]

[And though ordinary goods generally do not have enough force to necessarily cause an efficacious volition, since it is quite often possible to foresee more serious ills attached to them, nevertheless whenever an absolute or infinite good is clearly seen which carries no preponderating evil with it, it will necessarily give rise to desire and arouse an efficacious volition. Only wise and prudent men, therefore, have one ultimate end set before them to which they refer all their intentions to act. Other men live in a more *ad hoc* fashion, pursuing various things which are recommended by some appearance of good and fleeing the contrary, unless they see something attached to it which has the power to turn their minds in a different direction. But *all deliberation, whether about the ultimate end or about means, is to be referred in the last analysis to a certain immediate sense of pleasure or distress.*][5]

---

3. See de Vries, *Determinationes Pneumatologicae,* II, VI, p. 31.

4. The scholastic distinction between objective ends, about which there may be deliberation, and the formal end or happiness itself is found in Eustache, *Ethica,* 20–27, and Heereboord, *Collegium Ethicum,* pp. 13–22. See Carmichael, *Natural Rights,* p. 23, n. 7.

5. This paragraph was added in 1744. In the third edition of *Illustrations upon the Moral Sense* (1742), p. 318n. Hutcheson wrote: "In many Questions of this Nature we must have recourse with *Aristotle* to a *Sense,* which is the last Judge in particular Cases." (Also see *An Essay on the Nature and Conduct of the Passions and Affections, with Illustrations on the Moral Sense,* edited by Aaron Garrett, Liberty Fund, p. 189.) He appears to have had in mind (here, as in many other citations of Aristotle) Henry More, *Enchiridion*

3.

Where liberty lies

Since the sentiment of the mind after completing its deliberation does not depend on the will, but necessarily follows the evidence of truth which is put before it, and [since] no previous command of the will arouses simple wishing or the initial desire or aversion, there is no question of *liberty* here at all, whether liberty is taken as *the power of doing what we wish and omitting what we do not wish,* or *a certain indifferent power of the mind to turn equally in any direction.*[6] If therefore *liberty* is *a faculty which, given all the conditions for action, may act or not act, do one thing or its contrary,* it will only have place in an actual intention to act or in an efficacious volition, according to whether we can initiate [the volition] or suppress it by a previous decision of the will. But if this power pays no attention to the appearances of good or evil which are put before it or fails to follow them, it would seem to be a useless and capricious [power]. Anyone, therefore, who finds it absurd that our minds should be endowed with a power which in no way certainly follows our judgment will have to define it to mean merely *a power of doing what we wish and of refraining when we do not wish,* however much the mind may have been constrained to wish or not.[7]

[It seems to have been the position of the Stoics that the will is constrained and directed by each man's character, whether natural or artificial, together with the appearance of good or evil that is put before it, and that

---

Ethicum (1666) translated as *An Account of Virtue; or, Dr Henry More's Abridgement of Morals, Put into English,* p. 16: "The Philosopher having (in his great Morals [*Magna Moralia,* bk. 2, chap. 10]) brought in one who demands, what Right Reason was, and where to be found? The Answer is but darkly thus, *That unless a Man have a Sense of things of this Nature, there is nothing to be done.* . . . So that in short the final Judgment upon this matter is all referred to *inward Sense,* which I confess, I should rather have called, *The Boniform Faculty of the Soul.*"

6. The notion that the liberty of the will consists in indifference was defended by Eustache, *Ethica,* pp. 12–13, 64–65, and repudiated by the Reformed: Heereboord, *Collegium Ethicum,* pp. 4–5, 50. Locke dismissed the idea in *Essay,* II, 21, 73, pp. 238–84.

7. Hutcheson's note (1749): "See Part I, Chapter 4, Section 6," [pp. 97–99], where reference is made to Locke, "On Power." See also Part III, chap. 3, sec. 3, note 6.

it cannot happen otherwise. For they believe that there are certain natural laws set in the mind itself, or that the nature of minds is such that they are necessarily directed by what we have called causes. A great many things, they hold, have this power of constraining the mind and arousing certain feelings by themselves without any [process of] reasoning. For it is not only things which are useful or pleasant to someone which stir his desires, but closeness of blood, benefits received, evidence of virtues in others, and so on excite love and goodwill of themselves; and injuries arouse anger and a desire for vengeance. And under equally unchanging conditions each man's natural character is variously modified by its various encounters with things, as a result of custom, habits, and the complexion of the body itself. But given the character, the appearances presented to the mind necessarily direct it, so that all these circumstances being as they are, it cannot will otherwise; but it could act otherwise if it willed otherwise.

They hold that this condition of our nature is completely compatible with actions being good or bad, since in their view the goodness and badness of actions lie chiefly in our state of mind (*affectionibus*); some states, in accordance with the structure of our souls, are good and laudable in themselves, while others are disgusting and detestable however they may have been aroused in us. They also argue that this does not in any way detract from the force of laws, threats, and exhortations, since the power of these lies precisely in the fact that they offer a new image of good and evil. And though this reasoning shows that all anger is useless and unworthy of the ruler of all things as well as of the wise man, it will not make the threat or infliction of punishment useless or unjust provided that serious evils often cannot be averted without them, and men or other natures endowed with reason who are not very constant in virtue cannot be kept from their vices by any other equally ready means.

The Peripatetics and other learned and pious men, who find these views too harsh and not quite consistent with divine justice, take a different approach. They take the position that although minds always follow some appearance of good, still in situations where they are between two appearances of good, on the one hand *the right and the good,* on the other hand the *pleasant and the useful,* they turn themselves of their own accord in the one direction or the other. We linger no longer over this highly vexed question, which has always troubled the minds of the learned and pious.][8]

What control a man has over his desires

Whatever men's freedom may be, if adequate signs of superior goods are put before them, anyone who has carefully examined the things which arouse desire, and has directed the powers of his mind to this thing, [will find that] all his appetites and desires will be stronger or milder in proportion to the goods themselves. Everyone, therefore, who has seriously done this will be able to make all his desires for superior goods and aversion from the graver evils so strong that he will easily be able at need to suppress weaker desires for bad things and his aversion to lesser evils. Thus he will be able to shape the whole pattern of his life, so that he will pursue all the nobler goods and ignore all the lower things which are incompatible with them.

Joys and sorrows

Apart from desire and aversion, which are different from every sensation and incite to action directly and by themselves, *joy* and *sorrow* are commonly attributed to the will; but they are rather *reflex* and *secondary sensations*, which are different from the sensations which things at hand excite

---

8. It was a characteristic feature of the Neoplatonist philosophers of the third and fourth centuries A.D., some of them celebrated by Hutcheson ("Dissertation on the Origin of Philosophy," pp. 3–8), that they criticized Stoic fatality by insisting, with the Peripatetics, on the exercise of deliberation over appearances of good in acts of will. One of the most effective critics of Stoicism from this perspective was Nemesius of Emesa, remarked by Hutcheson, in *A Short Introduction to Moral Philosophy,* p. 4, as an author to be consulted on the subject of human nature, with Aristotle, Cicero, Arrian, Locke, Malebranche, and Shaftesbury. The text of Nemesius, "On the Nature of Man," is provided in an English translation with commentary in *Cyril of Jerusalem and Nemesius of Emesa,* edited by William Telfer; see especially pp. 389–423. The Cambridge Platonists also employed Peripatetic arguments against the Stoics on the question of the freedom of the will. See Henry More, *An Account of Virtue,* bk. 3, chap. 2, pp. 181–90.

directly, and may either precede or follow them.[9] For joy arises from the expected acquisition of a thing sought, or the expected avoidance of an evil presently threatening, and sorrow from the fear of a future evil or the expected loss of a good.

4.

Sensual desire and the passions

Very different from calm desire or aversion, which are concerned with our own or another's good or evil, and which follow the images of good that our understanding foresees, are the violent motions of the mind, which are called *passions* of the *will* and to be included in *sensual desire*. [They occur] when we are driven by a kind of blind but natural impulse to do certain things or to desire them, even when reason has not pointed to any appearances of good or evil, nor shown us that they are necessary or useful to our happiness or the happiness of those whom we hold dear. These motions are accompanied by a kind of confused and powerful disturbance of the mind which impedes the use of reason. They often agitate the mind when it is not moved by any pure affection or calm plan of action; often pure affections are found without these violent emotions; often they draw the mind in opposite directions at the same time, and *desire urges one thing, the mind another.*[10] Now calm plans of action suppress these passions, now they are overcome by them; this is the state of those who have not yet attained *continence* or the command of the lower regions of the mind.[11]

[There are four kinds of violent emotions (*motus*), as there are of calm emotions (*motus*): *desires, fears, joys, and sorrows,* and several divisions of

9. Locke considered joy and sorrow to be reflective or secondary sensations, which cannot otherwise make themselves "known to us than by making us reflect on what we see in ourselves." He also referred to these "modifications or tempers of mind" as "internal sensations." *Essay,* II, XX, 1–8, pp. 229–31.

10. *Aliudque cupido, mens aliud suadet:* Ovid, *Metamorphoses,* VII, 19–20, in *Metamorphoses,* vol. I, p. 342, from the soliloquy of Medea as she attempts to resist falling in love with Jason and betraying her father.

11. Hutcheson's note (1749): "All this has been more fully expounded by Cicero, in *Tusculan Disputations,* Book IV." See also *An Essay on the Nature and Conduct of the Passions and Affections,* sec. 3, p. 59 ff.

each, and some *tend to be frequently* associated with others and combined with them; it would take a long time to give a full account.][12]

They do not all aim at sensual good

Not all of these violent (*perturbati*) motions of the body aim only at pleasure or pain. The disturbances (*perturbationes*) and blind impulses of the mind in people who are reckless and intemperate are just the same, [though directed] toward a great variety of good and bad things. They are included with the sensual desires because they bring with them a very painful or violent sensation, which agitates the blood and often the whole body. Here we include not only the desires for eating or the pleasure of procreation, but also *ambition, anger, pity, envy, affection, favor, hatred,* and so on.

[*The cause of vices*

We should hold these violent motions primarily responsible for the various things that move and warp the mind without regard to their worth or usefulness. For just as there is *no desire for the unknown,*[13] so things that we barely perceive and rarely revolve in our minds make a feeble impression; and things that are far away (as to the eye so to the mind) appear small and insignificant unless they are brought closer by frequent and deep thought. Some disturbances also completely fill our minds so that we do not have the strength to follow anything by reason or design. This is how it comes about that earthly things, vile, fleeting, and transitory as they are, so often deflect men from the pursuit of noble, heavenly, and eternal things.][14]

12. This paragraph was added in 1744.

13. *Ignoti nulla cupido:* Ovid, *The Art of Love,* 3, 397 (p. 146), from Ovid's advice to a woman to get out and be seen by men if she wishes to find a lover. The same phrase appears in de Vries, *Determinationes Pneumatologicae* II, VI, p. 29.

14. This paragraph was added in 1744.

5.

The motives of the mind look either to one's own advantage or to another's

We should not neglect a remarkable distinction between the motives of our wills, whether calm or violent: in some of them we are ultimately pursuing merely *our own* pleasure or advantage, or protecting *ourselves* from evils, whereas in others we seek to bring about or preserve the happiness of *others* or to shield them from misery. For when we are not moved by envy or anger, or no conflict is seen between another's happiness and our own, we would desire happiness for every sentient creature, we would pray for every success and happiness for him, and we would strive to spare him all pains and troubles.

Whether violent or calm

This far-reaching benevolence corresponds to the calm *feeling* of *self-love (philautia),* which approves and desires the happiness of all men without distinction. For with most of our calm affections we desire the prosperity of our country, our friends, our family, and of all good men, just as we pursue the various goods which reason points to for ourselves.

Different from both of these, we also have violent movements of the will, or *passions;* certain of them seek some pleasure or advantage for ourselves, and some of them seek it for others. The natural reaction to benefits received is a grateful heart and a stronger motive of benevolence toward our benefactor. The performance of honorable and outstanding services toward any man or the practice of eminent virtue stirs our minds and often inflames us with strong emotion and an ardent zeal to advance men endowed with these virtues to higher dignities. Love of offspring is a very special thing, accompanied [though it is] by distressing sensations: all animals are prompted to procreate by a kind of blind impulse of nature. But anger, that brief madness,[15] and indignation are a natural reaction to in-

---

15. *Ira autem brevis ille furor:* Horace, *Epistles,* I, 2, 62 (p. 266).

juries whether committed against ourselves or against others who do not deserve it.

There is a kind of truly gratuitous goodness

Everyone who enters into his own mind and explores his own intentions and feelings in his actions will find that these kindly feelings of our hearts, whether calm or violent, are not aroused by a previous command of the will and do not ultimately look to any advantage or pleasure of our own. [This is] particularly [clear if] one surveys the counsels and deeds of famous men, sacred duties performed by dying men, voluntary deaths to save friends and country. We may also observe the ends of lesser men, how they commend their children and friends, remember and cherish old friendships, and maintain the highest standards of duty with their last breath! These show that probity and gratuitous goodness are innate in men, not prompted by pleasure or evoked by the prospect of reward.

[*Natural instincts*

There are also certain natural propensities of the mind, or instincts, to perform, pursue, or avoid certain things, without any preceding reasoning, and with no thought of their importance for our own or others' advantage. In the brute animals these things are more obvious; something very like the minds of men is implanted in them by the kindly design of God, for their individual or common advantage, so that they may show what things are suitable to nature and what things are to be sought for themselves, and so that each may use his own nature as a guide for living. I need not mention again our approval and praise of good men, our frequent commemoration of benefits received, our compassion for the afflicted, painful as it is, and the fact that we are ready to visit scenes of misery, even when we have no opportunity to do any good. What advantage for ourselves or others do we seek by lamentations for the dead or the funeral honors we give them, by the wishes of a dying man for a child who will be born after he is dead, by the avoidance of childlessness, or by our extreme aversion to physical deformity or abnormality even when there is no loss of function? Why do children have an itch to see and hear things which are no use to them, and why can they never sit still? What is the point of endlessly deploring disasters to which no relief can be given? And why do those who hold that human affairs are no concern of the dead give themselves so much pain and trouble to achieve an enduring reputation for themselves and their family?][16]

6.

Painful sensations (sensus) *either precede or follow motions of the will*

A painful sensation naturally precedes certain *passions* of the mind and accompanies or follows others. It precedes the passions which the scholastics quite properly ascribe to the sensual appetite, those which concern the nutrition of the body and the preservation of the species. Other passions or appetites are accompanied or followed by certain painful sensations, when the means to satisfy them are wanting. There are many such sensations, not very different from one other.

The mind's control of its violent emotions

Since all the lower desires get their special force from incautious *associations of ideas,* [17] from which without any natural cause to do so, we imagine that certain things have wonderful virtues or make some great contribution to a happy life, because these things are given a very high value by irresponsible people whom we associate with, or ambitious, self-indulgent, or immoral people (who by bad habits and long use have depraved or virtually destroyed their natural sense of things). If we are to achieve a just command of these desires and true freedom of mind, it would be very helpful to separate and take apart these notions which we have so carelessly put together, and take a long, hard look at those things that stimulate the appetite, stripping them

16. This paragraph was added in 1744.
17. See also *An Essay on the Nature and Conduct of the Passions and Affections,* pp. 95 ff., 136, 165, and so on, on "fantastic" and "foolish" associations of ideas.

of these stolen colors; so that we may discover and learn for ourselves what real good and evil is in each of them, and so that we may not seek or shun them beyond the measure of true good and evil.

7.

The passions not useless

Since men have not had sufficient force of reason or intelligence to get a clear idea of the fabric of their own bodies, and to understand what things are helpful and what do harm, or what it would be suitable for them to eat, we have had to be warned of need or hunger by a painful sensation; and useful things have had to be distinguished from harmful things by sensation rather than reason; and often we have had to be driven by a blind impulse of nature toward the things that are healthy for us or for the human race. By these things alone we have been driven, by strong stimuli of this nature, so that we would not remain mired in the ways of beasts; similar stimuli of distressing sensations are attached to many other appetites for things which reason would judge to be useful, so that the mind would be better strengthened against the enticements of the lower pleasures.

CHAPTER 3

Whether Spirit Is a Different Thing from Body[1]

I.

It is a celebrated question *whether thinking thing* (res cogitans) *is completely different from body,* or whether on the contrary *matter itself,* that is, extended thing (*res extensa*), [which is] solid, mobile, and made up of different parts, can understand and will and possess within itself all that we commonly call the properties of spirits.[2]

Whether substance is completely different from body

A number of respectable ancient philosophers adopted the latter view, believing that certain subtle bodies, whether air, fire, or aether, are the actual thing that thinks, though none of the denser bodies can have the power of reasoning or sense.[3]

[The subtleties of the Cartesians about the actual nature of the soul, which they choose to locate in *active thought,* which is also *general,* I de-

---

1. This chapter was located in Part II, chapter 1 of the first edition (1742). See note 2 to Part II, chapter 1, pp. 111–12.

2. In this chapter and the next, Hutcheson may be supposed to have had in mind the extended debate between Samuel Clarke, on the one hand, and Henry Dodwell and Anthony Collins, on the other, collected in *The Works of Samuel Clarke,* vol. 3, pp. 719–913, and the later defense of Clarke by Andrew Baxter in *An Enquiry into the Nature of the Human Soul.* For a review of eighteenth-century debates on the question whether it may be possible for matter to think, see John Yolton, *Thinking Matter: Materialism in Eighteenth-Century Britain.*

3. See Aristotle, *On the Soul,* I, 2, 405 a–b (pp. 24–28).

liberately pass over, because the inward natures of all bodies are hidden from us, and all thought seems plainly to be an action or passion or state of the soul. And the only sense in which we can understand "general thought" is as the general idea of thinking, and we make no assertion about whether or not the soul is always thinking.][4]

Our knowledge of things is imperfect

In this difficult question it will be well to remember that the eye of the mind is dull, and cannot penetrate to the inner natures of things, and therefore we are merely inferring likely conjectures about them from properties known by sense or experience. And it is not by arguments or reasoning based on the perceived nature of things that we are brought to adopt some of the most vital doctrines in philosophy, but rather by a certain internal sense, by experience, and by a kind of impulse of nature or instinct. Whoever sets out to settle the question before us, keeping this in mind, will find good reasons to believe that *thinking thing is completely different from body.*

2.

There is a great difference between the properties of the two things

For first he will see that every kind of thought is quite different from the properties which all agree are in corporeal things, so that it cannot arise from them or from any compound of them. The only apparent result of the motion or collision of several bodies is movement in different directions or damage to the bodies and fragmentation. Nothing can truly arise from the figures of bodies except a figure, either in the things themselves or in some compound formed from them: nothing that has anything in common with sense, understanding, and will.

4. This paragraph was added in 1744.

3.

Certain contrary properties show that things are different from each other

What [of the fact that] every body, if we are to believe men's reasoning, is a compound of things truly different which, however close they may be to each other, are in different places, and may easily be split apart by a suitably powerful force? And of the fact that the unique property which is in one part of a body cannot also be in another part, though it may have a similar property? The figure or motion of one part is not the figure or motion of another part, despite the fact that this other [part] has properties which are completely the same as those. By contrast, whatever properties the mind has of which it is conscious (and it has innumerable properties, including sensations, ideas, judgments, reasonings, volitions, desires, intentions), it also perceives that all these are properties of one and the same thing, which it calls its *self,* and it sees that they are unextended and indivisible. And it cannot doubt that it is one and the same thing which at different times feels, perceives, judges, and desires. But this cannot be the case with a corporeal system, each of whose parts has its own shapes, positions, and motions which are truly different from the qualities of the other parts.

4.

Every man's internal sense will show the same thing

Furthermore, the mind itself, under the guidance of nature, seems to have a consciousness of itself as distinct from every extension, indeed from the very body which it calls its own. For it seems to perceive that this body and its parts, however they may be connected with *itself,* are nevertheless subject to *itself,* to be ruled by *its* command, and are useful or distressing to *itself:* and perceives *itself* therefore to be distinct from that body.[5]

5. In the third edition (1749), a note was added: "See Plato, in Alcibiades I and *passim*" (Plato, *Alcibiades* I.129b–130e).

A threefold distinction between perceived properties

In order to better understand this argument, which comes from Plato or Socrates, we must not neglect a threefold distinction of perceptions. Some [perceptions], under the guidance of nature herself, refer to wholly external things, which belong to us only in the sense that they are perceived and whose changes do not affect us. There is a second kind of perception, namely, those which touch us more nearly, pervading us with a sense of pleasure or pain, and which, by a warning of nature, are always attributed to the parts of the corporeal system which we call our body, because they are associated with those places which the parts of the body occupy, and seem to arise directly from a certain motion, property, or change in those parts. These two kinds of ideas are involved in some way with corporeal properties, i.e., motion, extension, and space, and contribute nothing to the true dignity and excellence of man or to his depravity and baseness, and one would not put a lower or higher value on himself or another [person] on the basis of these ideas.

Finally, there is a third kind of perception, foreign to every corporeal property, which represents the very properties of man or of the human mind, and involves no ideas of space, extension, or motion, but depicts the true properties of each *self*, from which are fashioned all its dignity, goodness, and excellence on the one hand, and all its evil, depravity, and baseness on the other. Such are the notions of understanding, cognition, knowledge, reasoning, love, benevolence, faithfulness, and virtue, and of their contraries; none of them have anything in common with any kind of corporeal property.

5.

Thinking thing is a certain single thing, and is simple: body is an aggregate of several things

Moreover, every body is made up of parts which are really different, and every corporeal property is also divisible, so that a part of a property inheres in individual parts of a body, but the properties which, under the guidance of nature, are thought to be the properties of the mind itself are undivided and simple, and cannot be dissipated through the various parts of the body or diffused through the parts of space occupied by the body.[6] We are therefore right to conclude that *thinking thing is a simple substance, totally distinct from matter.*

6.

Thinking thing is active (actuosa), *body inert*

The human mind is also aware that it is endowed with a true power of acting. For it not only judges and desires, which are true actions, but also directs its attention wherever it may wish, and turns away from one thing and concentrates on another, entertains or ignores ideas it has received, and magnifies or minimizes them; it analyzes complex ideas or compounds simple ideas, and even sets the body in motion. But all body, if the physicists are correct, is inert, always retaining its own state or motion unless an external force impinges on it.

[Here should come a consideration of those divine powers which we see are in minds; there is memory, and that an almost infinite [memory] of innumerable things; there is invention and excogitation, which investigates hidden things; which has given names to all things; which has captured the almost infinite vocal sounds in a few marks of letters; which has brought together scattered men and summoned them to society of life; which has marked the various courses of the stars; which has discovered benefits, clothing, houses, cities, and the cultivation and protections of life; and has developed from necessary structures to more elegant things, whence so many delights/amusements have come, from poetry, eloquence, and the skills of painting, sculpting, and engraving. Why should I mention philosophy, a divine gift, which has educated us to the worship of God, to the

---

6. Compare the discussion in Hutcheson's *A System of Moral Philosophy,* p. 200: "The simplicity and unity of consciousness could not result from modes dispersed and inherent in an aggregate of different bodies in distinct places." The note to this sentence urges the reader to consult Aristotle, *De Anima,* I, i, Dr. Samuel Clarke, and "Mr. Baxter's ingenious book on the subject."

law of men which lies in community and society, to modesty and magnanimity, and every virtue: surely this power is divine and is not of the
heart or of the brain, or of the blood, or of the bile, bones, or muscles? can
it be in these crude elements of which bodies are composed?][7]

7.

There is no generation or corruption of spirit

These same [arguments] will show that spirit is neither generated in the
manner of bodies nor perishes. For bodies are generated when there is a
due formation, combination, and motion of previously existing parts, and
they die when this combination, formation, and motion is removed. From
this simplicity of the soul is derived what is called its *physical immortality,*
for the dissolution of the body is by no means necessarily followed by the
death of the thing which is quite different from it. But it needs a deeper
inquiry to determine whether human minds will survive and live after the
death of the body, and we will discuss it later.[8]

[*On the place of spirits*

The simplicity of minds offers a reason for doubting whether they occupy
space or have any relationship to space. One may make inferences about
unknown natures only from their properties. Now, the properties of minds
exclude all extension and figure. Indeed, in the present state of things, our
minds can act only on external things by way of the body, and their senses
are aroused by the movements of bodies; in fact, certain perceptions, in a
wonderful and inexplicable way, are related to parts of the body, and others
to things or places distant from the body. But the ideas which exhibit the
properties of the mind itself are not related to any place. It is not therefore
agreed whether a place should be assigned to the mind otherwise than by
mere *external denomination,* drawn from its body. Indeed in this question,

---

7. This paragraph was inserted at this place in the third edition (1749). There is also
a note to this paragraph: "See Cicero, *Tusculan Disputations,* I, 24–30."
8. See Part II, chap. 4, sec. 3, pp. 147–49.

as in others raised about the nature of the mind, the gaze of the mind has to be withdrawn from its habitual familiarity with the eyes and the other senses, as well as from hastily adopted opinions, lest we imagine that only those things are true which are perceived by the senses.

The conclusion of all this is that the human mind is "a thinking substance, endowed with reason, totally distinct from body, which desires knowledge and a diverse happiness; and it can find it chiefly in knowledge itself, in the kindly affections of the will, and in action consistent with them; it is normally joined in close union with a living body and is affected by its changes."][9]

9. These two paragraphs were added in 1744.

CHAPTER 4

On the Union of the Mind with the Body, and on a Separate State[1]

I.

The command of the mind over the body

The power of the soul to move the limbs of its body is familiar. But whether it is the action (*efficacia*) of the mind or will that moves the parts of the body directly by itself without the intervention of a superior nature has not been adequately explored. We feel a certain power of the mind, or energy, particularly in the initial moment, whenever we make an effort to move the limbs of the body in any manner. Reports of anatomists cast doubt on whether this action initiates these motions of itself. For it is well known that the movement of an exterior limb depends directly upon a certain movement of the nerves and muscles, of which we are barely conscious and which we never desire or will to exist. Similarly, in the other direction, the arousal of sensations in the mind follows directly upon a certain motion of the nerves which is connected with the brain, though the mind does not perceive this motion; it almost always feels that the motion exists in a certain part of the body at a distance from the brain or even outside the body. There are therefore pious and learned men who attribute all this to a certain divine force.[2]

---

1. The corresponding chapters in de Vries, *Determinationes Ontologicae,* are sec. 2, chaps. 9 and 10, pp. 37–45.
2. Malebranche, *The Search After Truth,* pp. 46–47, 59–60; and Baxter, *Enquiry,* pp. 395–407.

[It is also very well known by experience that perceptible motions of the blood and the finer humors accompany all the more intense actions and states of the mind, even those which are connected with barely perceptible things; but there is no sense of them in our tranquil thoughts. However, since thought, like all motions of the mind, is aroused, retained, put aside, and modified by command of the will, it is obvious that none of them is in any way wholly dependent upon the power of inert matter, which cannot change its state or motion.][3]

2.

The union of mind with body

Concerning the union of mind and body, we know nothing beyond those powers or constant intimations of powers, by which they seem to affect each other, so that certain bodily movements immediately follow decisions of the mind, and in turn sensations in the mind follow the movements aroused in the body, and they in turn stimulate various appetites and passions which are accompanied by internal and external motions. However, there are several parts of the body which the mind cannot directly move by its own will and whose movements it cannot stop or change, and the continual motions in the body on which life chiefly depends do not give rise to any sensations in the mind; and indeed this would not be at all useful but rather distressing.

[For this reason some believe that the soul does not move the body and the body does not affect the soul by its own powers or by a necessary connection between them, but by the intervention of a superior cause, since the power of the soul reaches only to certain parts of the body, and only certain parts of the body have the power of affecting the soul; and neither has been formed by our design. Nor does the great disparity between these substances seem to be consistent with such a natural and necessary mutual power. Accordingly, they believe that God himself unites souls with bodies at birth, and equally that he causes them to act upon one another in ac-

---

3. This paragraph was added in 1744.

cordance with a fixed law, as he is the same always, and is everywhere present and active.]⁴

<h1 style="text-align:center">3.</h1>

The survival of the soul after death depends on the will of God

Concerning the survival of the soul in separation from the body, all that has been securely established is that we have no awareness or memory of our existence or of any events before our birth, but we do have a probable expectation that the soul will survive the dissolution of the body.⁵ There is first the fact that we do not see any substance perishing, and cannot show by valid arguments that any substance does perish, and we cannot infer from the death of the body that a thing which is completely different from it will also perish. There is also the fact that the hope and longing for immortality has prevailed among all peoples in all centuries. [*The holiness and justice of God require it.*] And the government of the universe itself under a just and kindly God seems to require it, so that truly good men whom we often see oppressed by many external ills, and exposed to serious distress simply because they are good, may not fail to receive an appropriate reward for their virtues, and that wicked men, for whom all things turn out well and as they would wish, may not go unpunished. The kindly providence of our most holy governor would not permit either of these things, but for the happiness of his whole commonwealth will keep the majesty of his most excellent laws sacrosanct, safeguarded by fitting penalties.⁶

4. This paragraph was added in 1744. The authors involved in this paragraph are again Malebranche and Baxter. See Part I, chap. 5, sec. 5, p. 109 and note 15.

5. De Vries considered life after death to be a certainty; inasmuch as the soul is not material, it was therefore created by God from nothing, *Determinationes Ontologicae*, II, X, 3–4, p. 42. Hutcheson considered that we have only probable reasons to believe in the survival of the soul after death.

6. The argument that divine providence has made such provision for the happiness of the human race was developed at length by Hutcheson in *A System of Moral Philosophy*.

This is the only condition on which virtue deserves approval

All things in the physical world have been formed with so much art and skill by the supreme creator of all things, and so many features of the fabric of the human mind also show the benevolence and wisdom of the supreme creator. Yet many aspects of the government of this great commonwealth, which contains the whole human race, remain imperfect and need to be corrected, and if we regard only our present life, this is altogether unworthy of so great, so kind, and so powerful a ruler, and deserves universal condemnation. But all of this may easily be rectified if souls survive bodies, so that the whole fabric and government of the world become fully worthy of the great and good God. Who will doubt then that souls survive, and that the entire government of the whole universe is most perfect? We see considerable evidence of such a pattern even in the present state of things. For often things which in relation to a certain time would be blameworthy if viewed in isolation, because they appear to be sad, cruel, and unjust, and all the responsibility for them seems to rest on God himself, will be found in the end, when they are considered together with their necessary consequences even in this life, to have been planned according to a most intelligent and kindly design.

Immortality is especially desired and expected
by the best people

What too of the fact that the nearer a man's mind approaches the perfection of his own nature, as he looks toward the immense expanse of future time, and recognizes God as the creator and ruler of the world, and despises all things terrestrial and transitory, and at the same time views the common happiness of all men with a kindly intention, and embraces the whole human race with the greatest love and benevolence, how displeasing will the whole government of the world seem to him and all the design and providential plan of the supreme ruler, if all things are really to be destroyed by death? For it is not given to men to enjoy constant and unalloyed good, not even to the best of men for whom this life is often painful and passed amid sorrow and tears (not to speak of the many innocent children who die an early and tragic death), nor is it allowed to hope for other things for oneself or one's family or the human race beyond these brief and fleeting things soon to be snatched away by death, which human reason itself warns us to despise, bidding us love and long for immortal and eternal things. [And it is not credible that God, who has shown himself supremely intelligent and kind, should have willed to render empty and vain these ardent desires and prayers of the very best men which he himself seems to have implanted and to have specially commended to us.][7]

7. The final sentence was added in 1744.

On God

What natural theology is

All philosophy is pleasant and profitable, but no part is richer and more fertile than that which holds the knowledge of God, and which is called *natural theology*.[1] It exhibits what philosophers have perceptively uncovered or diligently argued in sole reliance on the powers of human reason; it does not touch those things which the great and good God in his supreme love for man has designed to teach those who have been inspired by his divinity with marvelous signs beyond man's normal reach. For imperfect as it is, this knowledge of the highest matters is not only delightful and worthy of a man in itself, but also offers supreme inducements to every virtue and to all honest modes of life, while at the same time laying firm foundations of true magnanimity, constancy, and peace.

In giving a brief synopsis of this science, we shall deal briefly with the most important topics which philosophers treat at length: first, that most serious question *whether there is a God*, next *the attributes of God*, and finally *the divine operations*.

---

1. This was the part of Hutcheson's metaphysics that he continued to teach at the University of Glasgow. He did not teach those parts of metaphysics that dealt with ontology and the human mind; those subjects were taught by the Professor of Logic. See the introduction, p. xxii. He taught natural theology because in the universities of Scotland and the Netherlands in the early eighteenth century it was considered that natural theology was the foundation of morality. See Gershom Carmichael, "Synopsis of Natural Theology," in *Natural Rights*, p. 230, and de Vries, *Determinationes Ontologicae*, III, 1, p. 47.

CHAPTER I

In Which It Is Shown That There Is a God

Who is the subject of the question whether there is a God?

In this part of our course, the question *whether there is a God* takes first place. But if we are to understand the force of the word, we must first say that God is *a certain nature much superior to human nature, governing this whole world by reason and design.* This summary is enough for now, as we shall soon give a more thorough account of the divine nature, after we have expounded the arguments which prove that there is a God and what his nature is. Whoever believes that this world and its major parts are governed by the reason and design of an intelligent nature believes that there is a God or gods, even though he may have formed many views rashly and falsely about the nature or attributes of God. The only people who are *atheists* are those who deny that the world is governed by the design of a wise ruler or that in the beginning it was made by him.

The intelligent fabric of the world shows that there is a God

That there is a God who formed this world in the beginning and rules it at all times is shown by the supremely intelligent design of the world and of all its parts, which have been so well made that they could not be more serviceable in use or more beautiful in appearance.

2.

Two kinds of action: by design and by brute force

We take it that there are two kinds of action: one, when we move bodies in an endeavor to put some specific shape or form into things by deliberate design; the other, when we stir bodies at random without any design, without concern to produce any special effect or form. From the latter kind of action we cannot expect anything that is beautiful or regular, or similar to previous things or usefully made, but from the former, all things beautiful, regular, similar, and useful readily arise.

The criterion of each and the reason for the difference

The reason for this difference is not hard to see: the ugly and useless figures and positions which the parts of any object may take are infinite in number, whereas there is only one form and perhaps only one position of things which tend to beauty or usefulness in any given kind. Without art, therefore, and design there can be no expectation that anything beautiful or similar or useful is likely to result from the use of brute force. Since, therefore, so many very beautiful forms appear in the world every day, things which have been fabricated on a similar pattern, whose innumerable parts have been most cunningly fashioned both for beauty and for use, anyone who believes that all these things could have been made without divine intelligence and reason must really be regarded as himself devoid of intelligence and reason.

3.

The movements of the heavenly bodies most cleverly devised

Anyone who wishes to treat this argument fully must surely survey the whole of natural philosophy (*physiologia*);[1] we shall only deal briefly with the more important points. Consider the immense size and power of *the heavenly bodies,* their certain motions and fixed orders, and especially the

---

1. In the third edition (1744) there is the following note: "Philosophers, ancient and modern, have fully explained this topic: Plato, Xenophon, Cicero, Arrian, and the writer of the very elegant little book, 'On the World' among the works of Aristotle. It would take a long time to enumerate the names of the moderns: the Cudworths, Stillingfleets, Nieuwentijts, Rays, Pellings, Derhams, Fenelons, Cheynes, Clarkes, Nyes." There is a notable duplication in this list with the names of natural philosophers cited by Carmichael in "A Synopsis of Natural Theology," in *Natural Rights,* p. 241.

grandeur and beauty of *the sun* and its effects: how in rising it brings in the *day,* diffusing everywhere a cheerful, healthy light, in setting gives place to *darkness* which is most suitable for rest, and in regular succession effects *the annual change of the seasons,* for the health and preservation of all animals and plants: anyone who has come to know these things will surely not be able to doubt that they are all caused by a preeminent and divine reason.

The fabric of the earth and of terrestrial things

Let us come to the *earth,*[2] surrounded by a living and breathable nature whose name is *air,* and clothed with *flowers, herbs, trees, and fruits,* the unbelievable multitude of which is marked by an insatiable variety. Add here the grandeur and usefulness of the *clouds* which are raised by the sun from the great ocean and the lakes and are held aloft by the weight of the air, *the height of the mountains, the power of the winds,* the *perennial springs* that flow from them, and the clear and health-giving water of the *rivers* that make this earth a fruitful, abundant, and pleasant home for all living things. No one looking at these things will fail to see the signs of a most benevolent God.

How wonderful is the structure of *those things that grow from the earth,* which are held by roots that draw nourishment from the earth: how great is their variety and beauty! How great is the force of all of them, so that from such little seeds they bring forth *grasses, plants, trunks, branches, leaves and flowers,* and then again *seeds,* distinguished by an infinite variety and providing so many uses to living creatures! And every one of them is so similar to all others of the same kind (whose number is infinite) that no hand or art could bring it about or mind imagine it.

4.

Signs of art and divine design in living things

How great is the variety of living things! How great a drive to reproduce and to persist, each in its own kind! And largely and abundantly has nature

2. Compare Shaftesbury, "The Moralists, a Philosophical Rhapsody," pt. 3, sec. 1: "Let us begin, then, said he, with this one element of earth. . . ." *Characteristics,* p. 310 ff.

provided *food* for living things, the proper food for each kind; and what differences in the shapes of animals so that they may get and consume their food, how cunning, how subtle! How admirable the structure of the limbs! And all of them so made and placed that none is superfluous, none not necessary for the preservation of life.

In their senses and appetites

Both *sense* and *appetite* have been given to living things, so that by the one they may endeavor to obtain healthy and useful things, and by the other distinguish the noxious from the healthful. Instinctive in the limbs are the powers that make possible a marvelous variety of *spontaneous motions,* so that they may get the things that will do them good and repel or avoid what will do them harm. These movements and senses are aroused according to specific conditions, by a wonderful artifice which men can scarcely learn even by long investigation. Specific sensations are caused by many movements in the body which are not known or observed by the animal itself; and in turn the desired movements immediately respond to a determination of the mind to move a certain part of the body. In both cases certain motions of the internal parts come into play which the mind does not perceive or command. And this mutual effect of the body on the mind and of the mind on the body extends as far as is useful and no further. For these continual motions of the inward parts on which the life of a living thing depends are maintained when we are asleep or doing something else, and even against our will. They excite no sense in the mind, which incidentally would be pointless and annoying. We cannot move at our will those parts of the body whose voluntary motion could not help us at all.

5.

In the preservation of species

With how provident a design are the kinds of animals and of things which grow from the earth preserved! Such power is in their seed that from one or two seeds many creatures are generated. Some living things are male, others female; some parts of the body are adapted for begetting and conceiving, and there are wonderful passions for bringing bodies together. As soon as the fetus of living things which are nourished by milk leaves the womb, the mother's nourishment begins to flow. And creatures which have only been born a moment before seek the breast under the guidance of nature, without any teacher, and are filled by its abundance. And that we may understand that none of these things is by chance, that all are the works of a provident and intelligent nature, there is innate in all animals whose offspring need their help an exceeding love and a special care to protect and raise what they have begotten right up to the time that the offspring can look after themselves, or in fact so long as the parents can provide help to them. But when the offspring no longer needs the help of the parents, and the parents' help is no longer useful, this love either disappears or remains inactive.[3]

Especially in the structure of the human body

What great evidence of supremely clever design there would be if the whole fabric of the human frame were thoroughly scanned? If the appearance and dignity of the whole body were considered? The organs of sense most subtly crafted and most aptly placed? Why speak of the eyes or ears of living things? Why of the internal organs? What of the human face which reveals all the motions of the mind? What works has not nature constructed for the purpose of speech? How apt are the hands she has given, the ministers of how many arts?

6.

And in the powers of the mind

Let us come to the powers of the mind whose aspect is still more glorious, and especially to the power of *reason,* which has given man empire over all the things of the earth, whether animate or inanimate. By men's reason and foresight so many arts have been invented which provide such a store

---

3. See also *A System of Moral Philosophy,* I, 9, p. 171.

of useful and pleasant things. Men's reason penetrates even to the sky and contemplates the beauty of the world, and surely comes to him not from chance nor by the design or skill of his parents but from the most wise God.

And in its nobler powers

Why should I mention the other powers of the mind? Why should I recall that it has been given virtually to man alone to discern the beauty of things, their order, the connection of their parts, and their use? Why should I say that men also sense in the intentions of their minds, and in their words and actions, what *beauty* and *goodness* are, what is *fitting*, what is *proper;* and that the feelings of our hearts and our plans for action meet with more approval from other men's sense of things, and are more universally praised, the more happiness in life they are likely to give to more people, even when those who approve and praise them have absolutely no prospect of any advantage for themselves.

What of the fact that men's desires are formed on a most benevolent design? For nature does not make a man love only *himself*, but also *his wife, his child, his family, his neighbors, his fellow-citizens,* all of whom we treat with spontaneous kindness, provided there is no reason for conflict; and good men love each other as if united by kinship and by nature. *Human love* goes even further, and sometimes *embraces the whole human race.* Why should I mention the natural approval of goodness even in those we have never seen, compassion for the wretched, and the pleasing memory of good deeds done? Nature has bound men to each other by these bonds which escape the sight of the eyes, and has inspired them to create companies, councils, and states, and equipped them for all the noble duties of life. If anyone thinks that all this has come about by chance, I do not know what works he would be able to leave to skill or design or foresight.[4]

[Assume that a corporeal structure can think (though we have shown this to be very much against probability),[5] yet, as even atheists admit, such

---

4. See the elaboration of the argument of this paragraph in "On the Natural Sociability of Mankind."
5. Note (1749): "Part II, Chapter 3," pp. 138–44.

a structure will have to have been constructed with the most subtle and exquisite art, to be adequate to think. Even so, no one would say, without the greatest perversity and determination to talk nonsense, that therefore brute and inert matter should, so frequently and regularly in a certain, determinate order, be so artfully composed that it rises to the power of thought, and does so in every single individual man who is born (not to speak of other living things), without the reason and design of a wise and powerful nature.][6]

7.

Arguments on the other side are refuted

We must take careful note in this inquiry that a nature endowed with reason and acting deliberately can act equally in both directions when it so wishes, and may make things either beautiful and similar and useful, or ugly, discordant, and useless. In fact, on occasion, even the most intelligent nature may try deliberately to make things crude and repulsive, and in other things not even attempt to create any distinction or beauty. Yet never will anything beautiful or uniform or fit for use be made by brute force. Therefore those things in the world which seem neglected and squalid do not afford a good reason why we should doubt the providential government of things, for there are so many more things most skillfully framed which argue that the world is governed by divine providence.

What of the fact that almost all those things that were regarded as faults in the world by the Epicureans, so that they denied that the world had been divinely made,[7] have been found by more careful observers of nature to be the best and most intelligent device after all, or to follow necessarily from the device which is altogether the best and most intelligent; and thus they are no small signs of divine wisdom.

6. This paragraph was added in 1744.

7. Lucretius, *On the Nature of Things,* II, 175; Bayle, "Epicurus," remark S, in *Dictionary,* 1737, vol. 5, pp. 56–59.

8.

Other reasons are adduced

From all this it is not rash to conclude that the world has been formed by the reason and divine power of a most wise and powerful nature. But we must not ignore the other arguments on this subject which have been acutely elaborated by philosophers, and which bring us to a fuller knowledge of God.

There is necessarily something which is first and independent

There are now very many things in existence; therefore there has also been something in all past time. There are now reason and prudence in the world; therefore they too have been there from eternity. For such genuine virtues could not have arisen by force of any things that were devoid of reason and design. And since an infinite series of causes operating deliberately cannot be conceived in the mind without some absolutely first and eternal nature which was not itself caused by any prior nature, we infer that God has been independent from the beginning and that he is endowed with the highest wisdom and power; only from him could these virtues derive; they could not have derived from the brute force of matter nor from ignorant parents.

Matter is not independent, nor is the material world

Metaphysical writers tell us that matter or body which receives no virtue or perfection is not a thing that was primary in itself or eternal but required a deliberately acting cause from which to receive figure and posture.[8] But suppose eternal matter without cause; it would still be a completely different nature from which matter received motion, one which is indifferent to motion or rest. Now, since we cannot conceive a motion or imparted force which does not tend in some direction, and all matter can be carried by motion in any direction equally, in such an ambiguous situation we cannot conceive that there is in matter either a natural or a necessary ability to

8. Baxter, *Enquiry,* p. 22 ff.

move, but all the ability that it has would have been imparted by force of an intelligent nature. Even suppose that matter moved in some way or had the power of moving, but had no design or foresight, there could never have come from that the magnificent order we see in the world.

New arguments from the discoveries of natural philosophers

What of the fact that those who have most carefully explored the causes of things in recent times, who see new traces everywhere of providential design, new reasons why we must have recourse to a divine power which moves all things? It is not unfamiliarity with nature and ignorance of causes which have compelled men to have recourse to God as the architect of the universe.

There are quite a few arguments for the newness of the world or for its recent origin, which show that this earth could not have existed from eternity and that a home fit for living things cannot last forever. For not to speak of the sun and the stars which must one day be exhausted by the perpetual outflow of light, and whose motions are gradually slowing in a space which is not completely empty, a great deal of matter is washed down daily in recent times from the higher parts of the earth into the seabed by the force of the rains and the winds. By this continual mutation, in a certain finite period of time, all the heights will be lowered and the hollows filled up, and the whole earth covered with the waters of the sea. Add to this the recent origin of the arts and sciences, the low antiquity of reliable history, the story of the recent origin of the world which almost all peoples preserve, and the universal consent about a deity that governs all things, which does not rest on a preconception of the senses.

A conflict of two beliefs

Relevant here is a comparison between the reasons that support this belief and those which can be adduced in favor of the other side. Contemplate also the problems involved for those who in declining the difficult notion of a first and most wise nature have recourse either to a world which is eternal in itself and most intelligently fashioned but without any reason or design to govern it, or to a fortuitous concourse of atoms. No intelligent man will fail to see which view an intelligent and serious person will approve.

9.

[I do not use the *Cartesian* arguments, because they suffer from obvious fallacies. Descartes first says that "there is a cause of every idea, endowed with at least as much perfection as is exhibited in the idea itself. But we have the idea of an infinitely perfect being; there is therefore some superior nature, infinitely perfect."[9] Both of the premisses of this argument are, to say the least, ambiguous. For men make for themselves obscure and inadequate ideas of virtues which are far superior to their own; and no one has a fuller or clearer idea of a supreme being than he has formed by amplifying the ideas of his own virtues and purging them of faults, unless God has given anyone a clearer sense of himself above the common lot of man. In vain does Descartes insist "that the progenitor of men had the same idea of supreme perfection; and since it was sufficient to him for existing, it sufficed also for attributing supreme perfections to himself." This affirms nothing, unless God is said to be the efficient cause of himself, which is absurd.

He continues, however, by saying "that necessary existence is contained in the idea of most perfect being; an infinitely perfect being therefore exists." However, anyone who has understood the nature of abstract propositions will see that one should only infer from this that *if* there is any most perfect nature, it necessarily exists and does not depend upon the will of another.][10]

---

9. Descartes, third meditation, in *Discourse on Method and Meditations on First Philosophy,* pp. 77–78. See also Carmichael's comment on the third meditation of Descartes in "A Synopsis of Natural Theology," in *Natural Rights,* pp. 246–47.

10. This section was added in 1744.

CHAPTER 2

On the Natural Virtues of God

I.

How the attributes of God are known

Since we seem to have shown clearly enough that a superior nature has existed from all eternity, we proceed to explain his *virtues* or *attributes*. [We understand well enough from logic that all our ideas arise from some sense either external or internal. What we derive from our external senses is supplemented by arguments from which we rightly infer that there is a God, and that he is endowed with every virtue; no external sense, however, can grasp the virtues of God themselves. All mental virtues therefore are understood by an internal sense or by internal consciousness of the self and its properties. This is the source from which at least the elements of all the notions which represent the divine virtues are engendered in the mind. But since it is agreed that the first and superior nature is free of all those vices and defects with which human virtues are tainted, we form the most perfect notions of the divine virtues of which our minds are capable by amplifying as much as we can these ideas of our own virtues or perfections, and removing all defects from them. [*Communicable and incommunicable attributes*][1] Hence in a certain manner all the divine virtues may be said to be *communicable,* because we find a certain resemblance to them or obscure intimation of them in created things. However, those names or attributes

---

1. For the distinction between the communicable and incommunicable attributes of God, see Heinrich Heppe, *Reformed Dogmatics,* chap. 5, p. 60 ff., and Carmichael, "A Synopsis of Natural Theology," *Natural Rights,* pp. 248–70.

that denote the supreme and highest degree of virtue which the virtues of God alone attain are called *incommunicable*.][2]

2.

Independent and necessary existence

Among the attributes which cannot be communicated, the first place is taken by *independence*, by which God is understood to have always existed in himself, the first of all things, so that he recognizes no other cause or force from outside to which he owes anything of himself. We should not, however, imagine from this that either God is cause of himself or that any attribute of his is the cause or effective reason of the other attributes. Independence always entails that God from the first and always necessarily *is*, and therefore depends on the will of no one. And we are not to ask any cause or *efficient reason* for the first cause; and a *necessity* of nature is not a cause or reason of the existence of the thing itself in which this necessity is, since no attribute can be prior to its subject.[3]

3.

Unity

Hence we also conclude that there is only one God, if by the word God we understand the first nature created by no one. For nothing suggests that there has been more than one thing of that kind, and indeed the notion is unintelligible. For when there is a certain number of any things, whatever they may be, we are simply compelled to think that the will or design of a spontaneous or free cause has intervened to decide on this number rather than any other. But this cannot be supposed in the case of the first nature.

The structure of the world shows this too: all the parts of the world that are known to us are so connected with each other and mutually dependent

---

2. All of the sentences between brackets were added in the second edition (1744).

3. Hutcheson's opinion that God does not require a cause and that the notion of self-creation or aseity is not a meaningful term or idea was shared by de Vries, *Determinationes Ontologicae*, III, 3, pp. 52–54, and Carmichael, *Natural Rights*, pp. 249–50.

that they seem to signal the design of a single maker. [*Polytheism does not preclude all piety.*] Not all piety, however, or religion would be abolished, nor would all the foundations of virtue be subverted by the belief that there are several gods, provided we retain a belief in the government of the whole universe by the harmonious counsel of benevolent and provident gods.[4]

4.

God infinite

From the fact that God is absolutely first and sprung from nothing, we conclude that the virtues or perfections of God are *infinite* in precisely the same way, and that he is endowed with every true and pure perfection. For when a thing enjoys only certain virtues but not all, or a merely finite mode and measure of perfection, these things seem to have been altogether determined by the will of an effective cause. We therefore rightly conclude that the first nature which recognizes no cause has all virtues and all superiority and that it is infinite.

5.

God is spirit

That God is not corporeal is shown by the same arguments that prove that human minds are things different from body and that matter cannot think or have a sense of itself.[5] And no thing devoid of sense can have any superiority or perfection. But all of these are to be attributed to the first nature of all.

4. As Hutcheson understood the Stoics, they made provision for the government of nature by "many inferior created spirits." See "The Life of the Emperor Marcus Antoninus," prefaced to Hutcheson's and Moor's translation of *The Meditations of the Emperor Marcus Aurelius Antoninus,* p. 35 ff. See also *A System of Moral Philosophy,* pp. 174 and 206.

5. Note (1740): "Part II, Chapter III," pp. 138–44 above.

6.

Simple

That God is a *simple* nature without parts and not made or composed of different things is inferred from the fact that he is spirit, and that primary and independent nature is most perfect. The perfections of God are not therefore adventitious but are all necessarily connected with the divine nature from the beginning. [*Immutable*] He is therefore *immutable,* whereas all adventitious things come in to make up a deficiency. Therefore God is rightly defined as *independent spirit, all of whose virtues are most superior.*

7.

In what sense he is immeasurable and eternal

Since all the things that we know *in time* seem to exist successively, and every action or passion of the mind of which it is itself aware appears to carry with it a certain notion or sense of this, and since all the corporeal things among which we live seem to fill a certain place or space, a difficult question arises about the divine nature: *does it exist successively, and is it diffused like space?* Serious thinkers have gone in opposite directions on this.[6] Some believe that God, like every thinking thing, is so simple that he cannot be coextended with space nor occupy any place. For these things cannot be understood without parts which are distinct, however similar or cohesive they may be. They also confirm this from the fact that the properties, virtues, and vices of spirits and all that seem to belong to the nature of mind itself, and which nature leads us to believe are properties of our own minds, appear incapable of being diffused through space or spread through an extended place. Likewise by a similar reasoning (which, however, seems to go beyond what the mind can see), some think that the simple and immutable divine nature, which understands and wills all the same

---

6. Note (1749): "Part I, Chapter III, Section 4 and Part II, Chapter III, Sections 4 and 5." See pp. 82–86 and 140–42. The "serious thinkers" whom Hutcheson had in mind were identified in his note to I, 3, 4 (p. 83, n. 10) and the note to *A System of Moral Philosophy,* p. 200, cited at II, 3, 5 (p. 142, n. 6).

things always in a single act, does not *exist successively* either. Other equally powerful thinkers, however, reject this belief and take the position that eternal duration is the very eternity of God, and that his immeasurability is infinite space itself. In this difficult question which altogether surpasses the powers of the human mind, we can hardly assert that anything has been fully made out, except this one thing: that *everything that happens in the whole of space is and always has been perceived and comprehended by God, and that in all places he can always bring about what he has willed.* The former position seems the more likely, though it is so obscure that it scarcely seems to come within the orbit of thought.[7]

8.

[*Incomprehensible*

From these natural attributes or virtues of God, which cannot be communicated with others, one may see above all that God is *uncomprehended,* not adequately grasped by any finite mind.[8] This is true of God not only in the sense in which it may be said of any other *substance,* namely that its inner nature is hidden from us and that no one has discerned and known its innumerable relations with other things, but also in the sense that our ideas of these attributes are not appropriate to depict or represent the things themselves, although they seem to go some way toward them. The moral attributes which are said to be *communicable* are another matter. For *our* ideas of these are appropriate, and they do truly depict them, however imperfect and inadequate [our ideas] may be; for all the evidence which proves

---

7. Hutcheson's view that "the former position seems the more likely" appears consistent with the line taken by Leibniz in his exchange with Clarke: "some have believed it [space] to be God *himself,* or, one of his Attributes, his *Immensity.* But since Space consists of *Parts,* it is not a thing which can belong to God." *The Works of Samuel Clarke,* vol. 4, p. 602. Carmichael had adopted a similar position: *Natural Rights,* p. 254.

8. Compare Joseph Butler, *The Analogy of Religion,* pt. 1, chap. 7, pp. 160–61: "The natural world then, and natural government of it, being . . . so incomprehensible, that a man must, really in the literal sense, know nothing at all, who is not sensible of his ignorance in it. . . ."

that God exists also proves that he is endowed with supreme wisdom, power, and goodness, and is the kind of evidence of which we can form distinct and suitable conceptions in our minds. We will now proceed to expound the virtues which we know from that inner awareness of our own virtues that we mentioned above.][9]

9. This paragraph was added in 1744.

CHAPTER 3

On the Divine Virtues Concerned
with Understanding

I.

God living and omnipotent

When we speak of the *living* God, we mean by this that he understands
and perceives all things, and moves and rules them by his own efficacious
will. In no other sense is he to be called *the soul of the world*.[1] For God is
not affected with a pleasing or displeasing sense against his will as a result
of the motions of matter, as men's minds are often affected by the motions
of their bodies. Further, since the divine nature is fully active and at the
same time absolute with every perfection, we cannot doubt that God can
effect whatever he has willed; all things are *possible* to him, as we defined
"possible" in our Ontology.[2]

1. The characterization of God as "the soul of the world" had become particularly
controversial in the early eighteenth century because of the identification of this Platonic
and Stoic idea with the philosophy of Spinoza. See, for example, Bayle's *Dictionary* article "Spinoza," remark A: "He was a systematical Atheist, and upon a scheme intirely
new, though the ground of his doctrine was the same with that of several other Philosophers, both ancient and modern. . . . The doctrine of the soul of the world, which was
so common among the ancients, and which made a principal part of the system of the
Stoics, is at the bottom that of Spinoza." Vol. 9, pp. 347, 351. See also Leibniz's second
letter to Clarke: "Will they say that [God] is *Intelligentia Mundana;* that is, the *Soul of
the World*? I hope not. However, they will do well to take care not to fall into that Notion
unawares." *The Works of Samuel Clarke,* vol. 4, p. 595.

2. Hutcheson's note (1749): "Part I, Chapter 1, Section 4." See p. 70.

2.

Wise and omniscient

That God is *most wise* and does not act by blind impulse is shown by the intelligent structure of the whole universe, and by the reason and prudence with which men are endowed; these must necessarily be more perfect in men's progenitor.

Divine ideas

The *divine ideas* which are prior to every external thing could not have been aroused either by an external exemplar or by a superior nature; and since all things have been made on their pattern, they adequately represent all things. Therefore we do not ascribe to God sensations and images or any inadequate ideas. And it is not credible that God himself once of his own will fashioned in his own mind, which had been ignorant at first of all finite things, the first ideas of all things, as obscure adumbrations of his virtues. For if from the first God himself and all his virtues had been clearly known to him, he would from the first also have known all the other things with which his wisdom, power, and goodness would one day be concerned. This receives rich confirmation from the fact that all notions, apart from the general notion of *being* itself, include in themselves some relation to other things, or something *relative;* hence the actual ideas of the divine virtues could not have been full and distinct in God unless ideas of other things had also been present. This is the probable answer to this difficult question.

3.

[Infinite knowledge

Little excellence would be found in ideas alone, if there were not also in them a knowledge or full perception of all the relationships and connections which hold between them. Hence we should attribute another operation of the mind to God, which logicians call *judgment,* or infinite *knowledge:* knowledge free from all doubt, error, ignorance, and forgetfulness, and from the laborious progress of inference from things known to things unknown, knowledge which extends to all things.

The knowledge of simple intelligence

The scholastics apply a twofold knowledge to God, namely, the *knowledge of simple intelligence* and the *knowledge of vision*.[3] By the former God is thought to view all abstract truths as well as his own nature and necessary virtues; these are all those things which they do not wish even the will of God to be the cause of, since among the eternal ideas themselves in the mind of God are the necessary relations and immutable connections which are expressed in these eternal and abstract truths. No one can conceive that these truths could be otherwise, or that the nature of things could be so changed that such propositions could become false.

The knowledge of vision

By the *knowledge of vision* God is thought to have foreknown from the first all absolute truths about the existences of all things and any changes which may happen to them, that is, the changes which are considered to depend on his decree that governs all things. All these things, therefore, God is thought to perceive not in their effects but in his own efficacious intention.

No place for mediate knowledge

Anyone who ascribes this twofold knowledge to God and holds that both kinds of knowledge extend to all things, will leave no room for the other kind of knowledge which they call *mediate knowledge,* by which *ex hypo-*

---

3. The distinction between knowledge of simple intelligence and knowledge of vision is found in the writings of Reformed scholastics. See Heinrich Heppe, *Reformed Dogmatics,* pp. 74–75; de Vries, *Determinationes Ontologicae,* pp. 68–69; and Carmichael, *Natural Rights,* pp. 259–61.

thesi God foresees what men will do.[4] Different views of divine knowledge correspond with different views of liberty. There is no dispute about events which depend on natural and necessary causes. The dispute is about free causes. Those who adopt the Stoic view of liberty hold that when all the agents' characters whether natural or artificial are thoroughly understood, and all the allurements and enticements are known which attract an agent toward one action rather than another, and all the support available to the agent is revealed, a sure foundation has been laid for divine foreknowledge to rest upon; and that foundation has been laid by God himself, who shaped all these things by his own decree. They will not grant that the supreme excellence of God allows one to say that divine knowledge may be said to increase gradually by fresh observation of events or that God may be said to make uncertain conjectures about future things.

The various views of the Peripatetics

Those who hold a contrary view about liberty think that this Stoic doctrine about foreknowledge and decrees, in decreeing and foreseeing evil actions as well [as good], is not consistent with the holiness and justice of God, and leaves no room for virtue or vice. There will be another opportunity, when we come to the divine operations, to discuss the reconciliation of divine holiness with a sure foreknowledge and decree of all events.[5] And we have already spoken above of virtue and vice in actions certainly foreseen.[6] Fairness itself, however, requires us to point out that the supporters of the Peripatetic position on liberty by no means deny to God a providence that extends to all things; and not all of them deny certain foreknowledge of all things. For some of them attribute also to man an indifferent liberty of turning himself in any direction, despite any attractions, and at the same time ascribe to God a sure foreknowledge of all actions from eternity: which

---

4. The doctrine of mediate knowledge was rejected by the Reformed as Jesuitical and Pelagian. See Heppe, *Reformed Dogmatics,* p. 78, quoting Voetius: "The Jesuits thought out *scientia media,* which to this day is the refuge of all Pelagianisers." See also Carmichael, *Natural Rights,* pp. 261–62.

5. Hutcheson's note (1749): "Part III, final chapter, Section 4." See pp. 183–84.

6. Hutcheson's note (1749): "Part II, Chapter 2, Section 3." See pp. 129–32.

indeed seems to us a completely inconsistent position. Others, in asserting this liberty in men, sharply deny that free actions have been certainly foreseen; they maintain that this is impossible, and that we no more detract from divine omniscience by denying it than we detract from divine omnipotence by denying that God can bring about the impossible. In any case, however, both sides hold that God has foreseen most things from certain causes, and that he has determined in himself from the beginning that as he is always present and aware of his own omnipotence, he will rule and govern all things by constantly interposing his power, and that he has always kept in view how far and in what directions men's freedom might stray and how easily he could check it.[7]

Since the supporters of contrary positions on this difficult question seem to be motivated by so much piety and such scrupulous care not to derogate from the virtues of God in any way, they should abstain from curses, insults, angry assertions, and personal resentment, and not hurl abuse at each other; this is unworthy of philosophy.][8]

7. See the introduction, p. xxv.
8. The paragraphs between brackets were added in 1744.

CHAPTER 4
On the Will of God

I.

What the will of God is

1. We also attribute to God a will which is similar to our own, though without our faults, weakness, and imperfection; no intelligent nature would be perfect which lacked a will. There are no violent emotions in God, analogous to human passions, and no disagreeable sensations or distress, since a most powerful and most wise nature is not liable to fatigue from his efforts to get a thing or from anxiety that he may not get it.

2. Although God is held to delight in external events, especially in the best and happiest state of the world, the divine happiness is not therefore made uncertain, precarious, or dependent on external things, since all external things and their entire condition depend upon his most powerful *self.*

3. There seems to be nothing that the most blessed God could seek as a result of self-love that would increase his happiness.

4. All intentions for his own actions seem to emanate rather from his unwavering benevolence and his natural and unchangeable will to share his felicity with others.

5. Of all the things that are pleasing to God in themselves and worthy to be sought by him, the greater are more sought and the greatest most sought.

[6. All ascribe liberty to God, but different kinds of it. However, hardly anyone would say that he could will anything contrary to his own innate virtues, or could fail to will anything consistent with them. God is not therefore to be thought to be *indifferent* to all those things that depend on his will, or favorable to both sides; for there is a certain necessary will.

7. Although some of the designs of God have the status of *ends* and others of *means,* since he sees that certain lesser things are a means to other, more excellent things, nevertheless the divine excellence precludes a progress like our own from conceiving the end to discerning the means: he sees all things at a single glance, and at the same time determines the whole sequence of all things with an unwavering will.][1]

2.

Arguments which show that God is good

We infer that God is wholly *good* and *benevolent* not only from the natural assumption that good men alone are happy, and that benevolence itself is a very great cause of happiness to its possessor and bars no other source of happiness, and because it is praiseworthy in itself and the supreme excellence and perfection of an intelligent nature, the very sense of which brings joy to such a nature, but also because no temptation to a contrary course could occur to a superior nature which needs nothing for its own sake.

[Arguments] *from the fact that the very fabric of the world is built to a benevolent design*

The whole structure of the world, all the things which have been fabricated by art and design, seem to have been built to a benevolent design and to have been intended to create or to preserve life and happiness. Nothing seems to have been made by art and intelligence for the purpose of causing pointless pain or misery. There is no trace of an evil intention or of a spiteful or cruel intention, which it would have been possible to see, frequently or regularly, in a world which was under the rule of a malignant deity. Let the structure of the world which shows that *God exists* be examined. How beautiful, clever, and kind it is! What a store of things has

---

1. The sentences between brackets were added in 1744.

kindly nature supplied which help one to live a comfortable and agreeable life! The senses of men and of all living things have been so fashioned that almost everything that is health-giving and useful is also pleasant to healthy people, and they are prompted by unpleasant sensations to avoid anything that would cause disease. All the appetites implanted by nature are useful, indeed necessary, for the preservation and happiness of the *individual* or of the species. By a kind of acute sense of the fitting and the beautiful, together with kindly and social feelings, men are prompted to be helpful one to another and to offer mutual assistance; by a most happy sense of the right and the good, those who have made an effort for the happiness of others are rewarded; and the approbation and approval of others fills them with the most honorable delight. But those who neglect these duties or do the opposite are punished by the bitter bites and unseen strokes of conscience.

From the preponderance of happiness in the world

All these things have that much greater weight because we see that there are far, far more good and happy things in life than there are sad and gloomy things, so that nearly everyone has a good reason to go on living; and even those who at some time feel it would be better to depart from life have had a happy and desirable life through far more years.

Various reasons which indicate that a kindly God had to mix evil with good

Even the evils which afflict many men seem to follow clearly from the fabric and structure of things and from the natural laws which are altogether necessary and most useful. The bodies of living things could not be preserved if they were not warned and compelled by a sharp sense of pain to avoid and repel things which would harm the fabric of the body and impair its integrity. If men cannot without much labor obtain what they need for food and clothing, and cannot enhance their lives without still further labor, still labor itself very much contributes to health and strength both of mind and body. In cultivating the arts, practice and thought sharpen men's minds, and should be called pleasures, not labors.

Disagreeable sensations often very useful

Who has grown so hardened against the feelings and promptings of nature that he finds fault with those motions of the mind by which we deplore the misfortunes of others and are prompted to give help to the distressed, even at some cost to ourselves? Or that bite or pain of the mind which we get from consciousness of wrongs we have done, which a kindly God intended as a remedy for vices? Who even will condemn all anger and indignation, especially that which stimulates us to protect ourselves, our family, and all good men from wrong, and to restrain evil men, and to advance good men to higher dignities?

Death too is desirable

What of the fact that death itself, from which we so fiercely shrink, also seems to be necessary, having regard to the whole system. For those who are satiated with all the pleasures of life and who do not know how to live well should give way to those for whom life will be happier and who can use it more fittingly. And an early death holds no sadness and grief for those who are departing from life, nor should God be thought to have had little regard for them. Death takes away the pleasures of life which they were expecting, but after death, either there will be for good men a happy experience or no experience at all. If the former, which right reason and the consent of all nations affirm, they will be much happier; if the latter, they will at any rate not be miserable. Nor do the brief pains of illness have so much importance that they deserve to be weighed against long years of health and the many pleasures of life.[2]

---

2. The argument that evil, disagreeable sensations, and death itself are consistent with the benevolent design of the world is developed at greater length in *A System of Moral Philosophy*, bk. 1.

The best system of the world requires various kinds of sentient natures

In even the best-constituted system of things there have to be different kinds of living things, higher and lower, so that there may be an opportunity to exercise the noble virtues of the mind. For compassion, doing good, generosity, courage, equanimity, patience, gentleness, and nearly all the duties that we freely do (the sense of which is by far the happiest and the memory the most agreeable) would be excluded if there were no weakness, no want, no vices and errors among men; and no honest duties would be performed. There would be no room for counsel, prudence, and industry, if there were no general laws in force in the nature of things, in the knowledge of which men could make their plans and promise themselves certain effects and consequences from certain actions; and from even the best-designed laws certain evils would necessarily arise. The things that are seen in a bad life will not have sufficient force to show that the world was not made by a good God. For under the rule of even the most benevolent God such evils would happen. And indeed the evils which we see, though many and various, do not seem to be built into the actual machinery or structure of things as the *proper end* of them, but appear to result from the weakness of the material, the error of inferior agents or chance, beyond the natural design or intention of the work, in accordance with laws which are altogether useful and necessary.

Evils often serve greater goods or are linked with them

And in the end it is only a small part of the world that we see and for a short space of time. In this corner and in this short time, there are far more goods than evils in life, so that it is better for nearly everyone to remain in life rather than to simply die, and the whole machinery of things shows the kindly design of the supreme artificer. Even in this life we see that very many evils bring great benefits, which often check and punish men's crimes, exercise and augment the virtues of the good, and convert men's minds from external things and lower pleasures to internal and true goods. Hence it is surely probable that even those evils whose use we do not now see have

been destined for the happiness and perfection of parts of the system remote from us, or of centuries to come, and of the whole world. At any rate
these things will not show that the government of the world is spiteful or
malignant.

God is very good

If therefore God is kind, and desirous of the happiness of all living things,
their greater happiness will be preferred to their lesser happiness. Despite
the fact, then, that many men are afflicted with grievous ills, we conclude
that since God is also most powerful, all things have been from the beginning made in the best way and are kept in the best condition they can be,
having regard to the whole world and its government through all the ages.[3]

3.

The justice of God

Justice is associated with goodness itself and is rightly thought to be a part
of it, since goodness expresses itself in making and promulgating laws per-
taining to conduct, which command all right things and which will benefit
the whole world, and also requires that these laws be fortified with strong
sanctions so that all men may be better held to their duty and due obedi-
ence. And that the force of these laws for the common happiness may be
all the greater, the same justice or goodness requires that fixed penalties be
attached to the laws and that there be no unfair indulgence or favor shown
toward evil men, which would harm the whole city of God.

And holiness

Holiness has almost the same nature as goodness and justice; in willing all
the best and in designing the best for the whole world, God is free of all

---

3. Hutcheson's note (1749): "On this whole question, read Leibniz, *Théodicée;* the
Earl of Shaftesbury, *Rhapsody* ["The Moralists, a Philosophical Rhapsody," in *Characteristics*]; Samuel and John Clarke; the Boyle lectures; and dissertations of others against
the Manichees."

evil or wicked desire, and rejoices in his own virtues and in all those who are like him, and condemns and turns his face from the opposite.

4.

God is truthful

Since there is no reason to doubt that God can teach men many things beyond the common lot of nature and declare his will through them, we conclude from the fact that he is both the best and the wisest, who neither can be deceived himself nor wishes to deceive men when it is not to their interest to be deceived, that God is *truthful* in keeping his words and promises.

5.

And blessed

From all the other virtues of God we conclude that he is *most blessed*. But the *blessedness* of God can by no means depend upon external things, since all these depend upon him. Rather the best and most benevolent God receives his supreme and unchanging joys from himself and the consciousness of his own virtues, and from the optimal state of the whole world which he has made and continues to preserve by his own virtue.

CHAPTER 5

On the Operations of God

I.

[Though we have little knowledge of the operations of God, we should make the following brief, general points. God's operations have no defects or faults; they follow his intention and his will, and therefore are completely free, though he cannot will anything that does not seem best to him in his wisdom. Never does God fail to achieve his expectation or intention, never does he change his design, nothing can obstruct him when he wills or impede his intention when he has determined in himself to act in a certain way. His power operates without any painful effort on his part; nothing can occur contrary to his will; and he does not borrow his force from any external power or need its help when he wills to do something without the intervention of others. However, things which are inconsistent with each other cannot happen, as we have already said.[1] And whether some action intervenes apart from the will of God itself, or whether on the contrary the actual volition is effective in itself, we may not say for certain.][2]

2.

Goodness is the cause of the divine operations

From what has been said above about the divine goodness, we shall not be likely to disapprove the view that the great and good God was moved by his own supreme and pure goodness to make this whole world and all its

---

1. Note (1749): "Part III, Chapter 3, Section 1," p. 168.
2. This section was added in 1744.

parts, in order that he might impart to things other than himself life, perfection, and happiness, and admitted no evils into the world other than those which appeared to be quite unavoidable to this end, because they are associated with the overriding good.

Among the operations of God the first place is taken by *the bringing into being of things different from himself, which before were not.* This is called *creation,* indeed the *first creation.* That is called the *second creation* which *gave matter its first forms, and created species out of matter which was not in itself suitable.* The first creation seems to be the work of God alone.[3] [It should not appear incredible to anyone that by his own power God caused things which previously were not to begin to be; human power could do nothing like this. One must reflect how small is man, how blind in seeing into the actual natures of things, so that he scarcely has any better understanding of how he recalls his own ideas and variously alters them and how he initiates new motions in his body when it is at rest.

Whether a nature active from all eternity could also have brought anything into being from the first, so that the duration of created things would have anteceded all finite time, has not perhaps been adequately investigated on the basis of the nature of things, but there is no reason to doubt that God can preserve created things forever.][4]

Preservation

There is no agreed view as to what sort of power on the part of God created things require in order to continue: that is, whether they need the same *continuous* force by which they came into *existence,* or whether in the beginning so much natural durability was given to them that they can endure by themselves, unless they once again perish by the hand of divine power. It is also unclear whether the attraction and communication of movement which we observe between bodies is effected by some divine force which is either continuous or applied from time to time by a fixed law, or on the

3. The distinction between first and second creation was made by Reformed theologians. See Heppe, *Reformed Dogmatics,* chap. 9, pp. 197–98, and de Vries, *Determinationes Ontologicae,* III, XVII, p. 79.

4. The sentences between brackets were added in 1744.

other hand whether so much force was given to the bodies themselves at the beginning and is preserved along with them. In either case, however, it is absolutely certain that God who gave *being* to things themselves can also destroy them when he wishes, and all their duration and power must be credited to God.

3.

All things are governed by the providence of God

That God governs the world by his providence we conclude from more or less the same reasons that show that God exists. It is simply not credible that a superior nature adorned with all wisdom, goodness, and power does not care about the world and its parts and especially about those parts that are endowed with reason and capable of so much happiness and misery, all of which he made with so much skill and intelligence; it is simply not credible that he has left them to the tender mercies of blind fortune.

[Besides, everything that happens is brought about by some adequate cause; for it seems that nothing can be effected except by a cause which is brought to effect this particular thing at this time either by its own nature and character (together, when it is a question of free causes, with the prospect of the things presented to it), or by some external force; for if indifference remains, nothing will be effected, unless we are to attribute some efficiency to *fortune* or *chance* as if they were real things. It is for this reason that some learned men[5] plausibly want us to conclude that all things happen through certain causes which had previously been moved by other things according to a certain law, and which will finally bring us back, if we trace it, to the first cause of all things, which set up the whole series of things and all their changes and causes as seemed best to himself at the beginning. This doctrine will not subvert the motives of piety, whether all things are said to be effected from the beginning or effected by the repeated intervention of divine power, provided that in both cases we maintain that in

---

5. Samuel Clarke, *A Demonstration of the Being and Attributes of God;* Baxter, *Enquiry.*

his counsels for ruling the world God took account of the virtues and vices which he foresaw would emerge in living beings endowed with reason, and adapted the outcomes of things to them.][6]

The question about the order of decrees is forestalled

Since nothing can happen without the knowledge or will of God, who in a single act surveyed the natures of all things, their powers and changes and all the links between them, and indeed everything that could happen, we must not think that God desires or decides different things at different times in the manner of men, and therefore that he first proposed the *end* and subsequently the *means* to obtain the end, but rather we must suppose that at the same time he both decided and effected in one unwavering decree the whole series of all things which seemed best to him. Hence any question about the order of his decrees is forestalled.[7] Notwithstanding, some things are rightly said to be sought by God for their own sakes, and some things for the sake of other things as means or supports. And we should not exclude the so-called *final* causes from physics.

4.

The whole question about free actions

[There is no dispute about the efficacy of what are called *natural* causes or how the movements and changes of the physical world are ruled by God, since they follow certain causes and necessary laws which God has made.][8] It is not so easy to explain, however, in what way a fixed providence relates to the actions and especially the vicious actions of *free* causes, without implicating God in a certain responsibility for evil actions. In governing and

---

6. This paragraph was added in 1744.

7. Reformed theologians distinguish between the "general decree," by which God created the world, and the "special decree," in which God predestined some for eternal life, others to be damned. See Heppe, *Reformed Dogmatics,* pp. 145–49. Hutcheson appears to preempt consideration of any distinction of this kind.

8. This sentence was added in 1744.

determining good actions there is no fear of attributing too much to God, because in that case he is rightly thought of as *the fount and head of every good and praiseworthy thing,* either because he has given a certain natural character to each man and keeps it subject to certain natural laws, which have such power even over free things that their feelings and characters are changed in a certain way as the result of certain causes, or because he put before them certain attractions, certain prospects of good and evil, or finally, because he attracts certain men to all things good by a divine instinct which is beyond the normal bounds of nature. But the control of evil actions is not so easily explained. Men are indeed prompted to do evil actions in a somewhat similar manner in certain conditions on the basis of objects presented to them and of their own character; and God is thought to have made all these causes of actions. However, he only permits those which he sees to be necessary and useful for the whole system, and does not allow human depravity too much scope because of his benevolent will toward all, and therefore, however depraved the passions are which move men to do evil, God permits them because of his most holy and benevolent will for the perfection of the whole system. Therefore no moral wrong is attributable to God.

[*God is free of all fault*

And there is no fault in the fact that God gave to each man natural and necessary appetites for the lower goods, nor are men therefore excusable, since he has also given to each man who carefully reflects on them more powerful attractions to all good things, and has implanted in men a sense of them and a desire for them, which will help them to govern and control their lower appetites, if they take them to heart. Nor should we consider it a fault in God that in his large bounty, he has also created inferior natures who can be depraved and turn to vices, since as we said before, this appears to be required by the most perfect state of the world, and from their very vices God has arranged, in his most intelligent design, to extract and obtain advantages and benefits for the whole universe of things, and these far outweigh the vices.

Concerning precursus and concursus

In explaining providence there is no need to follow the scholastics in combining with every action of men various, distinct actions of God which they call *precursus* or *premotions* and *concursus;* for it does not seem easy to reconcile these with divine holiness. For whatever may be said of external movements, in the motions of the soul it is barely possible, and perhaps not even barely possible, to separate *physical nature* from *moral nature,* so that God may be the efficient cause of the former and man of the latter. Similarly, whatever in any given circumstances moves one to the *exercise* of an action also impels one to the *appearance (speciem),* as they call it.[9]

Those who oppose the Stoic position should not say that many things are so evil and vile that they seem plainly unworthy of God's care. For we often see that the biggest things depend on the smallest; not only are the big things helped by small things, but all their hope often depends upon them. They should be careful they do not finish up eating salt in deriding the contrary opinion.][10]

The account of providence which we have given breathes the simplicity of nature and thus appears more worthy of God than the one which holds that God at the beginning is ignorant of very many things that will happen, but as he is always present he constantly forms new plans, according as things themselves and new events seem to require.

5.

The right of dominion and majesty

That God rightly assumes *government* or *majesty* over all things we conclude from his very perfections, namely, his wisdom and supreme goodness, which show that his government will benefit all men, and therefore should

9. The distinction between the preservation of all things by God (or *precursus*) and the manner in which God enters into the successive actions of creatures (or *concursus*) is found in Reformed scholasticism. See Heppe, *Reformed Dogmatics,* p. 250 ff.

10. The three paragraphs between brackets were added in 1744.

be approved by all men. The powerful inducement to encourage men to obey him is found in his omnipotence, which is capable of suppressing all resistance with the severest penalties. But the consideration which shows that it is always fitting and proper to conduct ourselves well toward God in all things and detest all resistance to him, lies in the innumerable benefits which he bestows upon us who gives us life and breath and all things.

6.

God can reveal his will beyond the normal means of nature

Finally, reason itself shows that God can, if he so wills, teach many things to those who are inspired by his divinity, which would otherwise have been hidden, and share his counsels and intentions with them, and by their ministry declare to mankind laws and guidance for the conduct of life. And trustworthy historians tell us that this has really happened. It will not, therefore, be beyond the bounds of philosophy to inquire what might be the means by which these inspired men can convince others of this fact. For God can make them as immediately aware and certain of his presence and divinity as each man is of himself thinking.

By what means we may be convinced of this

We scarcely seem able to understand how this can happen except by God predicting to them that events would occur which could not be foreknown by human foresight or intelligence, or by giving them the power to do *miracles* which are far above human capacity. The attributes of God which it particularly helps us to know are *wisdom, power,* and *goodness.* Prophecies will give signs of the divine wisdom, miracles of his power. It is vain to say of a *miracle,* "that it is a work that can only be performed by the omnipotence of God," because no one has sufficiently explored the powers of all created things so that he can assert that this or that was effected by God alone. Let us therefore be content with this description, that a *miracle is a work beyond the common tenor of things, far surpassing human powers, but done on the order of a man or at his will, or for his security and evident ad-*

vantage. For when such miracles are performed by a man so as to convince us that he is inspired by God, they plainly show that some superior nature is implicated in it. But what sort of powerful nature is it? Is it good and benevolent, that is, God himself, or is it one of the good angels at God's behest? Or is it on the other hand some spiteful and malicious demon? This will be determined by the laws and moral institutions he promulgates: if they are holy and conducive to man's happiness, we rightly believe that their herald or promulgator was inspired with the spirit of God in performing the miracles.[11] And thus *natural theology will lead us to the acceptance of what is called revealed theology.*

THE END

---

11. It was characteristic of the natural theologies of the Reformed scholastics that they eventuated in a discussion of miracles. See Heppe, *Reformed Dogmatics,* pp. 263–65; de Vries, *Determinationes Ontologicae,* p. 89; Carmichael, "Synopsis of Natural Theology," in *Natural Rights,* p. 277. Unlike Reformed natural theologians, however, Hutcheson considered it the criterion of a divinely inspired miracle that it must be conducive to human happiness.

Francis Hutcheson
Professor at Glasgow

On the Natural Sociability of Mankind
Inaugural Oration

Glasgow
At the University Press
1730

After I had devoted six years in this university to the study of humane letters and philosophy,[1] private considerations and duties called me away from this very pleasant place to Ireland, where I was involved in laborious and tedious business and had very little leisure for good letters or the cultivation of the mind.[2] It was therefore with no little joy that I learned that the university which had been my *alma mater* had after thirteen years proposed to restore me, its former student, to freedom;[3] and that the distinguished governors and professors, who once were as revered by me as parents, had now elected me to be their colleague.[4] Mindful of my former parents,[5] I was able to leave without too much sorrow my beloved native land,

> to seek the ancient mother . . .
> from whom I traced my lineage.[6]

For my heart longed to return to Scotland, venerable mother of brave and learned men, which has not grown feeble in our time, whose fertility will never be impaired by age.

I expected that I would be quite delighted (as indeed I am) to see again

---

1. Hutcheson registered as a student at the University of Glasgow in 1711 (*Munimenta Alme Universitatis Glasguensis,* bk. 3, p. 196) in the fourth or final year of the under-graduate curriculum (the natural philosophy year) in the class of John Loudon. He remained at the university for six more years as a student of divinity.

2. Hutcheson was the master of a dissenting academy in Dublin through the 1720s. It is indicative of the modest disposition he sought to cultivate on his return to Glasgow in 1730 (see Wodrow, *Analecta,* IV, p. 167) that he should have described his years in Dublin as intellectually unproductive; the works for which he was and remains best known, his two *Inquiries, Essay,* and *Illustrations,* were published in those years.

3. Metaphor from the manumission of a slave.

4. Hutcheson was elected Professor of Moral Philosophy on 19 December 1729 in a closely contested election, described by W. R. Scott, *Francis Hutcheson,* pp. 54–56. He was formally admitted to the university as Professor of Moral Philosophy at a meeting of the faculty on 3 November 1730: GUA 26647 fol. 22.

5. Virgil, *Aeneid,* 5, 39, in *Aeneid,* vol. I, p. 474.

6. Ibid., 3, 96, and 5, 801, in *Aeneid,* vol. I, p. 378.

the very places where, happy, cheerful, and free of care, I once passed my days, the very buildings, the gardens, the fields, and the river banks where we used to lie. But beyond all this, there rose before my mind the image of the university itself, of the learned and grave discourses delivered in this very auditorium and in the private classrooms of the professors. How I rejoice to see these places again, where I imbibed the first elements of the inquiry after truth; where I had my first taste of the immortal sublimities of Homer and Virgil, of the charm, the felicity and dexterity, the humor and wit of Xenophon and Horace, of Aristophanes and Terence; likewise the abundant grace and dignity of Cicero in every branch of philosophy and his eloquent and vigorous contention in pleading.[7] Here I first sought the nature and causes of virtue, and made my first attempts to trace those eternal relationships of numbers and figures on which this stupendous fabric of the universe rests; and beyond this, the nature, the power, the wisdom, and the goodness of the eternal God himself, by whose power, intelligence, and design all things are governed.[8] It was here too that all these things settled deeply in my mind and developed there, after they had been often weighed in gentle, friendly converse or in free and modest debate among friends and companions, as we walked in the gardens of the university or in the lovely countryside around the city, which the Glotta[9] washes with its gentle stream. As I recalled all these things, my departure for Scotland seemed happy and cheerful and full of joy.

One thing only troubled me, and still it causes me concern, that I might be found unworthy of the college of grave and learned men by whose votes I have been elected to be a professor, that I might be unequal to the task they have assigned to me and bring discredit on their generous judgment.

7. William Leechman, in his "Account of the Life, Writings and Character of the Author," prefaced to Hutcheson's *A System of Moral Philosophy* (1755), p. iii, records that while he was a student of natural philosophy, Hutcheson "at the same time renewed his study of the Latin and Greek languages."

8. Leechman, "Account," pp. iv–vi, also reports the youthful Hutcheson's exchange with Samuel Clarke on the eternal relations of things and their relevance for natural theology. See also pp. 152–61 (*A Synopsis of Metaphysics,* Part III, chap. 1).

9. The River Clyde. See also James Arbuckle, *Glotta, A Poem,* and M. A. Stewart, "James Arbuckle," *Thoemmes Dictionary of Eighteenth-Century British Philosophers.*

Though I still have this fear, I will freely confess that if there is any talent in me (and I feel how little it is), or if I have found a way of teaching true philosophy that is anchored in the study and discipline of the most excellent arts which I have never neglected at any time of my life, it is this university which seems to me to have the right to claim the fruit of my labors. For it was she who first led me to undertake and enter into the path of these studies; by her encouragement and instruction I have been formed, from her I have received what little I have that may allow me to be of use to the student body. Since this is what the university is now requiring of me, I have not allowed this fear of mine to deter me from coming here as a professor, and would not give a cowardly refusal to play my part in this task.[10]

Gentlemen, any scholar taking up a position of this kind is accustomed to give a public discourse. His topic is normally the origin, progress, dignity, and utility of his discipline. I too would have said something of this kind, if a number of learned men had not recently anticipated me in dealing with this whole subject.[11] It has seemed to me better, therefore, on this occasion to attempt a rather more careful consideration of human nature, and to inquire whether the seeds of perhaps all the virtues, or at least inducements to every kind of virtue, are found in our nature. This certainly was the view of the best of the ancients, who described virtue as the best and most perfect

---

10. The pressures which the Church and the University might impose upon a man of heterodox theological views, such as Hutcheson's, had been amply demonstrated in the trials of John Simpson, Hutcheson's former professor of divinity. See H. M. B. Reid, *The Divinity Professors in the University of Glasgow, 1640–1903*, chap. 6, and Anne Skoczylas, *Mr. Simpson's Knotty Case.*

11. Samuel Pufendorf, "On the Origin and Progress of the Discipline of Natural Jurisprudence" ("De Origine et Progressu Disciplinae Juris Naturalis"), in *Specimen Controversiarum;* Gottlieb Gerhard Titius, "On the Character and Context of the Discipline of Morals" ("De Habitu et Contextu Disciplinarum Moralis"), in *Observationes in Samuelis L. B. de Pufendorf De Officio Hominis et Civis;* Jean Barbeyrac, *Inaugural lecture on the dignity and utility of the law and history (Oratio inauguralis de dignitate et utilitate Juris ac Historiarum);* Gershom Carmichael, "On Moral Philosophy, or the Science of Natural Jurisprudence" (praefatio in *Samuelis Pufendorfii De Officio Hominis et Civis*), in *Natural Rights on the Threshold of the Scottish Enlightenment.* For discussion of these histories of morality, see T. J. Hochstrasser, *Natural Law Theories in the Early Enlightenment.*

life in accordance with nature.[12] It is also quite clear that I do not need to dwell on the dignity and utility of moral science, since it cannot be denied that whatever in life is good, lovable, or attractive, whatever makes a man useful and dear to his country, companions, friends, and even to himself, arises almost entirely from his moral character; it is hardly at all to be attributed to strength of body, to good health, or to material resources or wealth. Certainly there are more than enough who abound in the latter, yet are thoroughly disagreeable, sour, mean, and querulous, objects of shame to their friends and companions and even to themselves. And if jurists have received praise for books on praedial servitudes, or on the law of walls and runoff water,[13] and if the work of medical writers on secretions[14] has not been without reward or honor, then it is certainly not unworthy of a wise man to conduct inquiries on human morals, on the governance of all the passions and affections and on the tenor and order of life as a whole, and to inquire what may be the best and most perfect education in words and actions.

As we enter on our view of human nature, we shall not attempt the whole of the subject, which would be too long a task; instead we will discuss those parts of the human mind which make us sociable (*sociabilis*). Though many recent writers[15] have taken the position that sociability (*sociabilitas*) is the source of nearly all our duties, they do not seem to have sufficiently addressed the general question of what those things are which are properly

12. The Stoic idea of virtue as expressed by Cicero, *De Finibus Bonorum et Malorum,* IV, XIV, pp. 339–43, and in *The Meditations of Marcus Aurelius Antoninus* (in the translation by Hutcheson and James Moor), pp. 176n and 265–66n.

13. A servitude is a right over the property of someone else. Praedial servitudes refers to rural servitudes; the others mentioned are urban servitudes. Both are treated by Justinian in *Institutes,* III, 3. For a discussion of servitudes in Roman and Scottish law, see chap. 7 of *A History of Private Law in Scotland,* ed. Kenneth Reid and Reinhard Zimmermann.

14. George Cheyne, *A New Theory of Acute and Slow continu'd Fevers; wherein . . . the Manner and Laws of Secretion . . . are mechanically explained.*

15. It will be clear from what follows that Hutcheson had in mind recent editions of the writings of the early modern natural jurists, such as Hugo Grotius, *The Rights of War and Peace (De Jure Belli ac Pacis),* Prolegomena, sec. 7; Samuel Pufendorf, *Of the Law of Nature and Nations,* bk. 2, chap. 3, sec. 15; Richard Cumberland, *A Treatise of the Laws of Nature,* chap. 2, sec. 22, pp. 136–43.

to be called natural to man, or the particular question of what the sociality (*socialitas*) of our nature consists in, or, finally, with what part of our nature we are rendered apt and inclined to society, whether it be society without human government or civil society. While these questions have remained inadequately addressed, a whole battery of cavils and absurdities has been brought against them by certain writers,[16] who seem to vaunt and pride themselves on depicting human nature in the worst and most disgraceful light.

First, therefore, I will inquire what are the qualities which can rightly be said to be natural to man so far as concerns moral character; and then I will inquire how far human society, whether it be civil society or society without government, can be included among things natural.

Since we are conducting an inquiry about qualities which are natural to any kind of thing, or which come about naturally, it seems that one must first remark that any man to whom any natural thing or any artificial construction and all its parts are known, can easily discern for what end that design or construction, whether of nature or of art, is intended. And he can with equal ease distinguish between those things which happen to this natural entity by accident or by external force, and those things which are found in it by deliberate design in accordance with the nature of the thing. This distinction can be made on two grounds: first, if the construction which he is contemplating is whole and complete, he surveys all that is achieved by that design, and rightly infers that the device was constructed in order to accomplish precisely that. For no one, when he observes any structure in its integrity, whether of natural or of artificial objects, has any doubts about the ends for which each is naturally fitted. The eyes are surely designed for seeing, the teeth for chewing, buildings to live in, and ships for sailing. Secondly, even when the structure of a thing is not quite whole but faulty or disarranged by some accident, yet if all the parts remain, however worn, decayed, or disjointed, the spectator who is skilled in these things is not prevented from discerning for what end they were intended, the nat-

---

16. Thomas Hobbes, *On the Citizen, Leviathan;* Bernard Mandeville, *The Fable of the Bees;* Archibald Campbell, *Arete-logia: Or, an Inquiry into the Origin of Moral Virtue.* Mandeville and Campbell appear to have been very much in Hutcheson's mind as he composed his response to selfish moralists; see p. 206 ff.

ural constitution of the parts that are missing, and the aim and use of all of them.[17] For who, when he looks at a house, though it be ruinous, does not know that it was intended for habitation, to protect men from hardship from the weather? Further, who does not know how to distinguish what happens in accordance with the nature and fabric of the structure of which we are speaking from effects which result from some defect or depreciation? We see, for example, gaps and holes in the roofs of houses and the rain coming in, as a result of which human beings are assailed by the cold and contract illnesses; sometimes we see roofs falling in, walls collapsing, and poor unsuspecting men buried in a mass of rubble. But who will infer from these things that all this happened because of the structure itself, or that the builder intended these insidious assaults on human lives? Who does not know that these things happened by chance or carelessness, without intention, and from faults which are to be ascribed to the weakness of the material? The only thing which we can truly infer is that the builder either was not able or for some reason did not want the structure to be longer lasting. But our judgment about the end and proper use of the work itself is not changed.

And besides, once the true use of a device has become clear, if subsequently certain things seem, at first sight, to be contrary to its acknowledged end, one should not immediately have doubts about the general purpose of the contrivance until one has made a fuller investigation. It may be that the very parts which seemed contrary to the general purpose may serve this purpose by some other means, or be necessary to it in some other way. Or there may be certain other parts of the structure which remedy these apparent defects or mitigate their bad effects. So, in buildings, open windows might seem to be naturally fitted to let in shower and storm, until we see the panes of glass which can be easily lowered and admit all the light and heat but keep out the blustery gales.

Therefore you would not say that everything that happens to a thing is natural however it happens, even if it happens to each and every object of that kind, provided there is nothing in the structure of the object that was

---

17. See the argument from design and the analogy between the constitution of human nature and the construction of a house in Cicero, *De Natura Deorum,* 2.17.

designed to bring about precisely that effect. Or, as I would not want to argue about a word, I would call some things, in order to distinguish them, natural, because of their weakness. These are things which are the way they are because God, the maker of all things, did not wish them to be stronger or more enduring than they are. The weakness of our nature appears to have been willed by the good and great God in the excellent wisdom of his counsel; yet all our innate desires strive against that weakness and declare that such weakness is not the end of our duties, much less the goal which nature has set for our actions.[18]

I would say first of all, therefore, that those things are natural to man for which God has given our nature not only a natural desire but also the ability to obtain them. For a desire implanted by nature is perhaps the only conceivable faculty of an active nature that would allow us to distinguish between natural states or actions and their contraries; particularly if united with that desire is a sense, equally innate, which makes the actions or results sought agreeable and pleasant. But man is an intelligent animal, sagacious and endowed with memory, full of reason and counsel; an animal too, which not only can keep in view what is present, but also sees consequences and causes. He therefore desires not only things for which nature has implanted in him an immediate desire or which excite pleasure of themselves, but any number of other things which assist him in obtaining objects that are pleasing to the senses. Hence many things are said to be naturally desired which do not immediately give any pleasure at all, provided only that they are seen as useful or as a means to secure what is agreeable. Hence natural things are divided into those which are desired immediately and for themselves and those which we pursue for the sake of other things, or into primary and secondary natural things.[19]

Besides, there are many natural things of both kinds (that is, things which we desire for themselves and things which we desire for the sake of other things) for which we do not have a particularly powerful desire; our

---

18. Hutcheson's position, that "all our innate desires strive against that weakness," would have been perceived to be heterodox or, more specifically, Pelagian by strict Reformed or Presbyterian theologians. Compare Heppe, *Reformed Dogmatics*, p. 308.

19. See Hutcheson's *An Essay on the Nature and Conduct of the Passions and Affections* (1728) for a more extended account of natural desires.

desire for them may be easily checked and overcome by other equally natural desires. Thus there are many people who have a natural inclination to
love music, geometry, poetry, and other arts taken by themselves; however,
other appetites in them are so much more powerful that they quite over-
whelm and bury that love. In a similar way, aversion from work and a taste
for pleasures often get the better of an ambition to get rich. By contrast,
there are other natural desires which are so vigorous and backed by such
powerful forces of nature that they cannot be overcome except by other
natural desires. The former kind I would call natural, but not necessary;
examples of the latter, found in virtually all human beings, I would say, are
appetite for food, love of offspring, and the like.

Natural desires, then, I think I have sufficiently explained. It remains for
me to add this caution that the term "state of nature" (*status naturalis*) also
suffers from a serious ambiguity. I will not dwell on the utter abuse of words
by which the state of nature is not only opposed to the civil state, but is
also supposed to exclude all those things that are procured by human
strength, diligence, or sagacity, and therefore prevents the exercise not only
of our natural forces but also of some of our natural desires. In this usage,
so long as he preserves his natural state, man is depicted (may God forgive
the thought!) as a mute and naked animal, poor, solitary, nasty, dirty, rude,
ignorant, timid, rapacious, aggressive, unsociable, incapable of giving or
attracting love.[20]

> Great father of the gods, may it please you to punish inhuman tyrants
> in just this way![21]

I will not dwell, I say, on this abuse of words, which is an insult to our
nature, and blasphemy toward the great and good God, the father of men,
besides being despicable as philosophy. For it, long since, not only Hobbes
but Pufendorf himself have paid the penalty at the hands of such distin-

20. Hobbes, *Leviathan,* chap. 13.
21. Persius, *Satires,* III, 35–36, *Juvenal and Persius,* p. 76: Persius prays to the gods to
punish tyrants, the most evil of men, by making them conscious, by their wicked passions, of the virtue they have irretrievably lost.

guished men as Titius, Barbeyrac, Cumberland, Carmichael, and above all the most ingenious Earl of Shaftesbury.[22]

If we care at all about the use of words, "state of nature" should certainly denote either that condition of men which most encourages them to exercise all their natural aptitudes and desires, or that most perfect state to which men can rise by the intelligent use of all their forces and faculties, a state which seems to be recommended by the innate desire for supreme happiness and by whatever kindly and social (*communes*) affections are natural to man.[23] Hence state of nature will signify either the common condition of mankind or the most perfect condition which they can attain by the resources implanted in their nature. And certainly this most perfect state rightly takes the name of natural. For though certain parts of our nature, certain desires, carry us into many vices in the corrupt state of things in which we find ourselves, yet when we contemplate the whole fabric of human nature, disordered and corrupt though it be, and the different parts of our human nature, in particular the social and kindly (*communes et benignos*) affections and that moral sense which we may also call natural conscience,[24] we see clearly that vices are not natural to our nature; we see the faculties which ought to moderate and govern the lower desires. Therefore, though the strength and power of this sense or conscience may be so diminished that it is unable often to govern the lower desires, yet we see that by its own nature it is naturally fit to rule. Clearly it is *the ruling principle*[25] to which all things were made subject, and rightly so, in the integral state of our nature. Nor indeed can the true fabric of our nature as God disposed it be restored until conscience, seated on this its proper throne, crushes the bodily desires beneath its feet. And the Reformed theologians agree with

22. See references to the writings of Titius, Barbeyrac, Cumberland, and Carmichael in notes 12 and 16, above; also Shaftesbury, "Sensus Communis," in *Characteristics of Men, Manners, Opinions, Times,* pp. 42–45.

23. Shaftesbury, "Letters to Ainsworth," in *Several letters written by a noble lord to a young man at the university.*

24. Compare Joseph Butler, *Sermons.*

25. Hutcheson used the Greek term *to hegemonikon.* See Cicero, *De Natura Deorum,* II, xi, pp. 150–51: "I use the term 'ruling principle' as the equivalent of the Greek *hegemonikon,* meaning that part of anything which must and ought to have supremacy in a thing of that sort."

all these doctrines, very rightly pointing to the original fabric and construction of our nature as it once was.[26] And though in popular language they sometimes call our fallen and corrupt state natural, so as to distinguish it from the state which was superimposed from above by divine grace, they do not deny thereby that the original fabric of our nature was, by the divine art and plan, designed for every virtue, for all honest and illustrious things. And evident signs of this design and workmanship are preserved, they acknowledge, in the very ruins of its fabric.

We are therefore right to call that state which is most highly cultivated the *natural* state of the human race. But we must then ask what name we are to give to its opposite, the state which is not yet cultivated? Insofar as a condition which cannot last for long deserves the name of state, it is entirely appropriate to call it an *uncultivated* state, where our natural abilities have never been exercised. In things not endowed with intelligence, in an inanimate object, it is right to oppose the natural and uncultivated state to the state which has been cultivated by human art. And among men one may aptly distinguish the natural state from that artificial state which has been produced not by force of natural ability or human desire but by external force, by the cunning of men, by grievous and extraordinary need, or by any scheme which is clever and astute beyond normal human foresight. But an animal endowed with reason, which is always eager to learn something new and has a mind fitted to acquiring and practicing skills, in no way forsakes his natural state, but in every way follows his own nature and God his father and guide, when he forges and refines a variety of skills, when he seeks and offers help in a spirit of mutual affection, and with confidence in his fellowman preserves himself and the human race.

Since, then, we argue that political writers should unlearn the use of these words (*natural state*), what is that state to be called which is opposed to the civil state? This we can surely gather from those writers who thought it axiomatic that *"Any right granted to a ruler is subtracted from primitive*

---

26. Heppe, *Reformed Dogmatics,* 232–38: "In its original state the nature of man was the perfect image of God in creaturely form. . . ." Heppe goes on to cite Petrus van Mastricht, Johannes Marck, and others. See also Thomas Boston, *Human Nature in Its Fourfold State,* I, 1, on the state of innocence; chap. 1: "Man's Original Righteousness," p. 37 ff.

liberty."[27] That state, therefore, which is opposed to the civil state is best called a *state of liberty from human government.* We might seem to be lingering too long over these words, if there were not very serious matters contained in them.

I come now to what I had particularly in mind for my oration: and that is, to determine in what sense social life is natural to man, whether in the state of liberty or in the civil state; and first about sociability in the state of liberty.

Now, this warning would hardly have had to be given, if certain men had not gone astray in this matter. For in no philosopher does our natural sociability signify that "men desire the company of other men for its own sake, or that it is agreeable in itself for a man to pass his time in a crowd."[28] This is precisely what is desired for itself (perhaps by some instinct) by the other animals and, primarily, by those animals that live continuously in herds, although, so far as we are permitted to see, they have no common need, nor do they make a deliberate decision to protect themselves from dangers by means of their united strength. And it may be that this kind of herding together is desirable in itself for men, even though they very often congregate for other reasons; for example, they come together for mutual aid and assistance, or for common tasks or commerce; or when one, with kindly intention, seeks to care for and benefit others, or with crafty design, attempts to procure for himself fame, glory, power, or pleasure. The truth, however, which moral writers teach is that the natural sociability of man lies in the fact that "provided that all the forces and parts of man's nature are taken into view, he is inclined and naturally fitted to lead a harmless life, to give mutual assistance, to protect and preserve others; and therefore he is equally naturally fitted for everything that is obviously conducive to

27. Pufendorf, *On the Duty of Man and Citizen,* II, 5, p. 132: "In becoming a citizen, a man loses his natural liberty and subjects himself to an authority. . . .''; Locke, *Two Treatises of Government,* II, 4, 22, p. 301: "The *Natural Liberty* of Man is to be free from any Superior Power on Earth, and not to be under the will or Legislative Authority of Man. . . ." Hutcheson employed the construction "the state of natural liberty," in preference to "the state of nature," in *A Short Introduction to Moral Philosophy,* II, chap. 4, p. 139 ff., and in *A System of Moral Philosophy,* vol. 1, bk. 2, chap. 4, p. 283.

28. Mandeville, "A Search into the Nature of Society," in *The Fable of the Bees,* vol. 1, pp. 340–41.

these things."[29] And perhaps this has not been denied, and could not be denied, by anyone, even by Hobbes himself, who, of course, teaches that one may see by a very easy reasoning that peace and a harmless life are to every man's great advantage.

But the question about which there is substantial controversy is this: in what sense is this social life natural to man? Is it the case that all our benevolence toward the mass of mankind, that desires to protect whole peoples and do all that can be done for them, has its origin in each man's want, weakness, and indigence? Is it so that there may be others from whom each man may obtain what he wants for himself, so that by doing and receiving favors, he may get from another what he cannot get by himself? Or on the other hand, does benevolence arise from nature, and are we disposed to beneficence by nature, and not because we expect a favor in return or calculate the advantage our benevolence will obtain for us?

Pufendorf and most recent writers teach the doctrine of human nature which had been that of the Epicureans,[30] that is, that self-love (*philautia*) alone, or the desire of each man for his own private pleasure or advantage, is the spring of all actions, and they derive from it all the affections of the heart, even those that seem most kindly. Despite this, they insist that social life is natural to man on the ground that such is the nature of external things and such the nature of men, that we need the help of others to avoid almost all the human evils and to obtain almost all the external pleasures or advantages which human life affords. And we need others to such an extent that we are not able even to live, let alone to live well, without the company and help of others. They also teach that there is a resourcefulness in men, and abilities of mind and body, by which they can mutually help or hinder one another. Whence by an easy reasoning it is inferred that it is of the greatest advantage to each and every man so to conduct his life that he may procure for himself the help and assistance of others, and not provoke others to inflict harm on him. And since this cannot be achieved except by abstaining from all injury to others, and by helping them to the extent of

29. Pufendorf, *Of the Law of Nature and Nations,* II, III, IV, pp. 136–39; *On the Duty of Man and Citizen,* I, 3, p. 35.

30. Pufendorf, *Of the Law of Nature and Nations,* II, III, X, p. 130, citing Gassendi on Epicurus, and pp. 135–36.

one's ability, so far as the state of our affairs permits, they conclude that living in this way will be of the greatest benefit to each man; and this is what social life consists in. In fact Pufendorf ascends a little higher. He takes the position that knowledge of the great and good God and of the duty which he requires of us is easy for man; and that clear indications of this are given by the very constitution of our nature as creatures who desire happiness which can only be obtained in social life.[31] And hence it is clear that God has fashioned us for social life, and all the duties of this life are taught by divine law, sanctioned by rewards and punishments, and whatever is contrary to that law is forbidden. According to this view of Pufendorf's, although social life does not seem to be natural to man immediately and for itself, nevertheless it would be right to consider it as natural in a secondary sense and certainly as necessary. This whole position has been richly illustrated by him, and many profound observations have been added by the illustrious Richard Cumberland.[32] And indeed these writers have demonstrated correctly, perceptively, and copiously that social life is natural in this secondary sense. Without social life, such is the indigence of our nature, such the malignancy of external forces, that the human condition would be most miserable, yet by means of society our life can become safe, agreeable, happy, and in all respects desirable.

What Pufendorf taught is indeed true, but he omitted many of the most important observations that may be made on this subject. If one does not look into the matter more deeply, one will conclude that men were driven into society merely by external advantage and dread of external evils, contrary to the nature of their hearts, contrary to all their natural desires and affections; in the same way in which hunger, thirst, and the fear of cold often compel men to endure heavy labors from which our nature shrinks. But the fact is that there are many desires directly implanted by nature which do not seek either pleasure or physical advantage but things more sublime which themselves depend upon the company of others. These sublimer pleasures are prompted by no external sense, nor can any way be imag-

31. Pufendorf, *Of the Law of Nature and Nations,* II, III, XIX, p. 141 ff., and *On the Duty of Man and Citizen,* I, 3–4, p. 36 ff.
32. Cumberland, *A Treatise of the Laws of Nature.*

ined how they can be experienced outside society; particular instances of these are the pleasures of praise and honor. God gave us mind and sense, by whose help we see something beautiful, fitting, and honorable in intentions, words, and actions, whether our own or those of others; hence we bestow praise and favor upon those who have deserved well of the human race, and such is the character of all men that scarcely anything gives a man more happiness than to be praised and honored even though he expects no other profit from it. And by some wonderful provision of nature it happens that, though there is no small joy in the mere investigation of truth, yet that joy is immensely increased when there is another to whom one may communicate one's findings. And here I call as particularly suitable witnesses those happy souls, those lofty hearts, who

> have brought the distant stars before our eyes and
> subjected the upper regions of the sky to their understanding.[33]

Furthermore, by some wonderful sympathy[34] of nature, there are few or no pleasures, even physical pleasures, which are not augmented by association with others. There is no happy or cheerful frame of mind which does not demand to be shared and spread among others. Certainly, there is scarcely anything (and I could omit "scarcely") agreeable, joyful, happy, cheerful, or delightful, which does not boil up and bubble over from the human heart, and long to be poured out among others. Nor is there anything more cheering for a man than to share his happiness with others.[35] And therefore, though they claim that it is his own pleasure or advantage that each man seeks, yet such is the nature of certain pleasures, including the greatest of them, and of most of our desires, that they prompt us to seek social life by themselves almost without any reasoning; and by themselves they make the duties of social life agreeable and delightful. All these things the ancients seem to have discerned, nor does the illustrious Richard Cumberland altogether neglect them.[36] But they have been most eloquently

---

33. Ovid, *Fasti*, I, ll. 305–6, p. 22.

34. "Contagio": Cicero's translation of *sympatheia* in *De Divinatione* (*On Divination*), 2, 14, 33, in Cicero, *De Senectute, De Amicitia, De Divinatione*, p. 406.

35. Cicero, *De Amicitia* (*On Friendship*), 6.22, in Cicero, *De Senectute, De Amicitia, De Divinatione*, p. 130.

36. Cumberland, *A Treatise of the Laws of Nature*.

celebrated by the illustrious Earl of Shaftesbury, noble both by his family and by his genius, however correctly he has been criticized by theologians in other matters.[37] And I see nothing which can be said to the contrary.

Yes, and they have a higher teaching. For human nature is not sociable only in this secondary sense for the sake merely of our own advantage or pleasure, whatever it may be, but is in itself immediately and primarily kind, unselfish, and sociable without regard to its advantage or pleasure. And this is the rich explication they give of it. They declare their conviction that very many feelings and passions implanted in man by nature are kindly and unselfish and first and last look directly to the felicity of others. Such is the structure of the human mind, that when certain images (*species*) of things come before it, certain affections arise under the sole guidance of nature, without any art or deliberation, indeed without any previous command of the will. For just as a desire for private pleasure or advantage, a desire which is usually attributed to self-love, asserts itself as soon as a prospect of getting it arises, in the same way when images of other men and their fortune come to our attention, they excite public and unselfish feelings, even though there is no prospect of private advantage. For example, when the idea of a sentient nature tortured with serious pain is put before the mind, it excites commiseration and a simple desire to take away the pain. In the same way, the idea of a fortunate, happy, cheerful nature equally excites shared and social joy; and the continuance of that state is desired for itself. Nor is this concern for the condition of others only seen when they are present and before our external senses (in which case perhaps powerful reactions or emotions are visible) but whenever, in a quiet moment, we call up an image of others by reading histories or the narratives of travelers, or even when from the stories of drama we receive a certain image of human nature, even in the remotest nations or centuries where no advantage of our own is involved, with what heartfelt concern do we follow the fortunes of entire countries or honorable individuals? With what horror do we avert our minds from the major ills of human life, miserable slavery, the

37. Shaftesbury, "Sensus Communis," pt. 3, sec. 2, pp. 51–53, and "The Moralists," pt. 2, sec. 4, pp. 283–88, in *Characteristics;* and Isabel Rivers, *Reason, Grace and Sentiment,* vol. 2, for discussion of Shaftesbury on the higher pleasures of social life and on his differences with theologians.

arrogant devastations of conquerors, the cruelties of tyrants; and with what warmth of heart do we pray with the ancient choruses

That fortune may return to the wretched and desert the proud.[38]

But it is not the general kinship of human nature and the universal affection which embraces however feebly the whole human race which we should take note of, to illustrate our sociability. For most of the ties between human beings are narrower, and because of them some persons become far dearer to us than others. The appetite for procreation, and a certain special care for offspring, is common to all living creatures; and in desiring marriage itself men dwell not only upon those things which are sought also by the animals, but particularly seek out a good character in the spouse, many virtues, and above all a gentle, amiable, and kind disposition. And they cherish their offspring with the tenderest possible benevolence and concern. Hence arises the love of brothers and cousins, manifest always unless disrupted by wrongs, rivalry, or conflict of interest. Likewise most of those who are not bound by any tie of blood are commended to our love and more immediate benevolence by habitual association, familiarity, exchange of good offices, and collaboration in things serious or frivolous; and nothing binds closer than virtue itself. This is the origin of friendship and companionship, which indeed each man seeks for himself. This benevolent concern for the fortunes of friends, associates, and neighbors often endures apart from any consideration of advantage.

In addition, these writers[39] take the view that a sense of what is decent (*decorum*) and honorable (*honestum*) is natural to man; it is this sense which prompts us to esteem everything that is kindly, faithful, gentle, friendly; it is also the reason why we love men endowed with these virtues with a particularly intense love and goodwill. And when kindnesses are lavished upon us or upon those who are closely bound to us in affection, gratitude rises in our hearts; we feel a most tender love for those who have done us good; and we desire to return the favor. And because nothing can be more pleasing

38. Horace, *The Art of Poetry*, 201, in *Satires, Epistles, and Ars Poetica*, p. 466: one of the rules that Horace prescribes for a chorus in a tragedy is that they "pray and beseech the gods that fortune may return to the wretched and desert the proud."

39. Shaftesbury, Cumberland, Cicero, and others.

or more welcome to all men of lofty spirit than a mind that is conscious of its own integrity and of [other men's] approval and esteem, our benevolence expands and diffuses itself on all sides. We no longer take into account, in a mean and lowly spirit, those losses in external things caused by friendship or benevolence; all of that we hold not worth a straw, when right and integrity stand before our eyes. The kindly disposition of our hearts acquires new strength from this and is confirmed by use. Our zeal to deserve the praise of others in all good works burns more brightly. Those who enjoy these benefits, nay, all who see them, praise and commend them and desire to return them in kind. Hence too (though this is rarely in mind in the course of the action) humane and benevolent services of this kind, which are most welcome in themselves, are almost always attended by the greatest advantage to everyone.

The arguments which demonstrate this more amiable description of our nature I will perhaps publish more fully in another place.[40] Here I would simply like to suggest that each man must descend into himself and examine himself, to see and to feel whether he does not recognize many people as dear to him for themselves alone apart from any advantage to himself, such as his offspring, parents, friends, relatives, fellow citizens.[41] Or does he not find in himself an anxious concern for the condition of others, when he reads either tragedy or history, where no advantage to himself can be

40. It may have been Hutcheson's intention in 1730 to expand upon the theme of natural sociability in *A System of Moral Philosophy,* which was composed in the 1730s but published posthumously in 1755. In the event, Hutcheson also found it necessary to take into account the weaknesses and imperfections in human nature. See James Moore, "Hutcheson's Theodicy: The Argument and the Contexts of *A System of Moral Philosophy.*"

41. In the concluding paragraphs of this lecture, Hutcheson appears to have been responding to his critics, principally to Archibald Campbell (*Arete-logia; Or, an Enquiry into the Original of Moral Virtue*), who maintained that Hutcheson's various attempts to illustrate benevolence and disinterested affection could be reduced to self-love and desire for esteem. Campbell's argument that parental affection derives from self-love (from recognition that children are parts of oneself) appears on pp. 240–50. See also John Clarke, "The Foundation of Morality in Theory and Practice Considered," in *British Moralists,* vol. 2, pp. 229–30 and 245–46; and Luigi Turco, "Sympathy and Moral Sense," pp. 82–89.

detected?[42] What if God said to a man, "You are to die forthwith undisturbed by any sensation of pain or fear, and your soul will not survive your body, for so I have willed who can do all things.[43] Know, then, that whatever you ask with your last breath to be done for others, that I will be sure to effect for you. But no one will have or return gratitude to you however many good things you bestow by means of your prayer, nor will anyone detest or curse you if you invoke evils on them. Nor hereafter will you receive happiness or sorrow from the fortunes of others, since you will not feel anything more, for you will not be. In this state of things are all human things utterly foreign to you and indifferent? Your offspring, friends, fellow-citizens, I will make happy for you, or miserable, as you ask. They will flourish in virtue, health, friendship, wealth, and honor, or they will live wretchedly in vices, sickness, hatred, envy, poverty, infamy, shame, and slavery." Would all these things be indifferent to any man on earth? Nay, how many would not demand, in the very moment of death, for all those whom he holds dear, the very same things, with the very same passion of mind and the very same strength of will, as he had asked for them at any time previously, although all consideration of his own advantage would now be removed? There are, therefore, in man benevolent feelings which desire the happiness of others primarily and often uniquely.

Despite these considerations someone might perhaps ask: why do we say that a social life, that is, an innocent and kindly life, is more natural to man than a grasping, contentious, cruel, and savage life? For there are many appetites which seem to be natural, to wit, self-love, anger, and the desire for vengeance, which often incite men to inflict injuries on each other. How many things are done in lust, greed, wickedness, and crime! How many struggles for riches! How many intellectual disputes among the learned,

---

42. Campbell, *Arete-logia,* pp. 266–67, proposed that "we either secretly convey ourselves to that Part of the World, where he immediately acted, or we change the Scene of his Actions to those Places where we are." See also Clarke, "Foundation," pp. 229–30.

43. Campbell claimed that he could not conceive how any man of understanding could be ignorant of future rewards and punishments in an afterlife, *Arete-logia,* pp. 293–96. "We are all the Off-spring or Productions of the *Deity.* . . ." p. 305. See also Clarke, "Foundation," p. 228.

which are a fertile source of unjust and arrogant actions! How many different abuses would men inflict on one another if they were not restrained from wrongdoing by the civil government! All these vices arise from natural desires: are they therefore to be called natural?

To break the force of this objection, many learned men have rightly observed that many of the secondary desires and passions of the mind which particularly disturb our lives have been either introduced or massively increased by the civil state, whereas there was scarcely any occasion for their exercise in the state of unrestrained liberty. Such are greed and ambition and certain imperious and oppressive superstitions which encourage men to do evil. The remedies for these evils which arise from civil union are to be sought from civil government.[44] But I will not spend time on this response; it will not perhaps give satisfaction to all. It would perhaps be more acceptable to address one who was insisting on such arguments in the following way. Grant that men were created by the great and good God for the social life of which we speak. Will you not also at the same time admit that it is absolutely necessary that all these desires which have regard to private interest, even anger, were put into men by God himself when he was creating men for social life? One must not therefore conclude from these desires that men have not been equipped by nature for social life. Or would anyone say that the fabric of our nature is absurd and self-contradictory? Or that we are as naturally suited to vices as to virtues? Perish the thought that we should attribute to God a work so vain! Of course we have desires which seek satisfaction in private pleasure and advantage; we have equally, as I hope I have sufficiently shown, more creditable desires which make us sociable. Conflict often arises between these two, and desire prompts one way, and intellect the other. But he who has truly seen into himself and has experienced the whole of himself will find there is a part of his nature which is equipped to remedy these ills, and to reconcile these warring passions to peace. Certainly that divine providence[45] which is often called nature has not dealt malignantly with us. For God has given us un-

---

44. Barbeyrac, in Pufendorf, *Of the Law of Nature and Nations,* II, II, II, nn. 6–16, p. 105; Carmichael, *Natural Rights,* p. 127.

45. Hutcheson employs the Stoic term *pronoia* in Greek.

derstanding and discernment, and we may easily see that by a social and friendly life we can most effectively obtain and preserve all our pleasures, even private and sensual pleasures. Reason also instructs us that a modest and temperate enjoyment of pleasure which is not disruptive of human society is most advantageous and at the same time most agreeable. On the other hand, nothing will convince us that the endless accumulation of useful objects, or continuous soft and delicate sensual pleasures, for whose sake other people are hurt or honorable duties put aside, are necessary to any man for either a pleasant or a secure life. It certainly needs no long or laborious chain of reasoning to prove this. God gave us a sense of the fitting and the beautiful; associated with this sense, as moderator of all the grosser pleasures, is shame; he also gave the keen spur of praise. The effect of all these is to make life social and kindly, and to make all the duties which are honorable and beneficial to others most advantageous and at the same time most pleasant for the agent himself, and to make even the innate self-love of our nature in no way contrary to our common and benevolent affections.

There is a point of the highest importance which I think should be made here: to obtain a man's goodwill, it is not necessarily required that we should first have had an exchange of services with him.[46] Rather, we are favorably disposed to any harmless person, even if he has not commended himself to us by doing us some service. We are also favorably disposed to the most remote nations; we weep for their disasters, even though we only hear of them. By contrast, anger or any kind of malevolence can be excited only by a conflict of interests, rivalry, jealousy, or by some thought of previous injury or cruelty. This seems to demonstrate that benevolence is directly and in itself natural, but malevolence is only secondarily so, and often results from ignorance or accident.

Nor should we hold any part of our nature responsible for that laziness and inertia in controlling emotions and passions which takes possession of men's minds, or for the excessive inclination to the pleasures of the senses which throws all things into confusion. It is indisputable, to be sure, that our nature is fallen, weakened, and corrupt in very many ways. But who does not easily perceive the natural order of the human mind? Who does

---

46. Compare Campbell, *Arete-logia*, pp. 310–12.

not know what parts of it are naturally fit to rule even though they have been expelled from their position of power? To whom does it ever occur that natural conscience, that sense of the beautiful and the fitting, all the more noble affections, and that power of the mind itself which we call reason are only handmaidens of what are commonly called the sensual pleasures, are no more than the procurers of pleasure? On the contrary, we surely see that conscience and the sense of right, by whose side human reason sits as permanent counselor, is intended by nature to rule, and the bodily desires are born to serve.

Our adversaries are wonderfully ingenious and twist themselves into the six hundred shapes of Proteus to escape these conclusions. All these social inclinations, they say, are due to the daily care of parents and magistrates: students repeat by rote the clever indoctrination given them by the civil rulers. It is to this, they say, that one must attribute this human sociability and all those affections which either give an appearance of benevolence or actually are so.[47] Naturally, when we have been conditioned by the fear of punishment and years of habit to an external friendliness of manner, to politeness and affability, we believe that these manners are natural to us, just as someone from the lower classes accepts his vernacular speech as natural to him. And indeed it seems we must freely grant to our adversaries that all external duties and external civility can be achieved by respect for the laws and by the care of magistrates; for a calculation of simple advantage reaches this far and can effect this. But can the hope of advantage, can education or long habit also invent new internal affections and senses of things contrary to the structure of our nature? By education it can easily be brought about that we embrace the true for the false, and believe by false judgment that things that are particularly useless are useful. By long use too, perhaps the very organs of the body will be so changed that what at first was unpleasant becomes pleasant. Perhaps too we may believe things to be unpleasant before we take the risk of trying them, then after the risk is taken, receive the opposite sensation. In these matters, indeed,

---

47. Mandeville, "An Enquiry into the Origin of Moral Virtue," in *The Fable of the Bees,* I, pp. 41–57.

Is there anything that pleases or displeases that you would not think could be changed?[48]

But all these things happen in accordance with the very senses previously implanted by nature; no new sense of things arises, no new affections. Nor do these things appear to us under a different image from those which the senses implanted by nature allow us to perceive. By what art, I ask, or management could one commend to a blind man a piece of clothing or an ornament on the ground of its lovely color? If one had no other way of distinguishing good from evil than by calculating his own pleasure or advantage, then it is unlikely that any thing or event would be desirable unless it appeared to him in the image of his own pleasure or advantage. But in fact, we see that men think many actions honest, praiseworthy, pleasing, and good where no advantage of their own is indicated. We see anxious concern for others, and ready goodwill, even though the prospect of private advantage is totally absent.

I do not know how it happened, but since the famous Locke and other writers[49] demonstrated to the satisfaction of many, among them men both illustrious and honorable, that there are no ideas of things in the human mind from the very beginning, no conceptions of things, no judgments whether theoretical or practical (which alone they are determined to call innate), these men have virtually abandoned investigation into natural ideas, apprehensions, judgments, and the natural sense of anything whatever.[50] But the ancients, without exception, said that all the ideas, apprehensions, and judgments which we form about things under the guidance of nature at whatever stage this may occur, or which are received by any of the faculties of our nature more or less necessarily and universally, are innate. And certainly an investigation of these natural judgments, perceptions, and appearances of things offered by nature would be far more useful

48. Horace, *Epistles*, 3.1.101, in *Satires, Epistles, and Ars Poetica*, p. 404.

49. John Locke, *Essay*, I; Jean Le Clerc, *Pneumatologia seu de Spiritibus*, chap. 5, "On the Nature of Ideas, and Whether They Are Innate?"; Mandeville, *The Fable of the Bees*, II, 149, 168. See John W. Yolton, *John Locke and the Way of Ideas*, chap. 2.

50. Hutcheson's defense of innate ideas in this paragraph underlines the importance of such ideas for logic, as he understood it. See *A Compend of Logic*, passim, and the introduction, p. xii.

than to waste time on what is perceived or not perceived in that tiny little animal which eventually turns into a man, or by a few unfortunate men, born in some ill-favored corner of the earth to lead a hard and uncivilized life, ignorant of every art and of the human condition. Why would you tell a shipbuilder who was seeking material for the royal fleet what those tiny oak shoots are like which are put out by the acorn in the first or second year, in which of course for his purpose there is neither suitable height nor hardness, strength nor firmness? or to what purpose would you tell him what those oak shrubs are like which spring up in sterile soil or cling to craggy cliffs in the crevices of the rocks? There are many natural abilities in every species of thing, many senses and appetites in animals, and many devices of nature which are not apparent from the start. Nay, some will never become visible if due opportunity is lacking, or some condition required by nature is absent. Who has ever observed a desire for marriage among children playing with knucklebones and nuts? Yet what is more natural to every kind of animal than the union for procreation? Who will express anger when he has received no impression of injury, or love when there is no one to love? We see great, sheer, overhanging rocks clinging to mountains, finely balanced yet standing firm. Is there not in these, one may ask, an innate weight? When the moss is removed, when that firm cohesion is taken away, immediately we see a precipitous fall. Let them cease, then, to object that there are no innate ideas, and that passions or desires cannot be conceived without previous ideas. For this would just as well prove that all private passions and desires were not natural, since there would be no innate ideas of any private pleasure or advantage in the sense in which recent writers talk of a thing being innate.

Others have another objection: men are not desirous of the company of men as such; otherwise all would be equally desired who are equally men. As if anyone had denied that the bonds of nature are closer between some people than others. But they proceed: in every association between men, each man seeks his own advantage or pleasure or glory. If they meet in the marketplaces for trade, each one seeks his own profit; if they meet at banquets for mental stimulation, each seeks laughter for himself, in which, of course, he affirms his own superiority over those at whom he laughs, or carps at those who are absent, or boasts about himself and his affairs. And when conversation arises about serious matters, how many are there who do not think themselves superior and seek to make a reputation and claim the first place for wisdom, thus giving rise to squabbles and feuds? And those who have less confidence in themselves nonetheless desire to learn a little something from which their reputation may be made in the future.[51] To all these objections a reply is readily available. It often happens that good men meet together who are cultivated, witty, and kindly, among whom there is no expectation either of profit or reputation, no eagerness to brag of themselves or deride others or criticize them. And when they discuss serious matters in friendly conversation, each expresses his opinion freely and with humor, and asks others' advice, not seeking glory or the first place for wisdom. And though we confess that it is quite rare for men to meet without each expecting some advantage or pleasure, what will our adversaries make of that? Who ever denied that the private affections were implanted in man by nature? What if we also grant them that private affections are quite often stronger than public and social affections? Will they conclude from this that no affections are truly benevolent? From the fact that some bodies are heavier than others it could just as well be concluded that there are many bodies without weight. Moreover, if a man can pursue two objectives at the same time by the same means, how will anyone show that he was not aiming at one of the two objectives? And of course it is probable that men very seldom get together without any friendly and social feeling at all, whether in private associations or in states. If indeed benevolence were foreign to human nature, and equally foreign was that confident expectation of mutual benevolence, candid and free of suspicion, which is almost always the companion of a kindly character, then ambitious men, of the sort that are accustomed to assume political office, would not find the common people so easy and so tractable as to commit to their trust themselves and all their fortunes.

Finally, and most importantly: when men are said to be seeking profit, or their own advantage, they are surely quite often serving their offspring and family from the most benevolent motives and the most tender love.

---

51. Hobbes, *On the Citizen,* 1, 2; Mandeville, "A Search into the Nature of Society," in *The Fable of the Bees,* I, 337 ff.; Campbell, *Arete-logia,* pp. 315–16.

And indeed, by far the larger part of all the cares and worries of life is taken up by parental love and by our sense of duty toward parents, friends, or country. What grave, what continual worries arise from these affections? How intense are party passions in a country even among those who do not presume even covertly to seek for themselves honors or magistracies or salaried offices. With willing hearts they support the party which seems to them better and more beneficial to the country, not thinking at all of their own interest.

But they still insist: if the society of men is not sought for the sake of advantage or pleasure, why do we desire the company of the learned, the elegant, the affable, the liberal, the powerful and honored, if it is not that from them something advantageous, agreeable, or even honorable may come our way? And, they say, we avoid the ignorant, the gloomy, the sour, the boastful, the stingy, and the infamous.[52] As if we could be benevolent or have kind and sociable dispositions only toward those whom we would wish to choose as companions and intimates! As if, indeed, anyone had said that no other desire is implanted in the mind but that for society. Or as if there were no disagreeable and vexatious elements in the character of certain people which would deter us from taking men like that as our companions. Or, finally, as if there were no virtues in others, either natural or cultivated by art, which would render them more apt for friendship and better company.

I hope therefore, gentlemen, that I have made out an adequate case for my primary thesis that social life (in the state unrestrained by government) is natural to man for its own sake. Elsewhere perhaps I shall give an account of what seem to have been the most probable origin and causes of civil society.[53] But from what I have said, the divine benevolence toward the

52. Campbell, *Arete-logia*, p. 316: "How comes it to pass, that we enter into a more close and intimate Correspondence, with this Man rather than with that? . . . I see, that in his Choice of Friends, he overlooks the Clown of no Education, . . . he pitches upon one or more as his Bosom-Companions, and leaves all the Rest excluded from this Intimacy." Mandeville, "A Search into the Nature of Society," in *The Fable of the Bees*, I, p. 340.

53. Hutcheson's account of the origin and causes of civil society is found in *A Short Introduction to Moral Philosophy*, bk. 3, chap. 4, and in *A System of Moral Philosophy*, bk. 3, chap. 4.

human race which we should always recall with gratitude and adore is made manifest by the very fabric of man. For with such art and care, such deliberate ingenuity, has the most beneficent father of all things made us and equipped us for all things noble and good and indeed for everything that is most happy and delightful. Nor when we exhort men to live a good life, harmless, temperate, friendly, and beneficent, should anyone think that there is laid upon him anything sour, vexatious, repulsive, or sorrowful, which nature shuns. For in fact this is the only way by which nature herself directs us to the things we most desire, namely, security, tranquillity, felicity, and, I might even say, pure pleasure, untroubled by repentance or pangs of remorse. Go forward, then, in virtue, beloved young men, the hope of this generation and the glory, I trust, of the generation to come. Take nature and God as your guide, apply your minds to liberal studies, and lay down a varied store of useful knowledge which you may bring forth one day in all honorable, temperate, modest, and courageous service to our country and the human race. And even at this time, with hope and courage, take to yourselves the joyous sense of a mind conscious of its own integrity, the true dignity of life, the esteem [of others], the most honorable kind of fame, and the highest pleasures of life.

THE END

BIBLIOGRAPHY

Aldrich, Henry. *Artis Logicae Compendium.* Oxford, 1692.

Arbuckle, James. *Glotta: A Poem.* Glasgow, 1721.

Aristotle. *De Anima [On the Soul].* English translation by W. S. Hett. Cambridge, Mass.: Harvard University Press, 1935.

———. *Metaphysics.* Translated by John Warrington. London: Dent, 1956.

———. *Nicomachean Ethics.* Translated by F. H. Peters. London, 1891.

———. *The Organon; or, Logical Treatises of Aristotle with the Introduction of Porphyry.* Translated by Octavius Freire Owen. London, 1900.

Arnauld, Antoine, and Pierre Nicole. *The Art of Thinking: Port-Royal Logic.* 1662. Translated by James Dickoff and Patricia James. Indianapolis: Bobbs-Merrill, 1964.

Barbeyrac, Jean. *Oratio Inauguralis de Dignitate et Utilitate Juris ac Historiarum.* Lausanne, 1711.

Barrow [Barovius], Isaac. *Lectures on Mathematics* [Lectiones Mathematicae]. London, 1685.

Baxter, Andrew. *An Enquiry into the Nature of the Human Soul.* 1733. 2nd ed. London, 1737.

Bayle, Pierre. *A General Dictionary, Historical and Critical.* 10 vols. London, 1734–41.

Berkeley, George. *Works.* Edited by A. A. Luce and T. E. Jessop. 9 vols. London: Thomas Nelson, 1948–57.

———. *An Essay Towards a New Theory of Vision* (1709). Vol. 1 of *The Works of George Berkeley, Bishop of Cloyne,* edited by A. A. Luce and T. E. Jessop. Thomas Nelson and Sons, 1948. pp. 141–279.

Berman, David. "Francis Hutcheson on Berkeley and the Molyneux Problem," *Proceedings of the Royal Irish Academy* 74 (1974): 259–65.

Boston, Thomas. *Human Nature in Its Fourfold State.* Edinburgh, 1720.

Boyle, Robert. *Origin of Forms and Qualities.* London, 1666.

Bracken, H. M. *The Early Reception of Berkeley's Immaterialism 1710–1733.* The
    Hague: Martinus Nijhoff, 1965.

Brucker, Johann Jakob. *Historia Critica Philosophiae.* 6 vols. Leipzig, 1742–46.

Burgersdijk, Franco. *Idea Philosophiae, tum moralis, tum naturalis.* Oxford, 1654.

———. *Institutiones Logicae.* Leiden, 1632.

———. *Monitio Logica; or, An Abstract and Translation of Burgersdicius, His
    Logick.* London, 1697.

Butler, Joseph. *The Analogy of Religion Natural and Revealed to the Constitution
    and Course of Nature.* 1735. London, 1857.

———. *Sermons.* 2nd ed. London, 1729.

Campbell, Archibald. *Arete-logia; Or, an Enquiry into the Original of Moral Vir-
    tue.* London, 1728.

Carmichael, Gershom. *Natural Rights on the Threshold of the Scottish Enlight-
    enment.* Edited by James Moore and Michael Silverthorne. Indianapolis: Lib-
    erty Fund, 2002.

———. "On Moral Philosophy, or the Science of Natural Jurisprudence."
    Praefatio in *Samuelis Pufendorfii De Officio Hominis et Civis.* Edinburgh,
    1724. Reprinted in Carmichael, *Natural Rights on the Threshold of the Scottish
    Enlightenment.*

Chambers, Ephraim. *Cyclopedia, or An Universal Dictionary of the Arts and Sci-
    ences.* London, 1728.

Cheyne, George. *A New Theory of Acute and Slow Continu'd Fevers; Wherein
    the Manner and Laws of Secretion . . . Are Mechanically Explained.* London,
    1722.

Cicero, Marcus Tullius. *De Finibus Bonorum et Malorum* [On the Ends of Good
    and Evil]. Translated by H. Rackham. London: William Heinemann, 1931.

———. *De Natura Deorum* [On the Nature of the Gods]. Translated by H.
    Rackham. London: William Heinemann, 1933.

———. *De Senectute, De Amicitia, De Divinatione* [On Old Age, On Friend-
    ship, On Divination]. Translated by W. A. Falconer. Cambridge, Mass.: Har-
    vard University Press, 1923.

———. *The Speeches, with an English Translation: Pro Publio Quinctio; Pro Sexto
    Roscio Amerino; Pro Quinto Roscio Comoedo; De Lege Agraria, I, II, III.* Trans-
    lated by J. H. Freese. London: William Heinemann, 1930.

———. *Tusculan Disputations.* Translated by J. E. King. London: William
    Heinemann, 1927.

Clarke, John. "The Foundation of Morality in Theory and Practice Consid-
    ered." 1726. Vol. 2 of *British Moralists: Being Selections from Writers Principally*

of the Eighteenth Century. Edited by L. A. Selby-Bigge. Oxford: Clarendon Press, 1897.

Clarke, Samuel. "A collection of papers which passed between the late learned Mr. Leibniz and Dr. Clarke." Vol. 4 of *The Works of Samuel Clarke.* London, 1738. pp. 575–700.

———. *A Demonstration of the Being and Attributes of God.* London, 1705.

Clow, James. "A System of Logic." 1773. GUL MS DC 8.13.

Coutts, James. *History of the University of Glasgow.* Glasgow, 1909.

Cudworth, Ralph. *The True Intellectual System of the Universe.* London, 1678.

Cumberland, Richard. *A Treatise of the Laws of Nature.* Translated by James Maxwell. London, 1727. (For a modern edition, see *A Treatise of the Laws of Nature.* Edited by Jon Parkin. Indianapolis: Liberty Fund, 2005.)

Descartes, René. *Discourse on Method and Meditations on First Philosophy.* 3rd ed. Translated by Donald A. Cress. Indianapolis: Hackett, 1980.

de Vries, Gerard. *De Natura Dei et Humanae Mentis. Determinationes Pneumatologicae. Accedunt de Catholicis Rerum Attributis Ejusdem Determinationes Ontologicae.* 1690. 4th ed. Edinburgh, 1703.

Diogenes Laertius. *Lives of Eminent Philosophers.* Translated by R. D. Hicks. London: Heinemann, 1959.

Enfield, [William]. *The History of Philosophy from the Earliest Times to the Beginning of the Present Century: Drawn up from Brucker's Historia Critica Philosophiae.* 1791. London, 1819.

Epictetus, His Morals, with Simplicius His Comment. London, 1704.

Eustache de Saint Paul. *Ethica sive Summa Moralis Disciplinae.* 1609. London, 1693.

Gassendi, Pierre. *Institutio Logicae.* 1658. Edited and translated by Howard Jones. Assen: Van Gorcum, 1981.

Gravesande, Willem Jakob 's. *Mathematical Elements of Natural Philosophy, or, An Introduction to Sir Isaac Newton's Philosophy.* Translated by J. T. Desaguliers. London, 1726.

Grotius, Hugo. *De Jure Belli ac Pacis* [The Rights of War and Peace]. Edited by Jean Barbeyrac. Amsterdam, 1724.

———. *The Rights of War and Peace.* London, 1738. (For a modern edition, see *The Rights of War and Peace.* Edited by Richard Tuck. 3 vols. Indianapolis: Liberty Fund, 2005.)

Haakonssen, Knud. *Natural Law and Moral Philosophy: From Grotius to the Scottish Enlightenment.* New York: Cambridge University Press, 1996.

Heereboord, Adrien. *Collegium Ethicum.* London, 1658.

————. *Collegium Logicum Pneumaticae*. Leiden, 1659.

Heppe, Heinrich. *Reformed Dogmatics, Set Out and Illustrated from the Sources*. 1861. Translated by G. T. Thomson. Grand Rapids, Mich.: Baker Book House, 1978.

Hobbes, Thomas. *Leviathan*. 1651. Edited by M. Oakeshott. Oxford: Basil Blackwell, 1946.

————. *On the Citizen* [De Cive]. 1642. Edited and translated by Richard Tuck and Michael Silverthorne. New York: Cambridge University Press, 1998.

Hochstrasser, T. J. *Natural Law Theories in the Early Enlightenment*. Cambridge: Cambridge University Press, 2000.

Horace. *Odes*. In *Odes and Epodes*. Revised by Niall Rudd. Cambridge, Mass.: Harvard University Press, 2004.

————. *Satires, Epistles, and Ars Poetica*. English translation by H. Rushton Fairclough. Cambridge, Mass.: Harvard University Press, 1926.

Howell, W. S. *Eighteenth-Century British Logic and Rhetoric*. Princeton: Princeton University Press, 1971.

Hume, David. *A Treatise of Human Nature*. Edited by David Fate Norton and Mary J. Norton. Oxford: Oxford University Press, 2000.

Hutcheson, Francis. *The Correspondence and Occasional Writings of Francis Hutcheson*. Indianapolis: Liberty Fund, forthcoming.

————. *De Naturali Hominum Socialitate Oratio Inauguralis*. Glasgow: 1730, 1756. For another translation of this text, see *On Human Nature*. Edited by Thomas Mautner. Cambridge: Cambridge University Press, 1993.

————. *An Essay on the Nature and Conduct of the Passions and Affections, with Illustrations on the Moral Sense*. 1728. Edited by Aaron Garrett. Indianapolis: Liberty Fund, 2002.

————. *An Inquiry into the Original of Our Ideas of Beauty and Virtue in Two Treatises*. 1725. Edited by Wolfgang Leidhold. Indianapolis: Liberty Fund, 2004.

————. "Letter to William Mace." 6 September 1727. *The European Magazine and London Review* 14 (1788): 158–60.

————. *Logicae Compendium. Praefixa est Dissertatio de Philosophiae Origine, Ejusque Inventoribus aut Excultoribus Praecipuis*. Glasgow, 1756; reprinted 1759, 1764, 1772, 1778, and 1787.

————. "Logica et Metaphysica." 1746–49. GUL MS Gen. 872.

————. *Metaphysicae Synopsis: Ontologiam, et Pneumatologiam Complectens*. Glasgow, 1742; *Synopsis Metaphysicae, Ontologiam et Pneumatologiam, Complectens*. Editio altera auctior. Glasgow, 1744; *Synopsis Metaphysicae, Ontolo-*

giam et Pneumatologiam Complectens. Editio tertia, auctior et emendatior. Glasgow, 1749. There were four more editions in 1756, 1762, 1774, and 1780.

———. *Philosophiae Moralis Institutio Compendiaria. Ethices et Jurisprudentiae Naturalis Elementa Continens.* Lib. III. Glasgow, 1742; 2nd editio, altera auctior et emendatior, 1745; *A Short Introduction to Moral Philosophy, in Three Books; Containing the Elements of Ethicks and the Law of Nature.* Glasgow, 1747.

———. *A System of Moral Philosophy, in Three Books.* Glasgow and London, 1755.

——— and James Moor, trans. *The Meditations of the Emperor Marcus Aurelius Antoninus New translated from the Greek with Notes; and an Account of his Life.* Glasgow, 1742.

Huyshe, Rev. John. *A Treatise on Logic, on the Basis of Aldrich, with Illustrative Notes.* Oxford, 1847.

Justinian. *Justinian's Institutes.* Translated by Peter Birks and Grant McLeod. London: Duckworth, 1987.

Juvenal and Persius. Translated by S. M. Braund. Cambridge, Mass.: Harvard University Press, 2004.

King, William. *An Essay on the Origin of Evil . . . with Large Notes . . .* Annotated by Edmund Law. London, 1731.

Kneale, W. C., and Martha Kneale. *The Development of Logic.* Oxford: Clarendon Press, 1984.

Law, Edmund. *An Enquiry into the Ideas of Space, Time, Immensity and Eternity.* London, 1734.

Le Clerc, Jean. *Logica; sive Ars Ratiocinandi.* Amsterdam, 1692.

———. *Ontologia; sive de Ente in Genere.* London, 1692.

———. *Pneumatologia seu de Spiritibus.* London, 1692.

Leechman, William. "Account of the Life, Writings and Character of the Author." In *A System of Moral Philosophy in Three Books,* by Francis Hutcheson. Glasgow and London, 1755.

Leibniz, Gottfried Wilhelm. *Essais de théodicée.* Amsterdam, 1715.

Locke, John. *An Essay Concerning Human Understanding.* Edited by Peter Nidditch. Oxford: Clarendon Press, 1975.

———. "An Examination of Malebranche's Opinion of Seeing All Things in God." 1720. Vol. 9 of *The Works of John Locke.* London, 1823. pp. 211–55.

———. *Two Treatises of Government.* Edited by Peter Laslett. Cambridge: Cambridge University Press, 1960.

Loudon, John. "Compendium Logicae." 1729. GUL MS Murray 210.

————. "Logica, Pars Prima." 1712. GUL MS Gen. 406.

Lucretius. *De Rerum Natura.* Translated by W. H. D. Rouse, revised by M. F. Smith. London: Heinemann, 1975.

Malebranche, Nicholas. *The Search After Truth.* 1674. Translated from the French by Thomas M. Lennon and Paul J. Olscamp. Columbus: Ohio State University Press, 1980.

Mandeville, Bernard. *The Fable of the Bees; or, Private Vices, Publick Benefits.* Pt. 1, 1723; pt. 2, 1729. 2 vols. Edited by F. B. Kaye. Oxford: Clarendon Press, 1924.

Matriculation Albums of Glasgow from 1728 to 1858. Transcribed and annotated by W. James Addison. Glasgow, 1913.

Michael, Emily. "Francis Hutcheson's *Logicae Compendium* and the Glasgow School of Logic." In *Logic and the Workings of the Mind: The Logic of Ideas and Faculty Psychology in Early Modern Philosophy,* edited by Patricia Easton. Atascadero, Calif.: Ridgeview Publishing, 1997. pp. 83–96.

Moore, James. "Francis Hutcheson, 1694–1746." In *Oxford Dictionary of National Biography.* 61 vols. Oxford: Oxford University Press, 2004.

————. "Hutcheson's Theodicy: The Argument and the Contexts of *A System of Moral Philosophy.*" In *The Scottish Enlightenment: Essays in Reinterpretation,* edited by Paul Wood. Rochester, N.Y.: University of Rochester Press, 2000. pp. 239–66.

————. "The Two Systems of Francis Hutcheson: On the Origins of the Scottish Enlightenment." In *Studies in the Philosophy of the Scottish Enlightenment,* edited by M. A. Stewart. New York: Oxford University Press, 1990. pp. 37–59.

————. "Utility and Humanity: The Quest for the *Honestum* in Cicero, Hutcheson, and Hume." *Utilitas* 14 (2002): 365–86.

———— and Michael Silverthorne. "Protestant Theologies, Limited Sovereignties: Natural Law and Conditions of Union in the German Empire, the Netherlands and Great Britain." In *A Union for Empire: Political Thought and the Union of 1707,* edited by John Robertson. Cambridge: Cambridge University Press, 1995. pp. 171–97.

More, Henry. *Divine Dialogues, Containing Disquisitions Concerning the Attributes and Providence of God.* Glasgow, 1743.

————. *Enchiridion Ethicum.* 1666. Translated as *An Account of Virtue; or, Dr. Henry More's Abridgement of Morals, Put into English.* London, 1690.

————. *Enchiridion Ethicum: The English Translation of 1690.* New York: Facsimile Society, 1930.

Munimenta Alme Universitatis Glasguensis. 4 vols. Glasgow, 1854.

Nemesius. "On the Nature of Man" [De Homine]. In *Cyril of Jerusalem and Nemesius of Emesa,* edited by William Telfer. London: SCM Press, 1955.

Norton, David Fate. "Hutcheson on Perception and Moral Perception." *Archiv für Geschichte der Philosophie* 59 (1977): 181–97.

———. "Hutcheson's Moral Realism." *Journal of the History of Philosophy* 23 (1985): 397–418.

———. "Hutcheson's Moral Sense Theory Reconsidered." *Dialogue* 13 (1974): 3–23.

Ovid. *The Art of Love, and Other Poems.* Translated by J. H. Mozley. London: W. Heinemann, 1939.

———. *Fasti.* English translation by Sir James Frazer. Cambridge, Mass.: Harvard University Press, 1931.

———. *Metamorphoses.* Translated by F. J. Miller. Cambridge, Mass.: Harvard University Press, 1984.

Pemberton, Henry. *A View of Sir Isaac Newton's Philosophy.* Dublin, 1728.

Persius. See *Juvenal and Persius.*

Plato. *Alcibiades.* Edited by Nicholas Denyer. Cambridge: Cambridge University Press, 2001.

Pufendorf, Samuel. *Of the Law of Nature and Nations.* With notes by Jean Barbeyrac. 4th ed. London, 1729.

———. *On the Duty of Man and Citizen.* Edited by James Tully and translated by Michael Silverthorne. Cambridge: Cambridge University Press, 1991.

———. *Specimen Controversiarum.* Uppsala, 1678.

Reid, H. M. B. *The Divinity Professors in the University of Glasgow, 1640–1903.* Glasgow: Maclehose, Jackson and Co., 1923.

Reid, Kenneth, and Reinhard Zimmermann, eds. *A History of Private Law in Scotland.* 2 vols. Oxford: Oxford University Press, 2000.

Rivers, Isabel. *Reason, Grace and Sentiment.* Vol. 2: *Shaftesbury to Hume.* Cambridge: Cambridge University Press, 2000.

Ross, Ian Simpson. "Hutcheson on Hume's *Treatise:* An Unnoticed Letter," *Journal of the History of Philosophy* 4 (1966): 69–72.

Sanderson, Robert. *Logicae Artis Compendium.* Oxford, 1672.

Scott, W. R. *Francis Hutcheson: His Life, Teaching and Position in the History of Philosophy.* Cambridge: Cambridge University Press, 1900.

Shaftesbury, Anthony Ashley Cooper, third earl of. *Characteristics of Men, Manners, Opinions, Times.* Edited by Lawrence E. Klein. Cambridge: Cambridge University Press, 1999.

————. *Several letters written by a noble lord to a young man at the university.* London, 1716.

Simplicius. *On Aristotle's "Categories 1–4."* Translated by Michael Chase. Ithaca, N.Y.: Cornell University Press, 2003.

Skoczylas, Anne. *Mr. Simpson's Knotty Case: Divinity, Politics, and Due Process in Early 18th-Century Scotland.* Montreal: McGill-Queens University Press, 2001.

Stanley, Thomas. *The History of Philosophy: Containing the Lives, Opinions, Actions and Discourses of the Philosophers of Every Sect.* 3rd ed. London, 1701.

Stewart, M. A. "James Arbuckle." In *Dictionary of Eighteenth-Century British Philosophers.* Bristol: Thoemmes Publishers, 1998.

Titius, Gottlieb Gerhard. *Observationes in Samuelis L. B. de Pufendorf De Officio Hominis et Civis.* Leipzig, 1703.

Turco, Luigi. "Sympathy and Moral Sense." *British Journal for the History of Philosophy* 7 (1999): 79–101.

Virgil. *Aeneid.* English translation by H. Rushton Fairclough. Revised by G. P. Goold. Cambridge, Mass.: Harvard University Press, 1999–2000.

————. *Georgics.* Edited by Richard F. Thomas. 2 vols. Cambridge: Cambridge University Press, 1988.

Watts, Isaac. "Logick: Or, the Right Use of Reason in the Enquiry After Truth." 1725. Vol. 5 of *The Works of the Reverend and Learned Isaac Watts, D. D.* London, 1810. pp. 5–178.

Winkler, Kenneth. "Hutcheson's Alleged Realism." *Journal of the History of Philosophy* 23 (1985): 179–94.

————. "Hutcheson and Hume on the Color of Virtue." In *Hume Studies,* 22, 1 (1966): 3–22.

————. "Lockean Logic." In *The Philosophy of John Locke: New Perspectives.* Edited by Peter Anstey. London: Routledge, 2003. pp. 154–78.

Wodrow, James. "Letters to the Earl of Buchan." Mitchell Library, Glasgow, Baillie MSS 32225.

Wodrow, Robert. *Analecta; or, Materials for a History of Remarkable Providences.* 4 vols. Edinburgh, 1842–43.

Wolff, Christian. *Philosophia Prima sive Ontologia.* Frankfort, 1730.

Yolton, John W. *John Locke and the Way of Ideas.* [London]: Oxford University Press, 1956.

————. *Thinking Matter: Materialism in Eighteenth-Century Britain.* Minneapolis: University of Minnesota Press, 1983.

INDEX

This book is set in Adobe Garamond, a modern adaptation by Robert Slimbach of the typeface originally cut around 1540 by the French typographer and printer Claude Garamond. The Garamond face, with its small lowercase height and restrained contrast between thick and thin strokes, is a classic "old-style" face and has long been one of the most influential and widely used typefaces.

Printed on paper that is acid-free and meets the requirements of the American National Standard for Permanence of Paper for Printed Library Materials, z39.48-1992. ♾

Book design by Louise OFarrell
Gainesville, Florida
Typography by Apex Publishing, LLC
Madison, Wisconsin
Printed and bound by Worzalla Publishing Company
Stevens Point, Wisconsin